Artificial Intelligence: Models, Algorithms and Applications

Edited by

Terje Solsvik Kristensen

Department of Computing, Mathematics and Physics
Western Norway University of Applied Sciences
Bergen
Norway

Artificial Intelligence: Models, Algorithms and Applications

Editor: Terje Solsvik Kristensen

ISBN (Online): 978-1-68108-826-6

ISBN (Print): 978-1-68108-827-3

ISBN (Paperback): 978-1-68108-828-0

need for a court order if at any point you breach any terms of this License Agreement. In no event will any delay or failure by Bentham Science Publishers in enforcing your compliance with this License Agreement constitute a waiver of any of its rights.

3. You acknowledge that you have read this License Agreement, and agree to be bound by its terms and conditions. To the extent that any other terms and conditions presented on any website of Bentham Science Publishers conflict with, or are inconsistent with, the terms and conditions set out in this License Agreement, you acknowledge that the terms and conditions set out in this License Agreement shall prevail.

Bentham Science Publishers Ltd.
Executive Suite Y - 2
PO Box 7917, Saif Zone
Sharjah, U.A.E.
Email: subscriptions@benthamscience.net

CONTENTS

PREFACE

This book entitled **'Artificial Intelligence: Models, Algorithms and Applications'** consists of eight chapters. The book focuses on new achievements in AI and how AI may be introduced in different application areas, and how these areas may be changed when AI models and algorithms are used.

AI introduces new approaches to solve complex problems. It is interesting to note that AI introduces a significant shift in new models and algorithms. Advances in instrument technologies have seen a significant shift as far as the tools and techniques are concerned. Subsequently, it has made and is going to make equally powerful impact on the process and manufacturing industry through Industry 4.0.

The aim of this book is to give an introduction to the field of AI, its models and algorithms and how this may be used to solve problems in different application areas.

The book is primarily intended for students, researchers and engineers that are interested in AI and how it may be used to solve concrete problems. The structure of the book is organized as several different topics. We hope that technology developers and companies also find it interesting to be used in industry.

We do not yet have any chapter about how to use AI in Robotics and in Natural Language Processing (NLP). These are important fields where AI methods are very relevant to use and also give good results. NLP is also the field where I started to use AI algorithms for about twenty years ago. If there is going to be a new edition of the book it should be natural to extend it with these chapters.

The book consists of eight chapters which have been described concisely one by one below:

1. From AIS Data to Vessel Destination Through Prediction with Machine Learning Techniques by Wells Wang, Chengkai Zhang, Fabien Guillaume, Richard Halldear, Terje Solsvik Kristensen, Zheng Liu

The destination of vessels is an important decision maker in maritime trading. However, shipping companies keep this kind of data inclusively, which results in the absence of complete information of destination for every vessel. However, other information such as the position can be available due to Automated Identification Systems (AIS). Hence, predicting the vessels' destination port becomes possible. To give a baseline of how to make use of AIS data for vessel destination prediction with machine learning, several AIS data preprocessing approaches and machine learning approaches for vessel destination prediction are introduced in the literature. The chapter aims to give the audience an idea of how to link between AIS data, trajectories, and numerous machine learning models for the purpose of predicting arrival ports for maritime services. Furthermore, the discussion points out the current state of research on this topic and where the potential future work may possibly lie in.

2. AI in Mental Health by Suresh Kumar Mukhiya, Amin Aminifar, Fazle Rabbi, Violet Ka I Pun and Yngve Lamo

Managing the prevalence of mental health problems is both socially and economically challenging. Technological advancement in recent decades has provided potential solutions to this issue. In particular, Artificial Intelligence (AI) is one of the research areas that has expanded into behavioural, neurological and mental healthcare by fulfilling the main objectives of P4 medicine - personalized, predictive, preventive and participative medicine. In this chapter, we give an overview of recent applications of AI for screening, detection, and treatment of mental health problems; summarize the economic and social implications; present a systematic overview of which AI technologies are used for the different mental disorders and identify challenges for further development. Based on this, we identify some future research questions that could be solved with the use of AI in mental healthcare. The chapter concludes with an in-depth discussion on the key challenges of the application of AI in mental health interventions.

3. Deep Learning in Radiology by Madhura Ingalhalikar

Recent developments in artificial intelligence (AI), particularly deep learning (DL) algorithms have demonstrated remarkable progress in image recognition and prediction tasks. These are now being applied in the field of radiology on medical images to quantify, characterize, classify as well as monitor various pathologies. Such DL based quantifications facilitate greater support to the visual assessment of image characteristics that is performed by the physician. Furthermore, it aids in reducing inter-reader variability as well as assists in speeding up the radiology workflow. In this chapter, we provide an insightful motivation for employing DL based framework followed by an overview of recent applications of DL in radiology and present a systematic summary of specific DL algorithms pertaining to image perception and recognition tasks. Finally, we discuss the challenges in clinical implementation of these algorithms and provide a perspective on how the domain could be advanced in the next few years.

4. AI in Instrumentation Industry by Ajay V. Deshmukh

Artificial intelligence (AI) as the name suggests is a new way of automatically deciding upon the operation and control of real time machines and processes in industry. The advantages of using artificial intelligence in industry are many. First of all the decisions are dynamic and real time without any human intervention. Next, it is not based on any formula which in the past required updating for different process conditions and time. Operational technologies did not deploy complete intelligence systems and there used to be much more complexity in tuning the processes and systems together. Training of the operational people was very much crucial and required periodic updates from time to time as the operational technologies changed. AI can overcome most of these complexities, due to the fact that it obtains a data driven solution in real time. Intelligence could be distributed right from the sensory levels to higher levels of distributed computerized systems. Internet of Things (IoTs) and data analytics can provide dynamic information on the performance of machines and processes. Industries which would benefit from technologies based on Artificial Intelligence (AI), Machine Learning (ML) and Deep learning (DL) are in general any process or manufacturing industries including healthcare, petroleum, power sector, automotive etc. In fact, this would lead to applicability of Industry 4.0. In this chapter different concepts and applicability of AI in industry have been described. Off course it is possible due to the powerful computational tools, which help not only in doing computations, but also in terms of the capability of communication control, plus data storage, transmission and intelligent decision making.

5. *AI in Business and Education by Tarjei Alvaer Heggernes*

In recent years, the interest for artificial intelligence has gone from the computing department to the board room. Business leaders are in a rush to explore the possibilities presented by the abundance of data, processing power and the methods of AI to create business value and business opportunities. In this chapter we will adapt the view of a manager and explore some of technologies used in machine learning. We will also look at how managers should approach artificial intelligence. The chapter will close with a discussion of some use cases of the different technologies. On case will come from marketing and discusses the use of reinforcement learning in real-time bidding on an e-commerce platform. The next two cases are from the education industry, one case will discuss reinforcement learning in intelligent tutoring systems, and the final case will discuss neural networks in grading of tests and assignments. There are many exciting use cases for artificial intelligence, it is important for business managers to understand the possibilities, and equally important for programmers to understand how businesses create value.

6. *Extreme Randomized Trees for Real Estate Appraisal with Housing and Crime Data by Junchi Bin, Bryan Gardiner, Eric Li, and Zheng Liu*

Real estate appraisal plays a vital role in people's daily life. People rely on the estimation of decisions on buying houses. It is well recognized that the criminal activities around the house have significant impacts on house prices. House buyers can make more reasonable decisions if they are aware of the criminal activities around the house. Therefore, a machine learning-based method is proposed by combining house attributes and criminal activities. Specifically, the method firstly infers the intensity of criminal activities from historical crime records. Then, a novel machine learning algorithm, extremely randomized trees (ExtraTrees), is implemented to estimate the house price based on the extracted comprehensive crime intensity and real-world house attributes. The experimental results show that the proposed method outperforms contemporary real estate appraisal methods by achieving higher accuracy and robustness.

7. *The Knowledge Based Firm and AI by Ove Rustung Hjelmervik, and Terje Solsvik Kristensen*

Radical innovation is disruptive. It is a change that sweeps away much of a firm's, or an entire industry's, existing investment in technological assets, skills and knowledge. Such innovation has occurred throughout history and wealth has been accumulated in its wake. Companies have flourished as a result of such ingenuity, yet there is no evidence in the literature that radical innovation is a result of senior management's decision, rather it takes place through learning. In order to understand what drives a knowledge-based organization, one has to look at the inside of the firm where implemented structures and tools are supporting employees' empowerment to unleash their creativity. What the firm knows is stored in the employees' head and in the firm's procedural structure, and the firm learns in two ways - by its employees and through hiring new employees. Thus, development of radical innovation, such as artificial intelligence (AI), will either be learned by the firm's employees and/or through hiring experts. Whenever management prevents new methods from being applied, or employees refuse to acknowledge and learn new techniques, productivity suffers, resulting in firm and industry obsolescence. This is exactly what's happening in the case of AI. Almost eighty years after Alan Turing introduced AI theory, we see a world flabbergasted by its potential impact on productivity. Our case study is based on interviews of a dozen or so R&D managers in private and public sectors. Although our observations are not a guarantee to lead to a consistent agreement or interpretation, valid knowledge that can lead to better performance and organizational survival, may nevertheless provide useful learning for relevant readers.

8. *A Mathematical Description of Artificial Neural Networks by Hans Birger Drange*

After a short introduction to neural networks generally, a more detailed presentation of the structure of a feed forward neural network is done, using mathematical language, functions, matrices and vectors. Further, emphasis has been made on perceptrons and linear regression done by using ANN. Central concepts like learning, including weight updates, error minimization with gradient descent are introduced and studied using these simple networks. Finally, multilayer perceptrons are defined with their error functions and finally backpropagation is described precisely using composite functions and the concept of error signals.

The editor would also like to thank Bentham Science Publishers for all help during the writing of this book and specifically Asst. Manager for Publications, Mariam Mehdi, for all support during the publication process. I would also thank all the authors from different countries that have contributed to this book. At last, I would thank my prior student Kenneth Langedal for his help with the writing.

Terje Solsvik Kristensen
Department of Computing, Mathematics and Physics
Western Norway University of Applied Sciences
Bergen
Norway

List of Contributors

Amin Aminifar	Western Norway University of Applied Sciences, Bergen, Norway
Ajay V. Deshmukh	Phaltan Education Society's College of Engineering Phaltan, India
Bryan Gardiner	Data Nerds, Kelowna, BC, Canada
Chengkai Zhang	Intelligent Sensing Diagnostic and Prognostic Lab, Faculty of Applied Science, University of British Columbia, Kelowna, BC, Canada
Eric Li	Faculty of Management, University of British Columbia, Kelowna, BC, Canada
Fabien Guillaume	Spire Global Luxembourg, Luxembourg
Fazle Rabbi	Western Norway University of Applied Sciences, Bergen, Norway University of Bergen, Norway
Hans Birger Drange	Western Norway University of Applied Sciences (HVL), Faculty of Engineering and Science, Bergen, Norway
Junchi Bin	School of Engineering, Faculty of Applied Science, University of British Columbia, Kelowna, BC, Canada
Madhura Ingalhalikar	Symbiosis Center for Medical Image Analysis Symbiosis International University, Lavale, Pune 412115, India
Ove Rustung Hjelmervik	Biotech Innovation Center Bergen AS, Bergen, Norway
Richard Halldearn	Navarik Corp, Vancouver, BC, Canada
Suresh Kumar Mukhiya	Western Norway University of Applied Sciences, Bergen, Norway
Tarjei Alvaer Heggernes	Department of Strategy and Entrepreneurship, BI Norwegian Business School, Bergen, Norway
Terje Solsvik Kristensen	Department of Computing, Mathematics and Physics, Western Norway University of Applied Sciences, Bergen, Norway Biotech Innovation Center Bergen AS, Bergen, Norway
Violet Ka I. Pun	Western Norway University of Applied Sciences, Bergen, Norway University of Oslo, Norway
Wells Wang	Intelligent Sensing Diagnostic and Prognostic Lab, Faculty of Applied Science, University of British Columbia, Kelowna, BC, Canada
Yngve Lamo	Western Norway University of Applied Sciences, Bergen, Norway
Zheng Liu	Intelligent Sensing Diagnostic and Prognostic Lab, Faculty of Applied Science, University of British Columbia, Kelowna, BC, Canada School of Engineering, Faculty of Applied Science, University of British Columbia, Kelowna, BC, Canada

CHAPTER 1

From AIS Data to Vessel Destination Through Prediction with Machine Learning Techniques

Wells Wang[1], Chengkai Zhang[1], Fabien Guillaume[2], Richard Halldearn[3], Terje Solsvik Kristensen[4] and **Zheng Liu[1,*]**

[1] *Intelligent Sensing Diagnostic and Prognostic Lab, Faculty of Applied Science, University of British Columbia, Kelowna, BC, Canada*

[2] *Spire Global Luxembourg, Luxembourg*

[3] *Navarik Corp, Vancouver, BC, Canada*

[4] *Department of Computing, Mathematics and Physics, Western Norway University of Applied Sciences, Bergen, Norway*

Abstract: The destination of vessels is important decision makers of maritime trading. However, shipping companies keep this kind of data inclusively, which results in the absence of complete information of destination for every vessel. However, other information such as the position can be available due to Automated Identification Systems (AIS). Hence, predicting the vessels' destination port becomes possible. To give a baseline of how to make use of AIS data for vessel destination prediction with machine learning, several AIS data preprocessing approaches and machine learning approaches for vessel destination prediction are introduced in the literature. The chapter aims to give the audience an idea of how to link between AIS data, trajectories, and numerous machine learning models for the purpose of predicting arrival ports for maritime services. Furthermore, the discussion points out the current state of researches on this topic and where the potential future work may possibly lie in.

Keywords: AIS, Bayesian estimation, Deep learning, Destination prediction, Machine learning, Maritime analysis, Nearest neighbor search, Sequence to sequence, Similarity measures, Spatial-temporal data, Trajectory.

INTRODUCTION

Since ancient times, maritime transportation has been a major part of transporting passengers and commodities. According to United Nations, around 70-80 percent of world trade is carried through this mean. In 2016, the total volume of the worldwide seaborne trade had reached 10.3 billion tons.

* **Corresponding author Zheng Liu:** Intelligent Sensing Diagnostic and Prognostic Lab, Faculty of Applied Science, University of British Columbia, Kelowna, BC, Canada; E-mail: zheng.liu@ubc.ca

The global maritime transportation occupies around 90 percent of global trading by volume and 70 percent by value [1]. With the increasing demands of global shipping service, the naval transportation industry calls for a more reliable source of predicting vessels' destinations.

The advancement of technologies and availability of maritime data makes it possible to keep track of most vessels. Nowadays, automatic identification system (AIS) data are widely adopted for its capability in vessel tracking [2].

Furthermore, with the AIS data combined with computational intelligence, the destination of those vessels can be predicted [3]. Upon making the correct predictions for vessels' destinations, the efficiency of the overall supply chain management will boost.

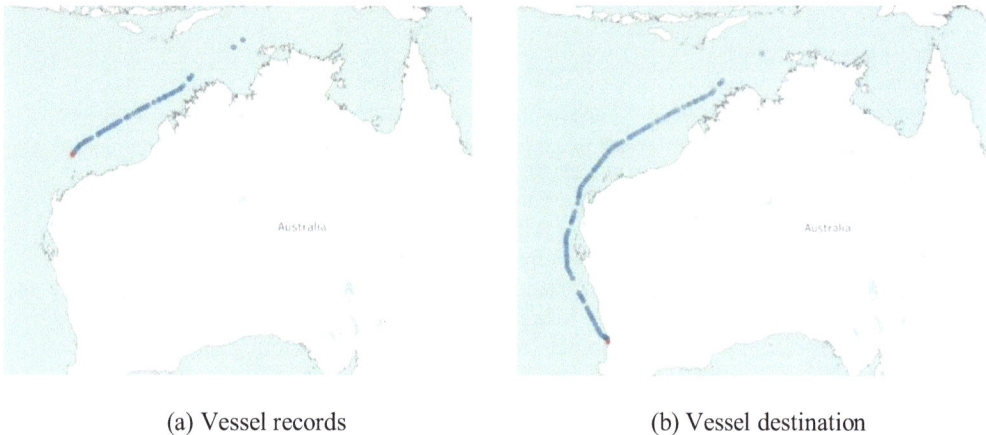

(a) Vessel records   (b) Vessel destination

Fig. (1). Illustration of vessel destination prediction.

To illustrate how vessel destination is predicted, this chapter uses an example of an on-the-way vessel on the northwestern side of Australia, which is shown in Fig. (**1**). Given a two-day record from the vessel (Fig. **1a**), the goal is to predict its destination (Fig. **1b**). The records on Fig. (**1a**) can be viewed as a part of a trajectory of the vessel, and the records on Fig. (**1b**) (from one port to another) can be viewed as a complete trajectory. To predict the destination of an on-th--way trajectory, machine learning techniques needs to be combined with historical trajectories for model training. With the help of AIS data, researchers can acquire enough historical trajectories around the globe as a source of constructing the model that is capable of predicting the destination of any new coming trajectories.

This chapter focuses on implementing trajectory data mining and machine learning techniques on AIS data-driven vessel destination prediction. In the context of this chapter, the discussion will introduce several AIS data preprocessing approaches and will elucidate some aspects of the existing machine learning approaches regarding vessel destination prediction.

AIS DATA PREPROCESSING APPROACH

The Automatic Identification System was initially designed for safety and security of navigation purposes [4]. As the messages transmitted by AIS systems are broadcasted in a non-secured channel, these AIS messages could be gathered by Vessel Traffic Services. Hence, AIS messages being collected could be used in other dimensions, such as destination prediction. However, with the nature of AIS data, some preprocessing procedures need to be done before conducting further analysis.

Among the 27 types of AIS messages, most of the messages are position reports (type 1, 2, and 3) or static reports (type 5). Discussion in this section lies in the position type AIS data, where some important parameters regarding destination prediction are listed in Table **1**. The complete version of Table **1** is in [5].

Table 1. Parameters of Position Type AIS messages regarding destination prediction.

Parameter	Description
User ID	Unique identifier such as MMSI number
Longitude	Longitude in 1/10000 min (±180°, East=positive (as per 2's complement), West=negative (as per 2's complement))
Latitude	Latitude in 1/10000 min (±90°, North = positive (as per 2's complement), South = negative (as per 2's complement))
Time stamp	UTC second when the report was generated by the electronic position system (EPFS)

The following introduces several approaches to turn raw AIS data into trajectory data for the purpose of training vessel destination prediction models. The data should be in the forms of vessel trajectories that are ready to be trained after procedures of trajectory extraction, trajectory resampling, noise filtering, and trajectory segmentation.

Trajectory Extraction

Raw AIS data contains various data points that represent the status of different vessels at different times. As mentioned in [6], trajectory data can be classified into four major categories: *mobility of people, mobility of transportation vehicles, mobility of animals, and mobility of natural phenomena*. The nature of AIS data falls in the *mobility of transportation vehicle*s category of trajectory data. With extracting trajectory for each vessel by its unique identifiers from the raw AIS database, some existing methods for processing and analyzing trajectories can then be implemented.

In terms of vessel destination prediction, the process of trajectory extraction may include filtering out the vessels without enough data points for model construction. Furthermore, considering there are usually more than thousands of vessels and that each vessel has thousands of data points (timestamps), saving extracted trajectories into separate files would be more practical regarding the cost of computation.

There are two major types of unique identifiers for vessels, IMO (International Maritime Organization) number and MMSI (Maritime Mobile Service Identity) number. The IMO number is part of the static type AIS messages that will permanently be associated to the vessel and will never be reassigned to another ship. On the other hand, the MMSI is part of the position type AIS messages that can be changed if the vessel is traded to different nations. Usually, trajectory extraction uses the MMSI number because it is within the position type AIS message (Fig. **2**).

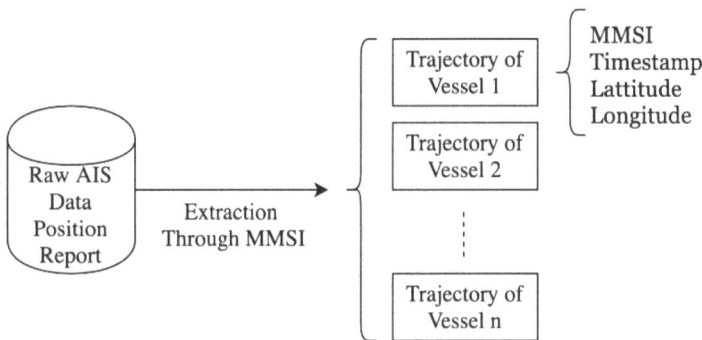

Fig. (2). Trajectory Extraction.

Trajectory Resampling

In most cases, trajectory data points are received within a unique time span (*i.e.* trajectory data of customers inside a mall might be received from the mobile devices that sent out locations of its owner every hour). However, for most of the vessel trajectories extracted from the raw AIS data, the time between two data points can vary from a few seconds to hours [7]. This character of AIS data creates a problem if it's directly put into training after extraction because every data point does not represent vessel position with the same time interval.

Moreover, keeping data of vessel positions that are too close to another makes the data redundant and would increase unnecessary cost of training time. Hence, the trajectory extracted from AIS data is recommended to be resampled.

In the trajectory resampling process, a threshold needs to be decided as the fixed time interval for each vessel trajectory. This threshold is dependent on how densely the data is distributed and the computational power. For vessel destination prediction on a global bases, resample trajectories to an hourly basis should be enough for training purposes. Additionally, resampling process map the non-identical timestamp into hourly bases. As a result, trajectories extracted from position reports would have the advantage to be combined with parameters from other types of AIS messages.

Noise Filtering

Noise in a trajectory could affect the accuracy in training destination prediction models. Sometimes the errors are acceptable when distances are small between the received position and true position, but that's not the case when the error gets too big. Fig. (**3**) shows a monthly trajectory with 541 data points that have been extracted and resampled, the orange point on the right of the image is an example of noise in a trajectory. The received position is too far away from the actual position that falls into the purple box. In a situation like this, the noise should be filtered before the training process. Existing methods to solve this problem fall into three major categories: mean and median filter, Kalman and particle filters, and heuristics-based outlier detection [6].

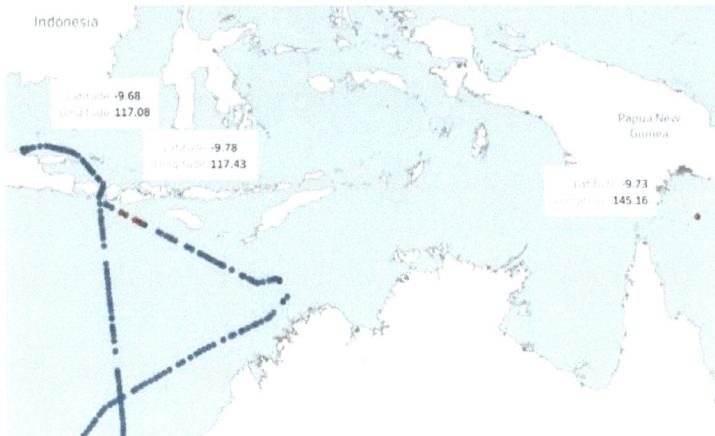

Fig. (3). Illustration of noise in a trajectory.

The discussion below gives an example of using median filter to solve the problem of the noise in Fig. (**3**). Median filter serves as a sliding window on the trajectory, where the threshold of the sliding window needs to be predefined. As it slides through each point in the trajectory, it generates a new point depending on the median value of all coordinates within the threshold.

Fig. (**4**) showcases parts of the process in median filter for the example in Fig. (**3**). As the median filter of threshold equals to 3 slides through observation 495, the noise at (-9.708, 145.162) (Table **2**) is filtered to (-9.708, 117.456) (Table **3**).

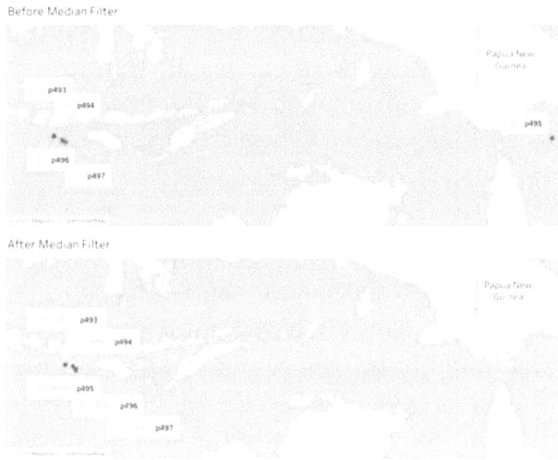

Fig. (4). Median filter for an example trajectory.

Table 2. Positions before median filter.

Obs	Lon	Lat
p493	117.000	-9.603
p494	117.004	-9.604
p495	145.162	-9.708
p496	117.456	-9.838
p497	117.635	-9.925

Table 3. Positions after median filter.

Obs	Lon	Lat
p493	117.000	-9.603
p494	117.004	-9.604
p495	117.456	-9.708
p496	117.635	-9.838
p497	117.635	-9.925

Trajectory Segmentation

A vessel may travel to multiple ports in a period of time. In other words, it may have different voyages within the trajectories extracted from the raw AIS data. In order to segment the trajectories to sub-trajectories as each voyage, the port that a vessel stays at in a trajectory should be detected.

In a trajectory, some points that denote locations where an object stayed for a while are defined as "stay points [8]." In terms of maritime trajectories, stay points can either occur at a port (port stay points) or in the middle of the sea (non-port stay points). Fig. (**5**) illustrates different types of maritime stay points and the process from port stay point detection to trajectory segmentation.

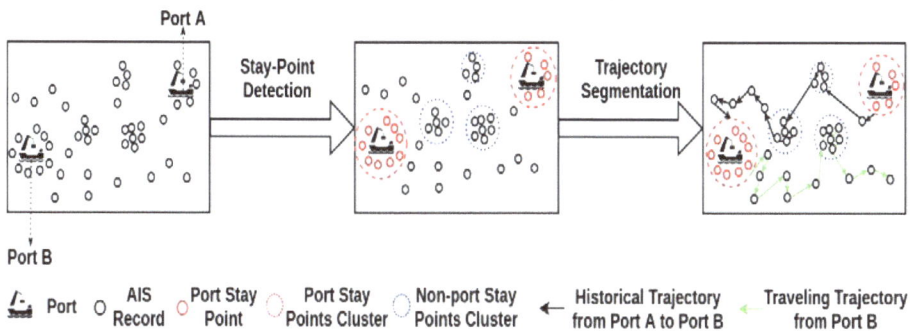

Fig. (5). Representation of trajectory segmentation.

If points concentrate on an area, the area will be labeled as a cluster. After labeling, the cluster that contains a port location will be regarded as a port stay-point cluster (red dashed circles in Fig. (**5**). Otherwise, the rest of the points will remain as a trajectory point. Finally, the trajectory points with timestamps between the timestamps of two stay-points are segmented to a sub-trajectory of a vessel. As shown in Fig. (**5**), the trajectory (black line in Fig. **5**) has been segmented as the sub-trajectory from Port A to Port B. The trajectory of the vessel that just departs from one port and has not arrived at the destination port is then regarded as the traveling trajectory (green line in Fig. **5**). Continued from the example of Fig. (**3**), Fig. (**6**) shows the example of the segmented trajectory where colors are different for different voyages.

With the preprocessing procedures being completed, the trajectory data can now be trained. In the next section, several machine learning-based approaches that are used for vessel destination prediction are reviewed. The approaches can be categorized into two major types, sequence prediction approach and classification approach.

VESSEL DESTINATION PREDICTION APPROACHES

Little research has been done in terms of vessel destination prediction with AIS data. Fortunately, The ACM International Conference on Distributed and Event-Based Systems (DEBS) launched a grand challenge that aims at predicting the vessels' destination. The participants provided several machine learning models as a result to the competition. In this section, the methods and the models regarding the prediction of vessel destination are reviewed and categorized into two categories, sequence prediction approach and classification approach.

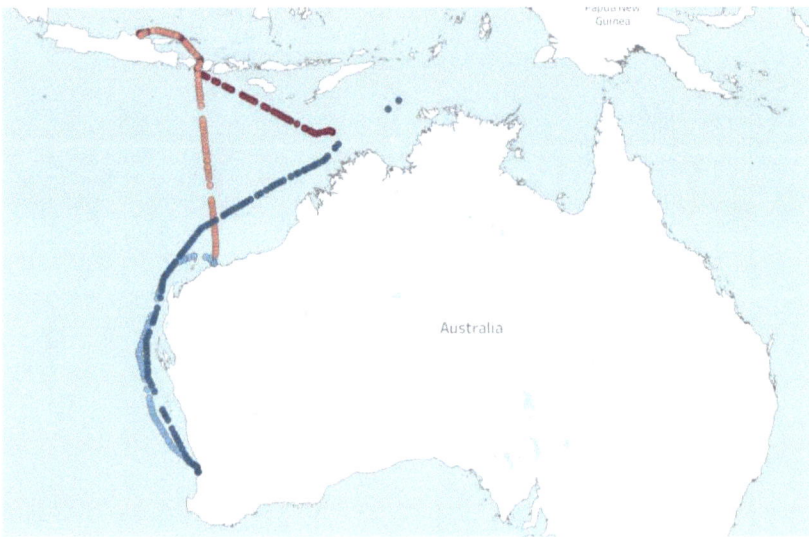

Fig. (6). An example of segmented trajectory.

Sequence Prediction Approach

A trajectory can be regarded as a sequence, more specifically, a spatial-temporal sequence [9, 10]. Numerous machine learning researches have been conducted on the prediction of sequential data. However, there are some restrictions mapping a trajectory prediction problem to sequences. Generally, recurrent neural networks (RNNs) are used for dealing with sequential machine learning problems. Nevertheless, RNN gets poor learning performances as the sequences needed to be predicted grow [11], which is the case for vessel destination prediction.

If a vessel's position of the next hour is to be predicted, regular RNN can solve the problem because the information gap between the wanted point and the known data point is small. However, it requires a different model that can handle "long-term dependencies" in terms of a larger information gap such as destination. Long

Short-Term Memory networks (LSTM) is a kind of RNN that is designed to deal with long term dependencies [12].

LSTM can be an ideal option for vessel destination prediction when the input and the output are the same. However, this case would only happen when the trajectories are in the middle of its voyage at the point where the predictions are made, which is not useful in practice. Fortunately, Google has proposed a sequence to sequence model with LSTM cells embedded that can deal with this problem [13]. This model has proven its usefulness in applications such as machine translation [13], speech recognition [14], and video captioning [15].

Sequence to sequence model has also been used in the case of vessel trajectory prediction [16] due to the reasons mentioned above. The research maps the position (latitude and longitude) of vessels to spatial grids on the world like in a king-chess game. Instead of sequence of coordinates, the inputs of the model are text that represents which grid the vessel falls in. This changes the context of this problem into a problem like machine translation, where input a sequence of text gets a sequence of text as output in different languages. While the output trajectory length varies by how close the vessel's position is to the destination, the advantage of this model is that it can deal with trajectories (sequences) at different lengths.

Classification Approach

Instead of directly predicting what would be the next in a trajectory, classification approach varies from classifying destination ports to classifying trajectories. The classification of arrival ports regards not the trajectory itself but the parameters like ship type, speed, course, *etc*. The classification of trajectory detects similarities between different trajectories [17].

Classification of Ports

Ships departing from the same port only arrive at a specific subsets of ports [18]. Thus, classifying ports could be a good option to reduce the solution space. A general flow of classifying arrival ports can be split into three steps:

1. Define the features important for port prediction
2. Define the algorithms to be used for the classification
3. Determine the decision strategy to decide the model output from the classification results.

In [18], the neural network classifier went through each position from the departure port to the current timestamp and recorded all predicted ports as a sequence. Next, an incremental major filter is implemented to form the final decision of the destination port. In [19], features of ship type, speed, longitude, latitude, course, heading, departure port name, and draught are included in the classification. Next, a combination of random forest, gradient boosting decision trees, XGBoost trees, and extremely randomized trees are used for classification. Finally, an ensemble learning method is conducted to decide the arrival port.

The classification of arrival ports does have the advantage of reducing solution space. However, the examples above consider only the prediction on a regional bases (40 ports) regarding the data given in the grand challenge. In a more general practice, where there are thousands of ports, the complexity of the classification would increase. As for the accuracy of the classification, though there are researches stating that possibilities exist for accuracy to increase with more classes [20], but in AIS case the rise or drop of the accuracy remains unknown.

Classification of Trajectories

In terms of vessel destination prediction on a more general case [21], proposed a model capable of dealing AIS data with 5,928,471 segmented trajectories that cover 10618 ports for vessel destination prediction. The research measures similarities between the on-the-way trajectory and all the historical trajectories departing from the same port. The haversine distances of each point in the trajectories being compared, are calculated and saved to a list as features [22]. Next, based on the features, a random forest [23] measure is implemented to figure out the similarity between on-the-way trajectories and every trajectory departing from the same port. Finally, the arrival port of the most similar trajectory will be predicted as the destination. The model eventually succeeded in predicting trajectories over 5 days duration at an accuracy around 70 percent.

CONCLUDING REMARKS

Researches on AIS data-driven vessel destination is limited to regional basis and requires a predefined framework as a baseline. The discussion in this chapter links AIS data to numerous techniques in formulating machine learning models for the purpose of predicting arrival ports for on-the-way vessels. With the example of different studies being listed as the basis of AIS data-driven vessel destination prediction, more research could be done in the future.

The future research may lie in several dimensions. First, the nature of sequence prediction approach maps the characteristic of Natural Language Processing (NLP). Hence, new models proposed in the field of natural language processing such as BERT [24] could be implemented. Second, as mentioned previously, the classification approach on arrival ports has the potential to be expanded to a global level with more classes. Finally, since vessel trajectory may be affected by weather, integration of AIS data with additional data could potentially increase the accuracy of existing models [25].

CONSENT FOR PUBLICATION

Not applicable.

CONFLICT OF INTEREST

The author declares no conflict of interest, financial or otherwise.

ACKNOWLEDGEMENTS

This research is supported by Mitacs Accelerate Program (IT13612).

REFERENCES

[1]   J.-P. Rodrigue, C. Comtois, and B. Slack, "The Geography of Transport Systems," 2013.
[http://dx.doi.org/10.4324/9780203371183]

[2]   K. Patroumpas, E. Alevizos, A. Artikis, M. Vodas, N. Pelekis, and Y. Theodoridis, "Online event recognition from moving vessel trajectories", *GeoInformatica,* vol. 21, pp. 389-427, 2017.
[http://dx.doi.org/10.1007/s10707-016-0266-x]

[3]   S. Hexeberg, A.L. Flåtent, B-O.H. Eriksen, and E.F. Brekke, "AIS-based vessel trajectory prediction", *2017 20ʰ Int. Conf. Inf. Fusion,* pp. 1-8, 2017.
[http://dx.doi.org/10.23919/ICIF.2017.8009762]

[4]   C. Iphar, A. Napoli, and C. Ray, "Detection of false AIS messages for the improvement of maritime situational awareness", *Ocean,* MTS/IEEE Washingt, pp. 1-7, 2015.
[http://dx.doi.org/10.23919/OCEANS.2015.7401841]

[5]   International Telecommunications Union (ITU), "Technical characteristics for an automatic identificationsystem using time-division multiple access in the VHF maritime mobile band", *Recommendation ITU-R M,* pp. 1371-4, 2014.

[6]   Y. Zheng, "Trajectory data mining: an overview", *ACM Trans. Intell. Syst. Technol,* vol. 6, p. 29, 2015.
[http://dx.doi.org/10.1145/2743025]

[7]   L. Zhao, G. Shi, and J. Yang, "Ship trajectories pre-processing based on ais data", *J. Navig,* vol. 71, pp. 1210-1230, 2018.
[http://dx.doi.org/10.1017/S0373463318000188]

[8]   Y. Ye, Y. Zheng, Y. Chen, J. Feng, and X. Xie, "Mining individual life pattern based on location history", *Tenth Int. Conf. Mob. Data Manag. Syst. Serv. Middlew,* pp. 1-10, 2009.
[http://dx.doi.org/10.1109/MDM.2009.11]

[9]   S. Wang, J. Cao, and P.S. Yu, "Deep learning for spatio-temporal data mining: A survey", 2019,

[10]   X. Shi, "Exploring deep learning architectures for spatiotemporal sequence forecasting", 2018,
[http://dx.doi.org/10.14711/thesis-991012671057603412]

[11]   Y. Bengio, P. Simard, and P. Frasconi, "Learning long-term dependencies with gradient descent is difficult", *IEEE Trans. Neural Netw,* vol. 5, no. 2, pp. 157-166, 1994.
[http://dx.doi.org/10.1109/72.279181] [PMID: 18267787]

[12] S. Hochreiter, and J. Schmidhuber, "Long short-term memory", *Neural Comput,* vol. 9, no. 8, pp. 1735-1780, 1997.
[http://dx.doi.org/10.1162/neco.1997.9.8.1735] [PMID: 9377276]

[13] I. Sutskever, O. Vinyals, and Q. V Le, "Sequence to sequence learning with neural networks", 2014,

[14] R. Prabhavalkar, K. Rao, T.N. Sainath, B. Li, L. Johnson, and N Jaitly, "A Comparison of sequence-to-sequence models for speech recognition", *Proceedings of the Annual Conference of the International Speech Communication Association,* Interspeech, pp. 939-943, 2017.
[http://dx.doi.org/10.21437/Interspeech.2017-233]

[15] S. Venugopalan, M. Rohrbach, J. Donahue, R. Mooney, T. Darrell, and K. Saenko, "Sequence to sequence - video to text", *Proceedings of the IEEE International Conference on Computer Vision,* pp. 4534-4542, 2015.

[16] D.D. Nguyen, C. Le Van, and M.I. Ali, "Demo: Vessel trajectory prediction using sequence-t--sequence models over spatial grid", *DEBS 2018 - Proceedings of the 12th ACM International Conference on Distributed and Event-Based Systems,* 2018pp. 258-261

[17] N. Magdy, M.A. Sakr, T. Mostafa, and K. El-Bahnasy, "Review on trajectory similarity measures", *2015 IEEE Seventh Int. Conf. Intell. Comput. Inf. Syst,* pp. 613-619, 2015.

[18] C.X. Lin, T.W. Huang, G. Guo, and M.D.F. Wong, "Grand challenge: MtDetector: A high-performance marine traic detector at stream scale", *DEBS 2018 - Proceedings of the 12th ACM International Conference on Distributed and Event-Based Systems,* pp. 205-208, 2018.

[19] O. Bodunov, F. Schmidt, A. Martin, A. Brito, and C. Fetzer, "Grand challenge: real-time destination and ETA prediction for maritime trac", *DEBS 2018 - Proceedings of the 12th ACM International Conference on Distributed and Event-Based Systems,* pp. 198-201, 2018.

[20] F. Abramovich, and M. Pensky, "Classification with many classes: Challenges and pluses", *J. Multivariate Anal,* p. 104536, 2019.
[http://dx.doi.org/10.1016/j.jmva.2019.104536]

[21] C. Zhang, J. Bin, X. Peng, R. Wang, R. Halldearn, and Z. Liu, "AIS data driven general vessel destination prediction: A random forest based approach," *Transp. Res. Part C Emerg. Technol.,* vol. 118, p. 102729, 2020.

[22] L. Shen, and E.C. Tan, "Reducing multiclass cancer classification to binary by output coding and SVM", *Comput. Biol. Chem,* vol. 30, no. 1, pp. 63-71, 2006.
[http://dx.doi.org/10.1016/j.compbiolchem.2005.10.008] [PMID: 16321568]

[23] K. Chatzikokolakis, D. Zissis, G. Spiliopoulos, and K. Tserpes, "A comparison of supervised learning schemes for the detection of search and rescue (SAR) vessel patterns", *GeoInformatica,* pp. 1-22, 2019.
[http://dx.doi.org/10.1007/s10707-019-00365-y]

[24] J. Devlin, M.-W. Chang, K. Lee, and K. Toutanova, "BERT: Pre-training of Deep Bidirectional Transformers for Language Understanding",

[25] C. Doulkeridis, Q. Qu, G.A. Vouros, and J.B. Rocha-Junior, "Guest editorial: special issue on mobility analytics for spatio-temporal and social data", *GeoInformatica,* vol. 23, pp. 323-327, 2019.
[http://dx.doi.org/10.1007/s10707-019-00374-x]

CHAPTER 2

Artificial Intelligence in Mental Health

Suresh Kumar Mukhiya[1,*], **Amin Aminifar**[1], **Fazle Rabbi**[1,3], **Violet Ka I. Pun**[1,2] and **Yngve Lamo**[1]

[1] *Department of Computing, Mathematics, and Physics, Western Norway University of Applied Sciences, Bergen, Norway*

[2] *University of Oslo, Norway*

[3] *University of Bergen, Norway*

Abstract: Managing the prevalence of mental health problems is both socially and economically challenging. Technological advancement in recent decades has provided potential solutions to this issue. In particular, Artificial Intelligence (AI) is one of the research areas that has expanded into several behavioural, neurological and mental healthcare areas by fulfilling the main objectives of P4 medicine - personalized, predictive, preventive, and participative medicine. In this chapter, we give an overview of recent applications of AI for screening, detection, and treatment of mental health problems; summarize the economic and social implications; present a systematic overview of which AI technologies are used for the different mental disorders and identify challenges for further development. Based on this, we identify some future research questions that could be solved with the use of AI in mental healthcare. The chapter concludes with an in-depth discussion on the key challenges of the application of AI in mental health interventions.

Keywords: Affective Computing, Ambient Intelligence, Artificial Intelligence, Cognitive Based Therapy, Deep Learning, Internet Delivered Treatment, Machine Learning, Mental health, P4 medicine.

INTRODUCTION

Recent studies conducted by WHO [1] as well as EU Green Papers [2, 3] reveal that the prevalence of having mental or neurological disorders has escalated over the past few decades. Dealing with mental health issues can be economically, physically, and emotionally challenging for the patients, their families and friends, and the society. For instance, the healthcare costs in the United States of America had a rise from 27.2 billion dollars (only 5 percent of GDP) in 1960 to 3200

* **Corresponding author Suresh Kumar Mukhiya:** DepaDepartment of Computing, Mathematics, and Physics, Western Norway University of Applied Sciences, Bergen, Norway; E-mail: skmu@hvl.no

Terje Solsvik Kristensen (Ed.)

billion dollars (17.8 percent of GDP) in   2015 [4, 5]. According to the report from World Economic Forum in 2010, the global cost of mental illness was approximated to be $2.5 trillion US dollars and is anticipated to be more than $6 trillion dollars by 2030 [6]. The same report justifies that mental health costs are the biggest health-related global economic burden. In addition to this, the patients' quality of life and standard of living are affected, they suffer from reduced productivity, problems with social interactions, and even suicidal tendencies.

It is not uncommon that healthcare systems operate on limited resources with a shortage of healthcare professionals and inadequate funding. Physicians do not have the luxury to spend much time investigating individual patients' cases. To cope with this situation, one must improve the existing healthcare system with efficiency and automation. We need a healthcare system that supports a flexible and interoperable information exchange that facilitates innovation in wellness and healthcare. However, this task is challenging due to the complex nature of health problems, which entails dynamic processes in terms of both the treatment being delivered and the cognitive process of the clinicians and the patients [7]. In addition to continuously observing the patients and evaluating the treatment decisions, the clinicians also need to prescribe different medications and adjust the treatments accordingly. Applying artificial intelligence (AI) in the mental health domain is a potential means to provide more efficient and adaptive treatments for mental health problems. The use of AI has the potential to reduce treatment time and cost and increase the effectiveness and the quality of the procedure. In brief, AI in mental healthcare provides exciting opportunities and benefits, including:

- Methodologies for learning, understanding, and reasoning to assist healthcare professionals with clinical decision-support, testing, diagnostics, and care management.

- To find a better correlation between the patient's symptoms and treatment outcome and adapt the treatment to the patients' needs.

- Introduction of self-management treatment programs using ambient intelligent m-health1 apps that can learn and adapt according to user preferences, user needs, and user contexts.

- Improvement in public health by assisting in the detection of health risks and intelligent recommendations of appropriate interventions.

In this book chapter, we give an overview of recent applications of AI for screening, detection, and treatment of mental health problems, we identify challenges for further development, and summarize the economic and social implications. We present a systematic overview of which AI technologies are used for different mental disorders. Based on this, we identify some future research questions that could be solved with the use of AI in mental health. Note that we have limited our work to discuss the use of AI for screening, and therapeutic interventions, hence the use of AI-related to psychopharmacology is out of the scope of this work.

The outline of the rest of this chapter is as follows: In Section Mental Health Treatment, we present some background information related to mental health treatments and artificial intelligence. Motivational factors of using AI in the mental health domain are further discussed in Section Motivation. In Section Data Collection and Preparation, we present an overview of data collection and preparation methods for AI in mental health. In Section Mental Health and AI, we outline some of the key AI technologies being used in the mental health domain. Section Challenges is dedicated to discussions and results. Finally, in Section Discussion about Future Development, we summarise our findings and propose potential future directions of research in AI and mental health.

MENTAL HEALTH TREATMENT

Current treatment approaches to mental health morbidities involve psychopharmacology, Cognitive Based Therapy (CBT), Cognitive Remedial Therapy (CRT), mindfulness, music therapy, gamification, and meditation, *etc.* All these approaches follow a common workflow where one starts by assessment and diagnosis in the form of a screening of the patient, then one decides and executes the treatment before one evaluates and monitors the treatment outcome [8]. The screening phase of the mental health practice includes the acquisition of relevant information from the patient and compare it with the current knowledge base for establishing a diagnosis and treatment paradigm. The elicitation of pertinent information involves the application of standardized psychometric questionnaires like PHQ-9^2, MADRS^3, MADRAS-S^2 for depression, in-person interviews, or use of ICT technologies including emails, chat, instant messaging, mobile phones and client peer support system.

MOTIVATION

Traditional medical practice has been reactive, meaning that doctors intervene when there is a disease [9]. However, the advancement in technologies, theories, and concepts over the last decades has preluded the transition towards anticipatory medicine centered on health and not disease. This is referred to as P4 medicine

(Personalized, Predictive, Preventive, and participatory) [9, 10]. P4 medicine is deeply rooted and connected to data science, especially AI. The use of AI in mental healthcare contributes to fulfilling the main objective of P4 medicine.

- *Personalized*: Personalization can be based on genomics and other biological high throughput data [10]; on bio-images (MRT, CT scans); Electronic Medical Records (EMRs); health claims; from other wearable sensors and mobile health applications.

- *Predictive*: Personalized information can assist in the prediction of risk factors and unusual patterns in each individual.

- *Preventive*: Provided the risk being predicted beforehand, prophylactic measures can be taken to decrease the risk.

- *Participative*: Medical interventions require the participation of the patients, therapists, and other medical practitioners.

In addition to these, the use of AI in the mental health domain offers the following benefits:

Adaptiveness and Adherence

The uniqueness of mental health problems makes it challenging to develop a technology that collaborates with human behaviour and creates positive outcomes and measurements. It is because screening and treatments for mental problems are patient specific. Thus, it is important for the technological solutions to be adaptive in order to provide personalized decisions both for screening and treatments [11].

Adherence and adoption of AI-based treatment systems depend on the patients trust in the technology, which in turn leads to trust-related behaviour [12].

In addition to trust in the system, other determinants of adherence include ease of use, availability and accessiblity of the system, structural assurance, perceived usefulness, ubiquity, system compliance to health standards, and privacy [12, 13].

Automation of the Treatment Process

The automation of treatments for mental health problems can enhance accuracy and efficiency, reduce cost and time consumption, improve coordination, and remove transportation barriers. An automatic treatment system could also improve communication between practitioners and patients. Moreover, AI powered systems are not susceptible to fatigue, boredom, forgetfulness, bias, or burnout [14]. People with mental health morbidity require continuous follow up in form of monitoring, screening, and treatment. Moreover, each patient's condition and screening data is different from another. There is no single clinical characterization of depression, anxiety, bipolar disorder, or any other mental or neurological disorders. These indicate that the diagnosis of mental health illness is time-consuming and subjective in nature. Hence, it is challenging yet technically required to automate this process of screening and treatment that can be done by deploying AI-powered treatment systems in the mental health domain.

Scalability

Advancement in AI has a positive effect on behavioural and mental healthcare fields. For example, computing techniques for learning, understanding, and reasoning can help healthcare practitioners with clinical decision making, testing, diagnostics, and care management. Moreover, AI-powered healthcare systems can provide remote monitoring of patients, collaborative consultation, early detection of health risks, and informed interventions. Such AI systems can be used in personalized treatment for mental health patients using a virtual therapist in everyone's pocket, hence, enforcing pervasive mental healthcare. In this context, pervasive healthcare refers to healthcare facilities for anyone, anytime and anywhere, without geographical, chronological, and other restraints. Pervasive healthcare aims to improve healthcare coverage with optimal quality. The use of AI in mental healthcare promotes such pervasiveness increasing scalability.

Personal Stigma (Self-aware Treatment Systems)

The study conducted by Sweeney [15] shows that people suffering from mental health issues undergo a fear of discomfort in facing a practitioner or choosing services, and fear of public opinions. This has direct consequences for the therapeutic relationship, engagement with services, and engagement with society. A similar conclusion has been drawn by a study conducted in the United States [16]; the potency of the stigma of mental problems is one of the reasons why some ethnic minority group members do not seek or adequately participate in the treatment process. Lack of such engagement has adverse outcomes on the treatment of mental health problems [16]. By offering an AI-powered medical technology that can give self-aware screening and treatment, one can help reducing discomfort associated with traditional face-to-face services. Moreover, according to the research by Gratch *et al.* [17], patients may prefer to encounter intelligent systems rather than a human therapist to overcome the experience of anxiety, discussion of intimate and private issues. The notion is justified by initial evidence indicating that patients may be comfortable disclosing information to virtual intelligent machines rather than medical staff [17].

AI for A Personalized Recommendation

One of the key components for increasing user adherence with AI technologies is reaching mental health patients with the most relevant personalized information at the right time. This can be realized in practice by the use of AI in a recommendation engine. The use of recommendation engines in mental healthcare raises intriguing possibilities like providing personalized behavioural counselling, finding the most appropriate, and affording care by searching a database of symptoms and causes like iTriage [18], proving personalized information in mental health domain and assisting clinicians with knowledge acquisition. These recommendation engines provide new ways to understand problems, causes, symptoms, and possible treatments in time. Fuelled by AI and data-driven predictive analytics, the recommendation made is proactive and personalized and with the potential to change the user behaviour and decision-making process about their healthcare.

DATA COLLECTION AND PREPARATION

Data collection and preparation are two major tasks in the application of AI techniques. With the phenomenal growth in the IoT industry, data collected *via* sensor devices and IoT allows substantial assistance in caretaking and diagnosis in the healthcare domain. For instance, with the movement data captured in wearable devices for Alzheimer patients, caretakers can be notified if they move outside of their known range of boundaries. In addition, the data collected can be utilized in AI to assist in making a decision on patient-specific treatment plans. In addition, edge/fog computing allows shifting data processing to a real-world environment, like mobile phones and wearable devices, which enables personalised self-adaptive home treatment for mental patients.

For data analysis, the idea of entropy, introduced by Claude Shannon in 1948 [19], has been adapted in the area of data science and machine learning and used as a means to calculate information gain and uncertainty in the dataset [20]. For example, dataset *A* has a higher degree of entropy if the predictions are more uncertain than dataset *B* where the predictions are less uncertain. The quality of dataset *A* can be increased, *i.e.*, the entropy could be decreased, by the data preparation process including noise removal, partitioning and/or combining, labelling, *etc.* For example, we wish to predict the suicidal incident of depressed patients from a dataset that contains various types of depressed patients, such as unipolar and bipolar. We will gain information (overall entropy loss) if we partition our dataset into two, as it is more likely for bipolar patients to commit suicide. Composing two datasets can also contribute to gaining information, *i.e.*, obtaining a lower degree of entropy if the composition reduces the randomness in the data. For example, the stress data of depressed patients could be found totally random but combining stress data of depressed patients with their activity data could provide useful insight into the behavioural patterns of the patients. This is the main reason why data preparation task has been taken into the main consideration of data scientists.

In a recent survey [21] conducted by CrowdFlower reporting on the most frequent tasks performed by 80 data scientists, it shows that the data scientists spend 79 percent of their time in non-machine learning algorithms selection, testing, and refinement. This includes 60 percent of the time in data cleaning and organizing, and 19 percent of the time in data acquisition and collection. In mental health screening and treatment, different types of data incorporate electronic health records (medical notes, electronic readings from medical devices, physical examination notes, clinical images), sensor data (heart rate, electrodermal activities, eyes movement data, brain activities, electroglottograph (EGG) data), audio and video data, virtual reality (VR) data and structured or unstructured text data.

A multitude of these datasets is generated by sensors, including external and wearable sensors. External sensors, incorporated in video cameras, microphones, motion sensors, and eye movement detectors (*e.g.*, Tobii[10]), are not necessary to be in immediate contact with the patients. Wearable sensors refer to portable devices that can be worn by the patients. The most common wearable sensors include heart rate monitors, gyroscopes, accelerometers, galvanic skin response monitors and eye movement detectors, and VR sets. Wearable devices come with embedded communication platforms with feedback and interaction capabilities. These capabilities can potentially be used for data acquisition, which can be consumed by AI algorithms to allow a deeper analysis of the users' conditions and provide personalized treatments. For example, using motion activities captured by smartphones for activity recognition has become an active research area. Activity recognition has a variety of applications ranging from personal biometric signatures, assistive technology, elderly care, health and fitness monitoring, indoor localization, and navigation [22, 23]. Moreover, the studies claim that smartphones are becoming the main platform for human activity recognition due to its low installation cost and unobtrusive feature. Smart watches, bands or bracelets can communicate with smartphones through microservices, this combination can facilitate multimodal data collection from patients. In addition to smartphones and smart watches, actigraphy devices [24] are used for monitoring activity patterns, sleep patterns, and predict sleep related disorders. Electronic textiles [25], with flexible sensors embedded in the clothes [26] tobe worn as patches on the skin, are used to sense the environment and utilized in data collection for mental health screening and diagnostics.

Challenges in Data Collection

With several heterogeneous types of sensing modalities from which patient's behavioural data can be procured into an analytic platform, it is essential to consider privacy, storage, data integrity, transmission process, and data labelling methods. Maintaining privacy during the data acquisition phase is necessary to protect the patient's integrity. This can be enforced by anonymizing all the collected data, encrypting them, and transmitting them to a secure server utilizing a secure communication channel. Moreover, it falls under ethical consideration to enlighten patients about the type of data being collected, intended use, implications, and hence get proper consent from them. Another aspect to consider during data collection is storage. The portable devices like tablets and smart-phones come with small internal memory that captures the data, whereas for smart watches data can be synchronised periodically to smartphones *via* Bluetooth and is further stored into a secured server.

MENTAL HEALTH AND AI

In this section, we outline various AI techniques and how they are used in assessment, detection, treatment, or monitoring of mental health morbidities. Table **1** provides a list of AI techniques applied in different types of mental health illnesses.

Natural Language Processing (NLP)

NLP is a sub-field of AI that combines linguistics with computer science to process and understand human language and is often referred to as *computational linguistics* or *statistical text classification*. NLP has been proven efficient in several behavioural and mental healthcare applications. In addition, NLP, together with machine learning (ML), enables interactions between computers and human users in terms of text and voice. Various conversational agents [27, 28] have been proposed for psychiatric counselling and mental health intervention. The study [29] conducted at Stanford School of Medicine concludes that conversational agents are a feasible, engaging, and effective way to deliver CBT.

NLP has also been used for scanning and semantic analysis for health surveillance; NLP combined with ML techniques is used to scan treatment sessions and identify patterns [30, 31]. This technique has been useful in training and fidelity monitoring in clinical trials.

Table 1. Different AI techniques used in various mental health illnesses; SAD = Social Anxiety Disorder; ADHD = Attention Deficit Hyperactivity Disorder; BD = Bipolar Disorder; SRA = Suicidal Risk Assessment; AD = Alzheimer's Disease; BCI = Brain Computer Interfacing; AmI=Ambient Intelligence, MP = Machine Perception, AC = Affective Computing; SVM = Support Vector Machine; BC = Bayesian Classification, CNN= Convolutional Neural Network, LSTM = Long Short-Term Memory, RNN = Recurrent Neural Network.

AI Techniques	Classification and Clustering Algorithms	Speech Analysis and Neural Network	AmI, MP, AC	BCI	Robotics	Augmented Reality	NLP and Conversational Agent
Depression & Stress		[60]	AC [39]	[47, 46]	[73, 5]	[74]	[28, 29, 31]
SAD		[64, 23]			[5]	[35]	[29]
BD	SVM [61]	[55]	MRI [67]				[75]
ADHD	SVM [62]		MP on MRI data [68]	[72]		[72]	AmI [76]
Schizophrenia		[56]	MRI [67]		[45]	[53]	[22 ,23]
Autism	[10, 63]		AC [69]	[46]	[40, 4]	[34]	[63]
SRA		[60]	AmI [22]				[77]
AD Mild Cognitive Impairment	[57]	[65], CNN and RNN [66], LSTM [66]	MP on MRI data [70]		[42]		[66]
Parkinson's Disease	BC [13, 78]	[15]	MP [71]	[47, 7]			

Virtual Reality (VR) and Augmented Reality (AR)

Augmented Reality or mixed reality includes virtual reality with the real world by superimposing computer-generated graphics with live video imagery [32]. The application of AR and VR in mental and behavioural healthcare include training and healthcare education [33], educating children with autism to learn facial emotions [34], creation of virtual stimuli for patients with Social Anxiety disorder [35], real-time therapeutic virtual coaching, and clinician training with real-time supervisions. Moreover, AR technologies have shown to be capable of projecting information and images into contact lenses [36] and directly into the retina of the human eye [37], allowing the user to view what appears to be a conventional video display drifting in the space in front of them. Such advancement in AR technologies helps in creating effective mental health intervention systems.

Affective Computing

Affective Computing refers to emotional recognition by machines, emotion modelling, affective user modelling as well as the representation and interpretation of emotion by robots and virtual agents. Understanding the emotions of mental health patients can help in two distinct perspectives:

- To understand the mental health state of a patient, which is strongly correlated with emotions, as suggested by the meta-analysis [38]; and
- To know the status of treatment provided to the patients.

Understanding the status of treatment allows us to evaluate the treatment provided and to comprehend whether the administered treatment is working or not. Affective computation incorporates NLP, ML, and computer vision to analyse linguistics, physical gestures, social signs, biological or physiological markers, as well as behavioural markers in humans to compute overall emotions. For example, DARPA (Defence Advanced Research Project Agency) created an affective detection system [39] to improve the psychological health of military personnel and detect distress in humans from inputs like sleeping patterns, voice, and data communication.

Robotics

Despite nascent in mental health, the potential of the application of robotics in healthcare is wide, including the administration of interventions for conditions ranging from cognitive impairments to autism spectrum disorder. Recent studies report the following applications of robotics in mental healthcare including: a survey article about the use of robotics for people with Autism Spectrum Disorders [40], robot-based intervention to encourage activity engagement and ambulation among a small number of participants with severe physical and cognitive disabilities [41], a review on the use of robotics in treatment of dementia [42], the use of robotics as a companion to improve psychosocial outcomes and decrease loneliness [43], the use of humanoid robots to train clinicians to better interact with patients during face-to-face interaction [44], and diagnosis of schizophrenia using robotics [45].

Brain Computer Interface (BCI)

The amalgamation of BCI and AI technologies has the potential to repair or improve cognition abilities in a human being, or to restore cerebral functions damaged by strokes, brain injuries, and even aging [46]. In addition, brain implant is a neurological procedure where electrodes are implanted into the brain to stimulate targeted areas of depression, chronic pain, OCD, Tourette's syndrome, and Parkinson's' disease [7, 47].

Machine Perception and Ambient Intelligence

Machine perception incorporates required hardware and software to recognize images, sounds, smell, and touch in order to provide the notion of interaction between humans and machines. Facial recognition is one of the hot topics buzzing these days. As discussed in Section 4, machine perception and sensing involve various types of sensors that capture the user motion and location information, GPS information, environmental information, physiological information (*e.g.*, Electro encephalography, Electro cardiography, electrodermal activity, blood pressure, *etc.*) and medical imaging like magnetic resonance imaging (MRI). These capabilities of ICT technologies give rise to a new paradigm in Information Technology, referred to as Ambient Intelligence (AmI).

In this computing paradigm, unlike traditional input and output, sensors and processors will be integrated into everyday objects that will work together to support inhabitants. AmI, in collaboration with AI, can provide interpretations of the contextual information obtained from embedded sensors and will adapt the environment to the user needs in a transparent and expected manner [48].

CHALLENGES

The practical use of AI technologies and its related offshoots in mental healthcare is swiftly propelling and shows many interesting opportunities and advantages. The advancement of hardware technologies and embedded systems has provided opportunities to capture, store, and understand human biological, physiological, and behavioural markers. These markers are used to create Ambient Intelligent systems that, by enhancing innovative human-machine interactions, give assistance to patients with mental/physical limitations. However, there are several challenges associated with it. In the following, we are going to explore some technical, design, ethical, and privacy issues.

Technical Issues

Despite the rapid advancement in technologies, a multitude of technological barriers remain rooted as a major challenge in the field of AI, such as computer vision and robotics. One of such issues related to cognitive reasoning is outlined in Moravec's Paradox asserting that high-level reasoning requires very little computation, but low-level sensorimotor skills require huge computational power [49]. Moreover, creating human like reasoning intelligence is still an intricate research topic for the field of AI. Some of the computational complexity and technological barriers are subjective to hardware resources, which are likely to be solved in a not-so-distant future [47].

Security and Privacy Issues

Privacy and security are among the most important concerns in the healthcare domain. This is due to the increasing amount of personal and medical records that are stored and transmitted electronically, particularly when it involves genetic information [50], and the growing number of medical devices and systems. To show the importance of privacy in these systems, consider, for instance, an IoT system in which a monitoring device sends the physiological signals of the patient to a server from which the doctor receives the patient's records on her/his computer. Then, the medicine is prescribed based on this data. An *adversary* may manipulate the medical data after sending it from the monitoring device and before arriving on the server. The physicians will then prescribe according to the manipulated medical data. This is a *man-in-the-middle* attack that, clearly, can have irreversible consequences and may even jeopardize the patient's life. Thus, privacy and security are among the most important components of healthcare systems that we should take into consideration the infrastructure of such systems. To this end, we may address such issues either from the machine-learning-fr-security or the security-for-machine-learning perspectives.

Today, companies suffer more economic loss through electronic theft than through physical theft [51]. Three important processes for attaining security are *threat prevention, detection*, and *response*. Threat prevention is a necessity to protect systems, infrastructure, and information from cyber-attacks; firewalls are a good example of prevention systems. In parallel, it is important to understand that not all the attacks can be averted in the beginning. These kinds of attacks are inevitable, and there should be a mechanism for identifying and responding to such attacks [52]. This stresses the importance of effective detection systems for maintaining computer systems along with preventive measures.

During the past two decades, the application of machine learning and data mining techniques for intrusion detection systems has been a topic of broad interest.

Surveys and reviews on this topic [53 - 55] indicate that artificial intelligence is being intensively used for intrusion detection systems. In such systems, learning algorithms can be trained to either distinguish between non-attack and attack situations or detect abnormal situations.

On the other hand, machine learning can be considered as a double-edged sword. Today, we intensively use machine learning to extract novel patterns from health data, and we are not fully aware of its pitfalls. The data breach of medical or health-related information can involve individuals' electronic medical records or medical billing information from patients' health insurance. The disclosed data may be sold in the black market [8, 9, 56, 57] or used against an individual, *e.g.*, against important politicians. According to the recent studies [58, 59], the output of machine-learning algorithms may reveal some individuals' sensitive information, and as a result, privacy will be violated. For instance, the output of a machine-learning algorithm may reveal the existence of an important politician's data among the data for patients with a special medical disorder using a membership inference attack [59]. Therefore, the possible medical data leakages from the result of machine-learning algorithms require further studies.

Moreover, the European parliament and the council introduced the regulations on the protection of natural persons with respect to the processing and movement of personal data. These regulations, General Data Protection Regulation (GDPR) [3], must be observed by businesses, organizations, and companies operating in the EU. Below are some requirements for data protection and information security set by GDPR:

- When they collect personal data, companies must specify what it will be used for, and it should not be used for anything else.

- Companies are supposed to minimize the amount of data they collect and keep, limiting to what is strictly necessary for those purposes—they're supposed to put limits on how long they hold that data, too.

- Companies must be able to tell people what data they hold on them, and what's being done with it.

- Companies should be able to alter or get rid of people's personal data if requested.

- If personal data is used to make automated decisions about individuals, companies must be able to explain the logic behind the decision-making process.

All these regulations pose challenges for applying AI specially in the healthcare domain. Since many machine learning algorithms are not rule based, it is hard to disclose algorithmic transparency to the user. Data anonymization is a way to get rid of the regulations, but there are some loopholes that allow re-identification of personal identification of users.

Ethical Issues

In earlier sections, we have mentioned that patients feel comfortable to communicate with artificial agents; however, this approach raises some ethical issues. Ethical issues in advanced artificial intelligence are among the important research areas which require special attention. Some philosophers argue that AI has the capability to bring about human extinction specially for the application areas where safety, security, and human's privacy is a concern.

With today's machine learning algorithms, it is not possible to achieve 100% accuracy to detect the mental condition of patients. Therefore, the application of AI should be limited to handle cases where the conditions of the patients are not very critical. Mental health professionals should be in control of providing care to patients with serious mental conditions. AI can ultimately enable them to do their jobs more effectively by treating a growing volume of patients.

Design Issues

To promote the use of Internet Delivered Treatment, it is essential to ensure good usability of the system. Chatbot or voice enabled applications are becoming more available nowadays and bring more potential in disseminating mental health treatment programs. However, it is important to ensure that the conversation with the patient takes place in such a way that the patients do not get upset or angry with the system. Therefore, a lot of design effort is required in order to develop AI enabled treatment programs.

The review done in [10] highlights three important challenges of using AI in the realization of P4 medicine objectives:

- *Insufficient Prediction Performance for the Clinical Practice:* ML methods describe complex correlations present in the dataset mathematically. Their success depends on the number of samples in the training data sets and the signal-to-noise ratio [2]. It is, therefore, essential to identify the right data modalities. Shortcomings in these datasets can result in loss of prediction performance.

- *Problems in Interpretation*: ML methods can precisely predict complex patterns in large datasets. However, they are unable to provide a deeper theoretical, mechanistic, or casual understanding of an observed phenomenon. ML models capture statistical dependencies, such as correlation in the datasets. However, correlation does not imply causation. Lack of such a mechanistic interpretation of predication hinders the acceptance of ML-based solutions despite the creation of an acceptable ML-based prediction.

- *Insufficient Validation for the Clinical Practice* Any ML-based models in clinical practice require rigorous validation, including internal validation during initial discovery; external validation based on an independent cohort, and validation to demonstrate the benefits compared to standard care. The entire process of validation is time-consuming and costly, hence creating a challenging task in AI-based interventions.

DISCUSSION ABOUT FUTURE DEVELOPMENT

Although, as mentioned in the previous section, detection and analysis of mental patients' conditions are not reliable and accurate enough to handle advanced critical cases, applying AI and ML techniques to the domain of mental healthcare are still beneficial in various aspects. From the perspective of clinicians: it allows early detection of mental illness, provides decision support regarding treatments, issues timely warning about abnormal behaviour of mental patients; from the perspective of the patients, it enables personalized self-adaptive home treatments, provides analytical reports to the patients and/or to the clinicians, which can raise the patients' awareness about the treatment progress and their own mental conditions before the next appointment with the doctors; for the caretakers, it gives an overview of the patients' mental conditions which allows the caretakers to give appropriate care and alerts them for further action, *e.g.*, contact the doctors.

One potential development in the mental healthcare domain with AI techniques is to use mobile applications, which are connected to wearable sensors, to collect biological markers. The biological markers can include voice, body movement, body temperature, and so on. With AI techniques like cognitive computation and machine learning, the collected data can provide insightful information about mental or neurological morbidity. This information can be used by clinicians to create personalized evidence-based treatments. If these treatments can be performed at home by the patients themselves, can be performed through applications like mobile, VR applications, and voice assistant, the continuous data collection and analysis with the AI techniques can be further employed to adapt the treatments accordingly. In addition, the analytical results also allow the patients to self-assess and evaluate their own mental conditions.

CONCLUSION

The diagnosis and assessment of mental health morbidities are difficult and time-consuming tasks; success often relies on the skill and experience of a clinician in extracting suitable diagnostic information from a patient, who, by definition, will have diminished outlook, motivation, and cognitive functioning. There is a substantial necessity for simple, inexpensive, and automated objective diagnostic aid for use in both primary care settings and specialist clinics. Such a tool could be game-changing in terms of patient assessment, monitoring, providing immediate feedback, and therapeutic mental health advice. AI can answer to the development of such game-changing tools.

The integration of AI for continuous monitoring, screening, and treatment of mental health morbidity is still clearly in its infancy. However, with the growth of AI, and associated ICT technologies in the facilitation of supporting complex computation, higher storage, and faster processing capabilities ensure a good future of AI in the mental health domain. Moreover, with the growing advancement in graphics and animation, speech recognition, natural language processing, and computing power, we can expect the creation of adaptive technologies closely coupled with AI to provide personalized screening and treatment in the mental health domain. However, there is a necessity for an interdisciplinary effort, including medical practitioners, physicians, patient advocates, data scientists, regulatory agencies, and health insurance organizations.

NOTES

[1]"mHealth | HIMSS." https://www.himss.org/library/mhealth
[2]"The PHQ-9 - NCBI." https://www.ncbi.nlm.nih.gov/pmc/articles/PMC1495268/
[3]"Comparison Between the Montgomery-Asberg Depression Rating ...." https://www.ncbi.nlm.nih.gov/pmc/articles/PMC4578910/. Accessed 6 May 2019.

CONSENT FOR PUBLICATION

Not applicable.

CONFLICT OF INTEREST

The author declares no conflict of interest, financial or otherwise.

ACKNOWLEDGEMENTS

This publication is a part of the INTROducing Mental health through Adaptive Technology (INTROMAT) project, funded by Norwegian Research Council (259293/o70).

REFERENCES

[1]   WHO, *World Health Report,* 2018.https://www.who.int

[2]   J. Fan, F. Han, and H. Liu, "Challenges of big data analysis", *Natl. Sci. Rev.,* vol. 1, no. 2, pp. 293-314, 2014.
[http://dx.doi.org/10.1093/nsr/nwt032] [PMID: 25419469]

[3]   GD Regulation, "Regulation (eu) 2016/679 of the european parliament and of the council of 27 april 2016 on the protection of natural persons with regard to the processing of personal data and on the free movement of such data and repealing directive 95/46", *Official Journal of the European Union (OJ),* vol. 59, no. 1-8, p. 294, 2016.

[4]   B. Scassellati, H. Admoni, and M. Matarić, "Robots for use in autism research", *Annu. Rev. Biomed. Eng.,* vol. 14, pp. 275-294, 2012.
[http://dx.doi.org/10.1146/annurev-bioeng-071811-150036] [PMID: 22577778]

[5]   S.M. Rabbitt, A.E. Kazdin, and B. Scassellati, "Integrating socially assistive robotics into mental healthcare interventions: applications and recommendations for expanded use", *Clin. Psychol. Rev.,* vol. 35, pp. 35-46, 2015.
[http://dx.doi.org/10.1016/j.cpr.2014.07.001] [PMID: 25462112]

[6]   DE Bloom, E Cafiero, E Jané-Llopis, S Abrahams-Gessel, LR Bloom, S Fathima, AB Feigl, T Gaziano, A Hamandi, M Mowafi, and D O'Farrell, "The global economic burden of noncommunicable diseases", *Program on the Global Demography of Aging,* 2012.

[7]   V.L. Patel, D.R. Kaufman, and J.F. Arocha, "Emerging paradigms of cognition in medical decision-making", *J. Biomed. Inform.,* vol. 35, no. 1, pp. 52-75, 2002.
[http://dx.doi.org/10.1016/S1532-0464(02)00009-6] [PMID: 12415726]

[8]   Mukhiya Suresh Kumar, Rabbi Fazle, Pun Ka I, and Lamo Yngve, "An architectural design for self-reporting e-health systems", *Proceedings of the 1st International Workshop on Software Engineering for Healthcare (SEH '19),* 2019pp. 1-8

[9]   P. Sobradillo, F. Pozo, and A. Agustí, "P4 medicine: the future around the corner", *Arch. Bronconeumol.,* vol. 47, no. 1, pp. 35-40, 2011.
[http://dx.doi.org/10.1016/S1579-2129(11)70006-4] [PMID: 21190770]

[10]   H. Fröhlich, R. Balling, N. Beerenwinkel, O. Kohlbacher, S. Kumar, T. Lengauer, M.H. Maathuis, Y. Moreau, S.A. Murphy, T.M. Przytycka, M. Rebhan, H. Röst, A. Schuppert, M. Schwab, R. Spang, D. Stekhoven, J. Sun, A. Weber, D. Ziemek, and B. Zupan, "From hype to reality: data science enabling personalized medicine", *BMC Med.,* vol. 16, no. 1, p. 150, 2018.
[http://dx.doi.org/10.1186/s12916-018-1122-7] [PMID: 30145981]

[11]   S.K. Mukhiya, J.D. Wake, Y. Inal, and Y. Lamo, "Adaptive systems for internet-delivered psychological treatments", *IEEE Access,* vol. 8, pp. 112220-112236, 2020.
[http://dx.doi.org/10.1109/ACCESS.2020.3002793]

[12]   W. Fan, J. Liu, S. Zhu, and P.M. Pardalos, "Investigating the impacting factors for the healthcare professionals to adopt artificial intelligence-based medical diagnosis support system (AIMDSS)", *Ann. Oper. Res.,* pp. 1-26, 2018.

[13]   A. Procházka, O. Vyšata, and M. Vališ, "Bayesian classification and analysis of gait disorders using image and depth sensors of Microsoft Kinect", *Digital Signal Processing: A Review Journal,* 2015.

[14]   D.D. Luxton, "Recommendations for the ethical use and design of artificial intelligent care providers", *Artif. Intell. Med.,* vol. 62, no. 1, pp. 1-10, 2014.
[http://dx.doi.org/10.1016/j.artmed.2014.06.004] [PMID: 25059820]

[15]   A. Sweeney, S. Gillard, T. Wykes, and D. Rose, "The role of fear in mental health service users' experiences: a qualitative exploration", *Soc. Psychiatry Psychiatr. Epidemiol.,* vol. 50, no. 7, pp. 1079-1087, 2015.
[http://dx.doi.org/10.1007/s00127-015-1028-z] [PMID: 25702165]

[16]   F.A. Gary, "Stigma: barrier to mental health care among ethnic minorities", *Issues Ment. Health Nurs.,* vol. 26, no. 10, pp. 979-999, 2005.
[http://dx.doi.org/10.1080/01612840500280638] [PMID: 16283995]

[17]   J. Gratch, N. Wang, J. Gerten, E. Fast, and R. Duffy, "Creating rapport with virtual agents", *International workshop on intelligent virtual agents,* 2007pp. 125-138
[http://dx.doi.org/10.1007/978-3-540-74997-4_12]

[18]   *Itriage,* Healthagen, 2014. https://itunes.apple.com/us/app/itriage-health-doctor-symptoms/id3046 96939?mt=8

[19]   C.E. Shannon, Notes and other formats., "A Mathematical Theory of Communication", *Bell System Technical Journal,* vol. 27, pp. 379-656, 1948.

[20]   *Hands-on machine learning with Scikit-Learn and TensorFlow: concepts, tools, and techniques to build intelligent systems. A. Géron.,* O'Reilly Media: Sebastopol, CA, 2017.

[21]   *Data   Science   Report,*   CrowdFlower,   2016.   https://visit.figure-eight.com/rs/416-Z-E-142/images/CrowdFlower _DataScienceReport_2016.pdf

[22]   G.R. Alam, R. Haw, S.S. Kim, A.K. Azad, S.F. Abedin, and C.S. Hong, "Em-psychiatry: an ambient intelligent system for psychiatric emergency", *IEEE Trans. Industr. Inform.,* 2016.
[http://dx.doi.org/10.1109/TII.2016.2610191]

[23]   P. Laukka, C. Linnman, F. Åhs, A. Pissiota, Ö. Frans, V. Faria, and T. Furmark, "In a nervous voice: Acoustic analysis and perception of anxiety in social phobics' speech", *J. Nonverbal Behav.*
[http://dx.doi.org/10.1007/s10919-008-0055-9]

[24]   A. Sadeh, and C. Acebo, "The role of actigraphy in sleep medicine", *Sleep Med. Rev.,* vol. 6, no. 2, pp. 113-124, 2002.
[http://dx.doi.org/10.1053/smrv.2001.0182] [PMID: 12531147]

[25]   M Stoppa, and A Chiolerio, "Wearable electronics and smart textiles: a critical review", *Sensors,* vol. 14, no. 7, pp. 11957-92, 2014.

[26]   L.Y. Chen, B.C. Tee, A.L. Chortos, G. Schwartz, V. Tse, D.J. Lipomi, H.S. Wong, M.V. McConnell, and Z. Bao, "Continuous wireless pressure monitoring and mapping with ultra-small passive sensors for health monitoring and critical care", *Nat. Commun.,* vol. 5, p. 5028, 2014.
[http://dx.doi.org/10.1038/ncomms6028] [PMID: 25284074]

[27]   S. D'Alfonso, O. Santesteban-Echarri, S. Rice, G. Wadley, R. Lederman, C. Miles, J. Gleeson, and M. Alvarez-Jimenez, "Artificial intelligence-assisted online social therapy for youth mental health", *Front. Psychol.,* vol. 8, p. 796, 2017.
[http://dx.doi.org/10.3389/fpsyg.2017.00796] [PMID: 28626431]

[28]   K.J. Oh, D. Lee, B. Ko, and H.J. Choi, "A chatbot for psychiatric counseling in mental healthcare service based on emotional dialogue analysis and sentence generation", *In Proceedings - 18ᵗʰ IEEE International Conference on Mobile Data Management,* 2017
[http://dx.doi.org/10.1109/MDM.2017.64]

[29]   K.K. Fitzpatrick, A. Darcy, and M. Vierhile, "Delivering cognitive behavior therapy to young adults with symptoms of depression and anxiety using a fully automated conversational agent (woebot): a randomized   controlled   trial",   *JMIR   Ment.   Health,*   vol.   4,   no.   2,   p.   e19,

2017.https://mental.jmir.org/2017/2/e19
[http://dx.doi.org/10.2196/mental.7785] [PMID: 28588005]

[30]   Z.E. Imel, M. Steyvers, and D.C. Atkins, "Computational psychotherapy research: scaling up the evaluation of patient-provider interactions", *Psychotherapy (Chic),* vol. 52, no. 1, pp. 19-30, 2015.
[http://dx.doi.org/10.1037/a0036841] [PMID: 24866972]

[31]   S.K. Mukhiya, U. Ahmed, F. Rabbi, Pun Ka I, and Lamo Yngve, "Adaptation of IDPT system based on patient-authored text data using NLP", *2020 IEEE 33rd International Symposium on Computer-Based Medical Systems (CBMS),* 2020pp. 226-232

[32]   T.P. Caudell, and D.W. Mizell, "Augmented reality: an application of heads-up display technology to manual manufacturing processes", *Proceedings of the Twenty-Fifth Hawaii International Conference on System Sciences,* 1992 .
[http://dx.doi.org/10.1109/HICSS.1992.183317]

[33]   E. Zhu, A. Hadadgar, I. Masiello, and N. Zary, "Augmented reality in healthcare education: an integrative review", *PeerJ,* vol. 2, p. e469, 2014.
[http://dx.doi.org/10.7717/peerj.469] [PMID: 25071992]

[34]   M.R. Kandalaft, N. Didehbani, D.C. Krawczyk, T.T. Allen, and S.B. Chapman, "Virtual reality social cognition training for young adults with high-functioning autism", *J. Autism Dev. Disord.,* vol. 43, no. 1, pp. 34-44, 2013.
[http://dx.doi.org/10.1007/s10803-012-1544-6] [PMID: 22570145]

[35]   I.A. Chicchi Giglioli, F. Pallavicini, E. Pedroli, S. Serino, and G. Riva, "Augmented reality: a brand new challenge for the assessment and treatment of psychological disorders", *Comput. Math. Methods Med.,* p. 862942, 2015.
[http://dx.doi.org/10.1155/2015/862942] [PMID: 26339283]

[36]   A.R. Lingley, M. Ali, Y. Liao, R. Mirjalili, M. Klonner, M. Sopanen, and B.A. Parviz, "A single-pixel wireless contact lens display", *J. Micromech. Microeng.,* 2011.
[http://dx.doi.org/10.1088/0960-1317/21/12/125014]

[37]   E. Viirre, H. Pryor, S. Nagata, and T.A. Furness, "The virtual retinal display: A new technology for virtual reality and augmented vision in medicine", In: *In Studies in Health Technology and Informatics,* 1998.

[38]   N.S. Schutte, J.M. Malouff, E.B. Thorsteinsson, N. Bhullar, and S.E. Rooke, "A meta-analytic investigation of the relationship between emotional intelligence and health", *Pers. Individ. Dif.,* 2007.
[http://dx.doi.org/10.1016/j.paid.2006.09.003]

[39]   "Defense applied research project agency (darpa, 2014), journey of discovery starts toward understanding and treating networks of the brain", https://medicalxpress.com/news/2014-05-journ-y-discovery-networks-brain.html

[40]   J.J. Diehl, C.R. Crowell, M. Villano, K. Wier, K. Tang, and L.D. Riek, "Clinical applications of robots in autism spectrum disorder diagnosis and treatment", In: *In Comprehensive Guide to Autism,* 2013.

[41]   G.E. Lancioni, J. Sigafoos, M.F. O'Reilly, and N.N. Singh, *Assistive technology: Interventions for individuals with severe/profound and multiple disabilities.* Springer: New York, 2012.

[42]   E. Mordoch, A. Osterreicher, L. Guse, K. Roger, and G. Thompson, "Use of social commitment robots in the care of elderly people with dementia: a literature review", *Maturitas,* vol. 74, no. 1, pp. 14-20, 2013.
[http://dx.doi.org/10.1016/j.maturitas.2012.10.015] [PMID: 23177981]

[43]   H. Robinson, B. MacDonald, and E. Broadbent, "Physiological effects of a companion robot on blood pressure of older people in residential care facility: a pilot study", *Australas. J. Ageing,* vol. 34, no. 1, pp. 27-32, 2015.
[http://dx.doi.org/10.1111/ajag.12099] [PMID: 24373064]

[44]   M.J. Gonzales, M. Moosaei, and L.D. Riek, "A novel method for synthesizing naturalistic pain on

virtual patients", *In: Simulation in Healthcare,* 2013.

[45] M. Lavelle, P.G.T. Healey, and R. McCabe, "Participation during first social encounters in schizophrenia", *PLoS One,* vol. 9, no. 1, p. e77506, 2014.
[http://dx.doi.org/10.1371/journal.pone.0077506] [PMID: 24465363]

[46] R. Kurzweil, "The singularity is near - when human transcends biology", *Viking,* 2005.

[47] D.D. Luxton, "Artificial intelligence in behavioral and mental health care",

[48] G. Acampora, D.J. Cook, P. Rashidi, and A.V. Vasilakos, "A survey on ambient intelligence in healthcare", *Proceedings of the IEEE,* 2013
[http://dx.doi.org/10.1109/JPROC.2013.2262913]

[49] H. Moravec, *Mind Children: The Future of Robot and Human Intelligence.* Harvard University Press: Cambridge, MA, USA, 1988.

[50] "Genetic Information: genetic information discrimination", https://www.eeoc.gov/laws/ types/genetic.cfm

[51] "Firms lose more to electronic than physical theft", https://www.reuters.com/article/us-crim- -fraud/firms-lose-more-to-electronic-than-physical-theft-idUSTRE69H25820101018

[52] S. Jajodia, and S. Noel, "Topological vulnerability analysis: A powerful new approach for network attack prevention, detection, and response", *In Algorithms, Architectures and Information Systems Security,* pp. 285-305, 2009.

[53] D. Freeman, J. Bradley, A. Antley, E. Bourke, N. DeWeever, N. Evans, E. Černis, B. Sheaves, F. Waite, G. Dunn, M. Slater, and D.M. Clark, "Virtual reality in the treatment of persecutory delusions: randomised controlled experimental study testing how to reduce delusional conviction", *Br. J. Psychiatry,* vol. 209, no. 1, pp. 62-67, 2016.
[http://dx.doi.org/10.1192/bjp.bp.115.176438] [PMID: 27151071]

[54] CF Tsai, YF Hsu, CY Lin, and WY Lin, "Intrusion detection by machine learning: A review", *Expert Systems with Applications,* vol. 36, no. 10, pp. 11994-2000, 2009.

[55] Z. Pan, C. Gui, J. Zhang, J. Zhu, and D. Cui, "Detecting manic state of bipolar disorder based on support vector machine and gaussian mixture model using spontaneous speech", *Psychiatry Investig.,* vol. 15, no. 7, pp. 695-700, 2018.
[http://dx.doi.org/10.30773/pi.2017.12.15] [PMID: 29969852]

[56] C. Jahshan, J.K. Wynn, and M.F. Green, "Relationship between auditory processing and affective prosody in schizophrenia", *Schizophr. Res.,* vol. 143, no. 2-3, pp. 348-353, 2013.
[http://dx.doi.org/10.1016/j.schres.2012.11.025] [PMID: 23276478]

[57] C. Aguilar, E. Westman, J.S. Muehlboeck, P. Mecocci, B. Vellas, M. Tsolaki, I. Kloszewska, H. Soininen, S. Lovestone, C. Spenger, A. Simmons, and L.O. Wahlund, "Different multivariate techniques for automated classification of MRI data in Alzheimer's disease and mild cognitive impairment", *Psychiatry Res.,* vol. 212, no. 2, pp. 89-98, 2013.
[http://dx.doi.org/10.1016/j.pscychresns.2012.11.005] [PMID: 23541334]

[58] K. Chaudhuri, C. Monteleoni, and A.D. Sarwate, "Differentially private empirical risk minimization", *J. Mach. Learn. Res.,* vol. 12, no. Mar, pp. 1069-1109, 2011.
[PMID: 21892342]

[59] R. Shokri, M. Stronati, C. Song, and V. Shmatikov, "Membership inference attacks against machine learning models", *2017 IEEE Symposium on Security and Privacy (SP),* 2017pp. 3-18
[http://dx.doi.org/10.1109/SP.2017.41]

[60] N. Cummins, J. Epps, M. Breakspear, and R. Goecke, "An investigation of depressed speech detection: Features and normalization", *Twelfth Annual Conference of the International Speech Communication Association,* 2011

[61] B. Mwangi, M.J. Wu, I.E. Bauer, H. Modi, C.P. Zeni, G.B. Zunta-Soares, K.M. Hasan, and J.C.

Soares, "Predictive classification of pediatric bipolar disorder using atlas-based diffusion weighted imaging and support vector machines", *Psychiatry Res.,* vol. 234, no. 2, pp. 265-271, 2015.
[http://dx.doi.org/10.1016/j.pscychresns.2015.10.002] [PMID: 26459075]

[62] J. Anuradha, V. Tisha Ramachandran, K.V. Arulalan, and B.K. Tripathy, "Diagnosis of ADHD using SVM algorithm",

[63] J. Yuan, C. Holtz, T. Smith, and J. Luo, "Autism spectrum disorder detection from semi-structured and unstructured medical data", *EURASIP J. Bioinform. Syst. Biol.,* 2016.
[http://dx.doi.org/10.1186/s13637-017-0057-1] [PMID: 28203249]

[64] A. Craig, K. Hancock, Y. Tran, and M. Craig, "Anxiety levels in people who stutter: a randomized population study", *J. Speech Lang. Hear. Res.,* vol. 46, no. 5, pp. 1197-1206, 2003.
[http://dx.doi.org/10.1044/1092-4388(2003/093)] [PMID: 14575352]

[65] A. König, A. Satt, A. Sorin, R. Hoory, O. Toledo-Ronen, A. Derreumaux, V. Manera, F. Verhey, P. Aalten, P.H. Robert, and R. David, "Automatic speech analysis for the assessment of patients with predementia and Alzheimer's disease", *Alzheimers Dement. (Amst.),* vol. 1, no. 1, pp. 112-124, 2015.
[http://dx.doi.org/10.1016/j.dadm.2014.11.012] [PMID: 27239498]

[66] S. Karlekar, T. Niu, and M. Bansal, "Detecting linguistic characteristics of Alzheimer's dementia by interpreting neural models", *The 16th Annual Conference of the North American Chapter of the Association for Computational Linguistics,* 2018
[http://dx.doi.org/10.18653/v1/N18-2110]

[67] H.G. Schnack, M. Nieuwenhuis, N.E.M. van Haren, L. Abramovic, T.W. Scheewe, R.M. Brouwer, H.E. Hulshoff Pol, and R.S. Kahn, "Can structural MRI aid in clinical classification? A machine learning study in two independent samples of patients with schizophrenia, bipolar disorder and healthy subjects", *Neuroimage,* vol. 84, pp. 299-306, 2014.
[http://dx.doi.org/10.1016/j.neuroimage.2013.08.053] [PMID: 24004694]

[68] X. Peng, P. Lin, T. Zhang, and J. Wang, "Extreme learning machine-based classification of ADHD using brain structural MRI data", *PLoS One,* vol. 8, no. 11, p. e79476, 2013.
[http://dx.doi.org/10.1371/journal.pone.0079476] [PMID: 24260229]

[69] R. el Kaliouby, R. Picard, and S. Baron-Cohen, "Affective computing and autism", *Ann. N. Y. Acad. Sci.,* vol. 1093, pp. 228-248, 2006.
[http://dx.doi.org/10.1196/annals.1382.016] [PMID: 17312261]

[70] X. Liu, K. Chen, T. Wu, D. Weidman, F. Lure, and J. Li, "Use of multimodality imaging and artificial intelligence for diagnosis and prognosis of early stages of Alzheimer's disease", *Transl. Res.,* vol. 194, pp. 56-67, 2018.
[http://dx.doi.org/10.1016/j.trsl.2018.01.001] [PMID: 29352978]

[71] A. Procházka, O. Vyšata, M. Vališ, O. Ťupa, M. Schätz, and V. Mařík, "Use of the image and depth sensors of the Microsoft Kinect for the detection of gait disorders", *Neural Comput. Appl.,* 2015.
[http://dx.doi.org/10.1007/s00521-015-1827-x]

[72] D.A. Rohani, H.B.D. Sorensen, and S. Puthusserypady, "Brain-computer interface using P300 and virtual reality: A gaming approach for treating ADHD", *In 2014 36th Annual International Conference of the IEEE Engineering in Medicine and Biology Society,* 2014
[http://dx.doi.org/10.1109/EMBC.2014.6944403]

[73] M.R. Banks, L.M. Willoughby, and W.A. Banks, "Animal-assisted therapy and loneliness in nursing homes: use of robotic versus living dogs", *J. Am. Med. Dir. Assoc.,* vol. 9, no. 3, pp. 173-177, 2008.
[http://dx.doi.org/10.1016/j.jamda.2007.11.007] [PMID: 18294600]

[74] C.J. Falconer, A. Rovira, J.A. King, P. Gilbert, A. Antley, P. Fearon, N. Ralph, M. Slater, and C.R. Brewin, "Embodying self-compassion within virtual reality and its effects on patients with depression", *BJPsych Open,* vol. 2, no. 1, pp. 74-80, 2016.
[http://dx.doi.org/10.1192/bjpo.bp.115.002147] [PMID: 27703757]

[75]   V.M. Castro, J. Minnier, S.N. Murphy, I. Kohane, S.E. Churchill, V. Gainer, T. Cai, A.G. Hoffnagle, Y. Dai, S. Block, S.R. Weill, M. Nadal-Vicens, A.R. Pollastri, J.N. Rosenquist, S. Goryachev, D. Ongur, P. Sklar, R.H. Perlis, and J.W. Smoller, International Cohort Collection for Bipolar Disorder Consortium, "Validation of electronic health record phenotyping of bipolar disorder cases and controls", *Am. J. Psychiatry,* vol. 172, no. 4, pp. 363-372, 2015.
       [http://dx.doi.org/10.1176/appi.ajp.2014.14030423] [PMID: 25827034]

[76]   R. Håvik, J.D. Wake, E. Flobak, A. Lundervold, and F. Guribye, A Conversational Interface for Self-screening for ADHD in Adults.*Internet Science. INSCI 2018.,* S. Bodrunova, Ed., vol. 11551. Springer: Cham, 2019.Lecture Notes in Computer Science
       [http://dx.doi.org/10.1007/978-3-030-17705-8_12]

[77]   B.L. Cook, A.M. Progovac, P. Chen, B. Mullin, S. Hou, and E. Baca-Garcia, "Novel use of natural language processing (nlp) to predict suicidal ideation and psychiatric symptoms in a text-based mental health intervention in madrid", *Comput. Math. Methods Med.,* vol. 2016, p. 8708434, 2016.
       [http://dx.doi.org/10.1155/2016/8708434] [PMID: 27752278]

[78]   A. Tsanas, M.A. Little, P.E. McSharry, J. Spielman, and L.O. Ramig, "Novel speech signal processing algorithms for high-accuracy classification of Parkinson's disease", *IEEE Trans. Biomed. Eng.,* vol. 59, no. 5, pp. 1264-1271, 2012.
       [http://dx.doi.org/10.1109/TBME.2012.2183367] [PMID: 22249592]

CHAPTER 3

Deep Learning in Radiology

Madhura Ingalhalikar[1,*]

[1] *Symbiosis Center for Medical Image Analysis Symbiosis International University, Lavale, Pune 412115, India*

Abstract: Recent developments in artificial intelligence (AI), particularly deep learning (DL) algorithms have demonstrated remarkable progress in image recognition and prediction tasks. These are now being applied in the field of radiology on medical images to quantify, characterize, classify as well as monitor various pathologies. Such DL based quantifications facilitate greater support to the visual assessment of image characteristics that is performed by the physician. Furthermore it aids in reducing inter-reader variability as well as assists in speeding up the radiology workflow. In this chapter, we provide an insightful motivation for employing DL based framework followed by an overview of recent applications of DL in radiology and present a systematic summary of specific DL algorithms pertaining to image perception and recognition tasks. Finally, we discuss the challenges in clinical implementation of these algorithms and provide a perspective on how the domain could be advanced in the next few years.

Keywords: Artificial intelligence, Convolutional neural nets, CT, Deep learning, MRI, Radiology, X-rays.

INTRODUCTION

Recent discoveries in Artificial Intelligence (AI) have illustrated exceptional performance in complicated tasks by allowing machines to better characterize and interpret the underlying complex information. These discoveries include the area of deep learning (DL) that is loosely inspired by how the human brain works during learning and execution [1, 2]. DL algorithms usually employ a large number of interconnected neurons that learn the complex data patterns to create a "trained" model which can then be applied to perform the task under consideration on new data. DL algorithms have a specialty that they do not require pre-programmed instructions, have the ability to extract features and learn

* **Corresponding author Madhura Ingalhalikar:** Symbiosis Center for Medical Image Analysis Symbiosis International University, Lavale, Pune 412115, India; E-mail: head@scmia.edu.in

Terje Solsvik Kristensen (Ed.)

these automatically from a large amount of data. Results from multiple performance tasks have demonstrated that DL algorithms perform better than humans. For example, DL based creation of automated image captions is highly efficient [3, 4]. Similarly, many other problems such as localizing objects in images [5], sentiment analysis [6], language translation tasks [7], planning and control of autonomous vehicles [8, 9] *etc.* have been resolved more effectively using DL. Moreover, with the power of modern computational hardware, DL learning frameworks can be built effortlessly. Overall, this has led to major advances in applications ranging from natural language processing [10], web searching [11], self-driving vehicles and creating automated systems and support in every possible field of work that includes agriculture [12, 13], military [14] as well as medicine [15, 16]. Within the healthcare and medicine domain DL has been driving multiple applications such as virtual assistants in hospital management, patient monitoring [17], and drug discovery [18 - 20] as well as is used in medical diagnostics and imaging [21 - 23]. Further, bioinformatics studies that include large datasets pertaining to genome, RNA and DNA employ a plethora of AI techniques for analysis and to gain an understanding into the pathological genotypes [24 - 26]. Medical imaging is at the forefront of using AI techniques as these not only support precise processing and quantification of images, but hold promise to overcome the limitations of subjective visual inspection [27]. In addition, the predictive power of these methods can facilitate finding specific markers that relate to the pathology under consideration. These models are being integrated into clinical workflow as a tool to assist clinicians.

As mentioned earlier, unlike earlier AI techniques, DL models are non-deterministic where explicit feature extraction is not required. These algorithms learn directly by maneuvering through the data space and therefore can be considered as a fundamentally different paradigm in machine learning [2]. Although the techniques have existed for a while, only with the advent of state-o--art computational hardware and collection of enormous amounts of digital data these have become relevant and are being applied. To this end, multiple DL algorithms have been developed in the past few years; however convolutional neural nets (CNNs) are the most prevalent type of architecture when working directly on images [28]. CNNs are a modern adaptation of the traditional artificial neural network with multiple neuronal layers that act directly on the images through millions of 2D or 3D convolutional filter parameters where each layer is followed by a pooling operation that down-samples the image (Fig. **1**). These filter parameters are computed for each hidden layer that helps extract fine, intermediate as well as coarse imaging features. Finally, these are connected to fully connected layers that provide high level reasoning before the output layer facilitates the predictions. The complete model is transformed into the desired output by using end-to-end optimization [28]. The CNN can therefore be considered as a multi-layer automated feature extraction tool with a classifier in the final stages. To this date, CNNs have demonstrated ground-breaking performance in image classification tasks often becoming the new state of art in several use cases. For example, the ImageNet competition proved that on a database of 14,000,000 images of cars, buildings and multiple other categories, the CNN based architectures dramatically improved the error-rate to be comparable or even better than human performance and also at a very high computational speed [28]. The ability of CNNs in extracting such discriminative pixel based features, automatically, is striking as it often accounts for better classification performance, especially on large datasets, when compared to a similar task on empirically drawn features. Other than CNNs, other DL models such as auto-encoders, recurrent neural nets, generative adversarial networks, deep belief nets *etc.* have also been employed in radiology. Some of these have been described in the following sections.

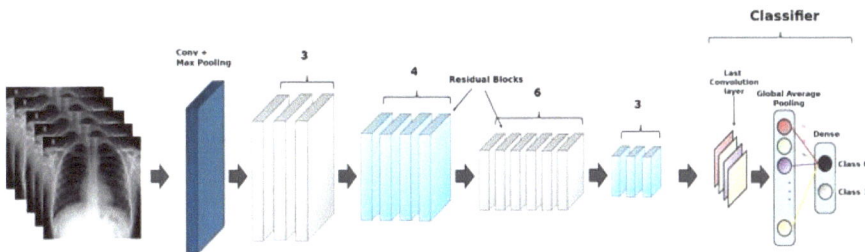

Fig. (1). A schematic representation of a CNN architecture showing chest X-rays as input that are being classified either as normal (class 0) or abnormal (class 1). The convolutional layers filter the input images at multiple-resolutions and extract features that are optimized via end-to-end optimization.

Overall, this chapter aims to provide an overview of the recent applications of AI in radiology – that include image pre-processing, segmentation, registration and prediction of pathology. Section 2 discusses the underlying motivation for AI in radiology while section 3 presents applications for various problems with diverse imaging modalities and organs. In section 4 we discuss about the confounding factors, challenges and limitations of AI in radiology and potential solutions for the way forward.

MOTIVATION

Radiology is a medical specialty that employs medical images such as X-rays, ultrasound sonography (USG), computed tomography (CT), Positron emission tomography (PET) and magnetic resonance imaging (MRI) for detection, diagnosis, and characterization of disease (diagnostic radiology) as well as guiding procedural interventions (interventional radiology). Radiologists are medical doctors who has undergone years of training to visualize and interpret the images to generate a report of their findings based on which the next treatment plans are usually decided.

It is important to note multiple aspects about the practice of radiology and why AI could be a valuable tool in aiding radiographic medical diagnosis: **(1)** Radiological imaging data is growing exponentially while the numbers of trained doctors that can read these images are inadequate in comparison, which in turn dramatically increases the workload of the radiologists. **(2)** The radiologists perform visual inspection and qualitative interpretation of data that does not involve any quantitative illustrations. Qualitative characterization may give rise to uncertainties, errors especially under stress of finishing the workload. Moreover, such subjective decision making based on visual perception may create inter-reader variability whereas a machine may provide more reproducible results, Finally, **(3)** unlike most other branches of medicine, the imaging data created is digital in nature thus automatically facilitating straightforward quantitative analysis where AI techniques can be effortlessly implemented. These techniques will not only use predictive models for diagnosis but also can be employed to quickly process the images for better visualization, structure measurements, noise removal, image acquisition protocols, data simulation to higher resolutions *etc.* that can increase the efficiency and reduce errors and uncertainties of the radiology workflow.

DEEP LEARNING IN RADIOLOGY

In this section we provide an overview of the applications of deep learning in radiology. The section is organized based on the task performed followed by subsections that give examples of tools developed on certain modality and organ to perform that particular task.

Diagnostic Predictions

Predictive tools created using DL methods, usually learn the underlying patterns of abnormality on a given set of images to create a mathematical model, which in turn can be employed on new images to distinguish if the abnormality is present or absent. A generalized framework that uses CNNs to distinguish various abnormalities is shown in Fig. **(1)**. These models have been used in a plethora of radiographic applications that include automatically detecting bone fractures from

X-rays, classifying abnormalities on chest X-rays such as pneumonia, pleural effusion, pneumothorax *etc.*, determining the presence of abnormality on a given scan, delineating malignancies from benign tumors on mammography, USG or MRI, classification of cancerous lesions based on their histopathology, predicting neurological disorders, disease staging in chest CT for smokers, discriminating overlapping, noisy data for radiological database cleanup *etc.* [15, 29 - 31]. The applications are inexhaustible; however in the following sub-sections we have illustrated a few prominent ones.

Detecting Abnormalities on Chest X-rays

Chest X-rays are one of the most common radiological diagnostic tests wherein the appearance of abnormalities such a pneumonia could be fuzzy and can have common characteristics with other thoracic disorders making the process of reading chest X-rays complicated with a high inter-reader variability. Moreover, a high percentage of chest X-rays go unreported every year especially in areas with no access to an imaging specialist [32]. To mitigate these issues, recent works in DL-CNN models have demonstrated potential to make this process more efficient with reasonable predictive accuracies that can quickly facilitate the diagnosis. The software framework can be delivered to populations with inadequate access to radiology clinics.

The CNN models built on chest X-rays are generally trained on thousands of datasets to learn the patterns in multiple thoracic disorders [29, 33]. Most of the chest X-ray algorithms developed use 14-15 thoracic diseases that include pneumonia, pneumothorax, cardiomegaly, effusion, infiltration, mass, nodule, atelectasis, consolidation, edema, emphysema, fibrosis, hernia, pleural thickening, combinations of multiple disorders and normative data. For example, the Stanford CheXNet is trained on 112,120 frontal view chest X-rays and employs a 121-layer dense CNN that demonstrates higher accuracies than other existing models [34]. Currently, multiple products are also available to discriminate the chest pathology.

Screening for Lung Cancer on Low Dose CT

Lung cancer screening using low dose CT has been effective as early treatment has shown to reduce mortality [35]. Current challenges include high inter-reader variability and high false-positive rates. To alleviate these issues, CNN model based on patient's prior scan and latest scan has been developed to predict the risk of lung cancer [36]. A recent study trained a CNN on 6716 scans and validated it on 1139 test subjects. When prior computed tomography imaging was not available, the proposed model outperformed the radiologists while where prior computed tomography imaging was available, the model performance was at-par with the radiologists [36]. Screening tests are generally performed on masses and having a tool that can automatically detect the risk can increase the adoption of lung cancer screening ultimately saving lives.

Genotype Detection in Gliomas on Multi-Modal MRI

Gliomas are the most common type of neoplasms of the brain. The 2016 World Health Organization (WHO) classification of brain tumors recognized several new entities based on genotypes in addition to histological phenotypes [37]. Amongst these, mutations in isocitrate dehydrogenase 1(IDH1) were considered crucial as these are associated with longer overall survival [38]. Currently, the IDH genotype is identified *via* immuno-histochemical analysis following biopsy or surgical resection. Therefore, developing non-invasive pre-operative markers for IDH genotype has been clinically important as it can not only aid prognosis but also support treatment planning and therapeutic intervention. Visually, radiologists cannot diagnose the IDH genotype on a MRI scan. It is therefore important to use computational techniques that can learn the imaging patterns and distinguish the mutants from wild type. Recent studies have employed deep neural networks such as convolutional neural nets (CNNs) [8] that operate directly on the images and eliminate manual feature extraction and selection steps. Studies using CNNs have demonstrated higher accuracies in delineating gliomas with IDH mutation from IDH wild type [31, 39, 40] on large datasets.

ResNets (residual networks) have been commonly used in this application illustrating superior predictive power than other architectures [39, 41]. ResNets not only enable training of deeper architectures but also are robust to the vanishing gradient problem. The introduction of a shortcut connection supports learning of the residuals and ensures that subsequent layers have essential information to learn additional features. Fig. (**1**) shows the ResNet 16 architecture.

Prostate Cancer Detection

At a radiological level, prostate cancer detection is performed using multimodal MRI usually using a standardized approach to image interpretation called PIRADS [42] (Prostate Imaging Reporting and Data System) that has been developed for radiologists. However, PIRADS suffers from inter-reader variability issues as well as is not the best diagnostic tool for differentiation between clinically relevant and low grade tumors. It is therefore crucial to employ multi-variate predictive models to extract features from multi-modal MRI images and characterize the tumor types accordingly. To this end, CNNs have illustrated great potential in delineating the tumor type and therefore assisting radiologists for accurate diagnosis, decreasing the diagnosis time as well as the cost of diagnosis. Current models that have been applied to demonstrate approximately 90% accuracy with equal sensitivity and specificity and outdo the classification accuracies using PIRADS, multivariate PIRADS as well as other machine learning algorithms. Recent work has illustrated high accuracies of 88-94% [43 - 45] using DL models either on diffusion MRI [44] or using multi-modal MRIs [45].

Segmentation

Measuring the size, shape and volumes of different organs, tumors or other tissues is a standard practice in radiology that supports the diagnosis in majority cases. Usually the radiologists measure the minor and major axes and compute the area/volume of the organ under consideration. When the volume/area does not lie in the normative range it typically gives an indication of pathology. For instance, in cardiac imaging, automatic segmentation of the heart chambers is necessary for computing the cardiac volume and ejection fraction [46, 47]. In brain MRI, tumor segmentation is required for surgical planning [48, 49], hippocampal volume estimate can provide the possibility of dementia [50, 51], lesion segmentation for patients with multiple sclerosis [52] and so on. These measurements on the image are usually carried out manually by the physician and are laborious and time consuming. Moreover, they only provide a ball-park assessment.

In the past two decades, there has been an enormous focus on automated extraction or segmentation of the structure of interest that could facilitate precise volume/area quantification in turn increasing the efficiency in radiology workflow. Traditionally, this has been performed using standard image processing techniques such as region growing, edge detection, histogram based thresholding, active contours and other morphological operations [53]. However, in recent years the procedures for segmenting the region of interest are being performed using deep learning methods. These methods can learn the location and accurate shapes of the region of interest and are more flexible on varied imaging protocols and contrasts. Moreover, once the model is trained the computational power and time for segmenting new incoming images is insignificant. Multiple models have been created until now and applied to various radiographic problems. Further sub-sections will discuss a few popular models such as CNNs and U-nets and their effective applications. Models such as recurrent neural nets (RNNs) and its variations are also employed for segmentation however these are not discussed.

2d and 3d Cnns

As described in the earlier sections, CNNs have demonstrated promising capability in performing image classification tasks where we can predict a certain abnormality or pathology from radiological images. On similar lines, many researchers have explored the idea of applying CNNs to medical image segmentation problems. In image segmentation problems, the CNN is typically trained on patches of images, where each patch is labeled either as a structure or the background. The CNNs learns the underlying patterns to distinguish between the structures of interest *vs.* the background. Once the CNN is trained, the patches have to be connected together to create the complete binary mask of the segmented structure. CNNs have been employed for efficient skull stripping on brain MRIs [54], multi-region identification in bladder cancer [55], segmentation of spinal cord [56] *etc.* The biggest issue with using CNN for segmentation includes the laborious post processing part where the image has to be reconstructed back from the learned patches. Many researchers instead of fully connected layers at the end, prefer to employ fully convolutional network (FCN) [57] as it allows the network to have a dense pixel-wise prediction. Moreover, to achieve better localization performance, high-resolution activation maps are combined with upsampled outputs and passed to the convolution layers to assemble more accurate output.

U-Nets

One of the most popular network in medical image segmentation is the U-net that was initially proposed by Ronneberger *et al.* [58] using an encoder-decoder type architecture. The U-net as illustrated in Fig. (**2**), where it includes two paths of analysis and synthesis. The analysis path follows a structure similar to the CNN (Fig. **1**). The synthesis path, commonly known as expansion phase, consists of an upsampling layer followed by a deconvolution layer. The most important property of U-Net is the shortcut connections between the layers of equal resolution in analysis path to expansion path. These connections provide essential high-resolution features to the deconvolution layers. The expansion path facilitates a direct binary segmented output making it simpler than using only a CNN type architecture where patches are typically used to classify them into a certain structure or non-structure. Multiple variations of 2D and 3D U-nets have been developed to this date that boost the segmentation accuracies [58 - 60] as well as require less computational time and power. U-nets have been successfully implemented in cell segmentation and counting [61], brain extraction on MRI [62], detecting lung nodules on CT [63], lesion detection on PET [64], segmenting arterial walls on intravascular USG [65], hippocampal subfield segmentation [66] *etc.* Moreover, many applications have now started using transfer learning where the weights of a trained model are transferred as initial weights to train another that expedites the process of training another model.

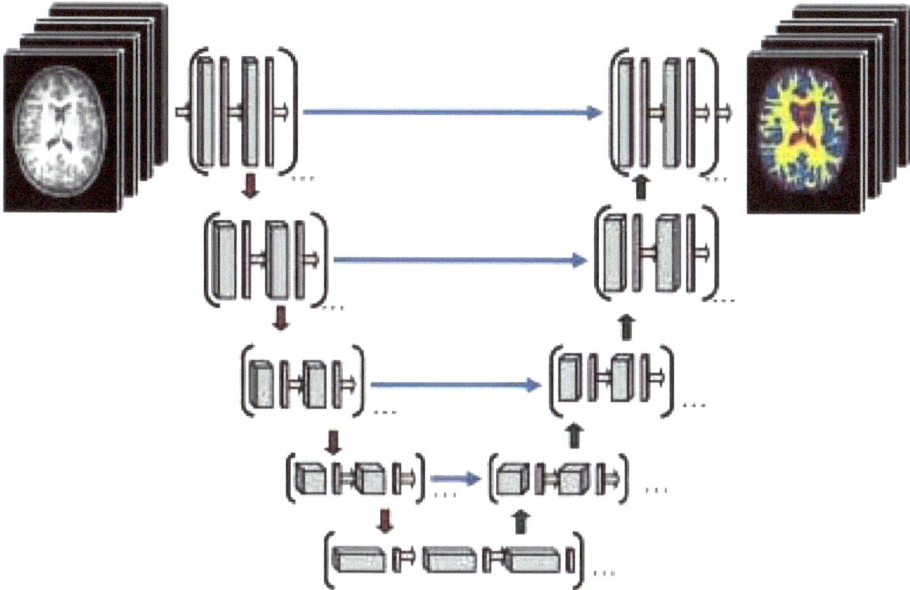

Fig. (2). A U-net architecture where the first leg downsamples the image while the second leg upsamples it. The blue lines are called the shortcut connections. The application demonstrated in this case is of tissue segmentation in brain MRI.

Registration

Building image correspondence between various imaging modalities or between various subjects is a non-trivial task and is generally performed using a process known as image registration. Automatic intensity-based image registrations can be divided into linear and non-linear transformations. In the linear type, the complete image undergoes translation, rotation as well as skew and stretch to match another image. In non-linear transformations, each pixel or voxel undergoes non-similar transformation and therefore can more accurately map one image co-ordinate frame with another [67]. All these registration methods typically require both a metric that quantifies the similarity between a moving image and a fixed image and an optimization algorithm that updates the transformation parameters such that the similarity between the images is maximized. With the advent of deep learning algorithms, these are now being employed either to compute the similarity metric [68, 69] between the two images or to perform the complete registration using models such as reinforcement learning [70].

Image Generation

There are many instances in radiology, where the radiologist would want to enhance the image, represent in a different manner or even compare it to image from another scanner. For example, the visualization of diffusion MRI of the prostate is superior as compared to on a 1.5T MRI. However, majority radiology clinics utilize 1.5T scanners that do not provide the enhanced features as in the 3T. Therefore, if we can acquire images from 1.5T and computationally can simulate or represent the image as it would appear on 3T, this would benefit the radiology community as well as lower the expense involved. With the advent of generative models using deep learning, reconstructing data from poor quality images into images that is noiseless, with more contrast, with higher resolution or ones that manifest similar to an image acquired from advanced acquisition protocol is now a possibility. The current focus is only on one of the most interesting recent breakthroughs in the field of deep learning - generative adversarial networks (GANs) [71]. GANs are a special type of a neural network where two separate networks are trained simultaneously, with one focused on image generation and the other centered on discrimination. The generator creates fake images while the discriminator distinguishes these into real and fake. Through- and-through optimization makes the generator produce better and better images which at one point are indistinguishable from the real dataset, thus creating a trained model that can generate newer images. The adversarial training scheme has gained attention due to its effectiveness in counteracting domain shift, and efficacy in generating new image samples (Fig. **3**). Applications include synthesizing MRI from CT [72], CT from MRI [73], various contrasts of MRI [74], low resolution MRI to high resolution MRI images [75] and so on.

Other Applications

The applications of DL in radiology are limitless and earlier sections discussed the most prominent ones. However, some other areas where DL has been successfully used or has a potential to develop include the following: **(1)** content based image retrieval, where the algorithm finds the most similar images in a given dataset. For instance, the work by Yan *et al.* automatically annotates type, location *etc.* of the lesion by modeling their similarities [76]. **(2)** Compressed sensing in MRI: Recent work in the area of MRI image acquisition has focused on accelerating the process of acquisition. Compressive sensing MRI uses only a small fraction of data that is needed to generate full reconstruction *via* a computational method. Earlier, techniques such as wavelet transforms, cosine transforms *etc.* were proposed for computing the sparse transformation. Recent work has demonstrated that DL algorithms such as GANs can facilitate optimal sparse encoding which in turn improves the image quality significantly [77, 78]. **(3)** Image quality check: Qualitative assessment (QA) of medical images is crucial to classify the image to be either satisfactory or unsatisfactory for subsequent tasks. Images can be corrupted by artifacts, motion of the patient, magnetic field inhomogeneity in MRI *etc.* Manual QA of images is time consuming and laborious. To this end, DL models can automatically delineate low quality images for other the ones that are satisfactory with a high accuracy. For example, T2-weighted liver MRIs were discriminated into diagnostic or non-diagnostic quality by CNNs [79] **(4)** Finally, DL models such as GANs have also been applied to enhance image quality, reduce noise and remove artifacts [80].

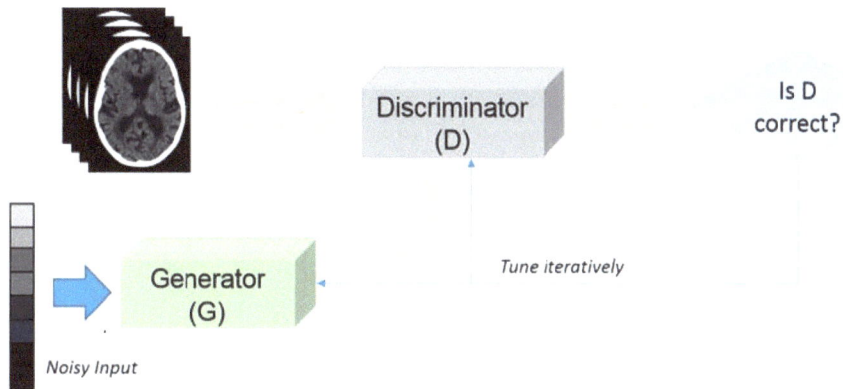

Fig. (3). displaying a schematic of the working of GANs.

LIMITATIONS AND WAYS FORWARD

The area of medical imaging has become one of the most important pillars in standards of care, diagnostics as well as in intervention. Even with current advances in medical imaging with higher resolutions and sophisticated modalities, minute details may yet be difficult to identify by visual inspection. In such cases, DL based algorithms may provide powerful solutions with increased accuracy and a significant reduction of time and effort.

However, it is important to understand the challenges faced when applying these algorithms. Firstly, DL methods are designed to work on large amounts of datasets (more the better). Nonetheless, many applications trained for radiological diagnosis use small datasets, which may overfit the classifier thus providing a rather inferior performance on the test cases. However, to acquire bigger datasets more imaging is required – which may not be cost-effective. Also, larger datasets are more complicated to curate and label manually. Massive effort from trained doctors is needed for manual labeling of the data, which may be difficult due to time constraints and high clinical workload. To mitigate this, there has been a push to employ algorithms with least amount of labeling or no labeling at all (unsupervised) [81]. For example, state-of-art segmentation techniques such as few-shot segmentations require the label to be drawn only on a few slices and few subjects [82].

Multiple metrics such as reproducibility, generalizability, effect of acquisition protocols, noise in images *etc.* need to be evaluated for each model under consideration for clinical use. For example, the CNN architecture designed to diagnose the chest X-rays may not perform with the best accuracy on X-rays scanned from the other parts of the world, on noisy and low contrast X-rays or on images acquired on a different brand of machine. It is therefore crucial to benchmark these algorithms and perform rigorous testing before bringing them into clinical use. Finally, it is important to understand that each algorithm is developed to perform a single task with only a few performing better than humans. These algorithms have no insights into the patient history and other factors such as symptoms, clinical tests *etc.* that the human is capable of associating quickly for diagnosis. It is therefore unlikely that AI will replace the radiologists and their complete workflow. However, it can be safely assumed that it certainly will play an important role in radiology. Majority of the times, the role of deep learning in diagnostic predictions will complement the radiologist by providing validation to subjective inferences. It may also support complete diagnosis on problems that are well-defined and where the trained model is highly accurate and benchmarked to standards. Such solutions can be implemented in remote regions where imaging specialists are scarce. Usage of these models can also generate more time for radiologists to perform more demanding tasks where DL solutions are not yet applicable. Furthermore, other applications such as automated segmentation, registration, data generation, image denoising *etc.* will increase the workflow efficiency significantly in radiology.

CONCLUSION

In summary, it is incredible to see the achievements in AI in the past 5 years, and the amount of effort that researchers and clinicians are putting in to create data repositories for training and testing these techniques. As a community we have achieved preliminary results on many tasks however, on limited data. Now the next phase will include rigorous testing and benchmarking these techniques such that these can be built into a generalized framework that can work across different populations, scanners, acquisition protocols and standards of care.

CONSENT FOR PUBLICATION

Not applicable.

CONFLICT OF INTEREST

The author declares no conflict of interest, financial or otherwise.

ACKNOWLEDGEMENTS

I would like to thank my research assistants Sumeet Shinde and Tanay Chougule for help with creating Figs.

REFERENCES

[1]   Y. LeCun, Y. Bengio, and G. Hinton, "Deep learning", *Nature,* vol. 521, no. 7553, pp. 436-444, 2015.
[http://dx.doi.org/10.1038/nature14539] [PMID: 26017442]

[2]   I. Goodfellow, "Deep learning", *MIT press Cambridge,* vol. 1, 2016.

[3]   X.D. He, and L. Deng, "Deep learning for image-to-text generation a technical overview", *IEEE Signal Process. Mag.,* vol. 34, no. 6, pp. 109-116, 2017.
[http://dx.doi.org/10.1109/MSP.2017.2741510]

[4]   X.X. Liu, Q.Y. Xu, and N. Wang, "A survey on deep neural network-based image captioning", *Vis. Comput.,* vol. 35, no. 3, pp. 445-470, 2019.
[http://dx.doi.org/10.1007/s00371-018-1566-y]

[5]   Q. Abbas, M.E.A. Ibrahim, and M.A. Jaffar, "A comprehensive review of recent advances on deep vision systems", *Artif. Intell. Rev.,* vol. 52, no. 1, pp. 39-76, 2019.
[http://dx.doi.org/10.1007/s10462-018-9633-3]

[6]   Q.T. Ain, "Sentiment analysis using deep learning techniques: a review", *IJACSA,* vol. 8, no. 6, pp. 424-433, 2017.

[7]   L. Deng, "Deep learning: from speech recognition to language and multimodal processing", *APSIPA Trans. Signal. Inf. Process.,* p. 5, 2016.
[http://dx.doi.org/10.1017/ATSIP.2015.22]

[8]   S.D. Pendleton, "Perception, planning, control, and coordination for autonomous vehicles", *Machines,* vol. 5, no. 1, 2017.

[9]   H. Nguyen, "Deep learning methods in transportation domain: a review", *IET Intell. Transp. Syst.,* vol. 12, no. 9, pp. 998-1004, 2018.
[http://dx.doi.org/10.1049/iet-its.2018.0064]

[10]   T. Young, "Recent trends in deep learning based natural language processing", *IEEE Comput. Intell. Mag.,* vol. 13, no. 3, pp. 55-75, 2018.
[http://dx.doi.org/10.1109/MCI.2018.2840738]

[11]   W. Serrano, "Neural networks in big data and web search", *Data (Basel),* vol. 4, no. 1, 2018.
[http://dx.doi.org/10.3390/data4010007]

[12]   J. Boulent, S. Foucher, J. Théau, and P.L. St-Charles, "Convolutional neural networks for the automatic identification of plant diseases", *Front. Plant Sci.,* vol. 10, p. 941, 2019.

[http://dx.doi.org/10.3389/fpls.2019.00941] [PMID: 31396250]

[13]   A. Kamilaris, and F.X. Prenafeta-Boldu, "A review of the use of convolutional neural networks in agriculture", *J. Agric. Sci.,* vol. 156, no. 3, pp. 312-322, 2018.
[http://dx.doi.org/10.1017/S0021859618000436]

[14]   Y. Li, "Deep learning for remote sensing image classification: A survey", *Wiley Interdiscip. Rev. Data Min. Knowl. Discov.,* vol. 8, no. 6, 2018.
[http://dx.doi.org/10.1002/widm.1264]

[15]   H.J. Jang, and K.O. Cho, "Applications of deep learning for the analysis of medical data", *Arch. Pharm. Res.,* vol. 42, no. 6, pp. 492-504, 2019.
[http://dx.doi.org/10.1007/s12272-019-01162-9] [PMID: 31140082]

[16]   V.S. Parekh, and M.A. Jacobs, "Deep learning and radiomics in precision medicine", *Expert Rev. Precis. Med. Drug Dev.,* vol. 4, no. 2, pp. 59-72, 2019.
[http://dx.doi.org/10.1080/23808993.2019.1585805] [PMID: 31080889]

[17]   A. Davoudi, K.R. Malhotra, B. Shickel, S. Siegel, S. Williams, M. Ruppert, E. Bihorac, T. Ozrazgat-Baslanti, P.J. Tighe, A. Bihorac, and P. Rashidi, "Intelligent icu for autonomous patient monitoring using pervasive sensing and deep learning", *Sci. Rep.,* vol. 9, no. 1, p. 8020, 2019.
[http://dx.doi.org/10.1038/s41598-019-44004-w] [PMID: 31142754]

[18]   H. Chen, O. Engkvist, Y. Wang, M. Olivecrona, and T. Blaschke, "The rise of deep learning in drug discovery", *Drug Discov. Today,* vol. 23, no. 6, pp. 1241-1250, 2018.
[http://dx.doi.org/10.1016/j.drudis.2018.01.039] [PMID: 29366762]

[19]   G. Urban, K.M. Bache, D. Phan, A. Sobrino, A.K. Shmakov, S.J. Hachey, C. Hughes, and P. Baldi, "Deep learning for drug discovery and cancer research: automated analysis of vascularization images", *IEEE/ACM Trans. Comput. Biol. Bioinformatics,* vol. 16, no. 3, pp. 1029-1035, 2019.
[http://dx.doi.org/10.1109/TCBB.2018.2841396] [PMID: 29993583]

[20]   L. Zhang, J. Tan, D. Han, and H. Zhu, "From machine learning to deep learning: progress in machine intelligence for rational drug discovery", *Drug Discov. Today,* vol. 22, no. 11, pp. 1680-1685, 2017.
[http://dx.doi.org/10.1016/j.drudis.2017.08.010] [PMID: 28881183]

[21]   G. Litjens, T. Kooi, B.E. Bejnordi, A.A.A. Setio, F. Ciompi, M. Ghafoorian, J.A.W.M. van der Laak, B. van Ginneken, and C.I. Sánchez, "A survey on deep learning in medical image analysis", *Med. Image Anal.,* vol. 42, pp. 60-88, 2017.
[http://dx.doi.org/10.1016/j.media.2017.07.005] [PMID: 28778026]

[22]   L. Carin, and M.J. Pencina, "On deep learning for medical image analysis", *JAMA,* vol. 320, no. 11, pp. 1192-1193, 2018.
[http://dx.doi.org/10.1001/jama.2018.13316] [PMID: 30422287]

[23]   D.G. Shen, G.R. Wu, and H.I. Suk, "Deep learning in medical image analysis", *Annu. Rev. Biomed. Eng.,* vol. 19, pp. 221-248, 2017.
[http://dx.doi.org/10.1146/annurev-bioeng-071516-044442]

[24]   F. Wang, P. Chainani, T. White, J. Yang, Y. Liu, and B. Soibam, "Deep learning identifies genome-wide DNA binding sites of long noncoding RNAs", *RNA Biol.,* vol. 15, no. 12, pp. 1468-1476, 2018.
[http://dx.doi.org/10.1080/15476286.2018.1551704] [PMID: 30486737]

[25]   J. Zhou, C.Y. Park, C.L. Theesfeld, A.K. Wong, Y. Yuan, C. Scheckel, J.J. Fak, J. Funk, K. Yao, Y. Tajima, A. Packer, R.B. Darnell, and O.G. Troyanskaya, "Whole-genome deep-learning analysis identifies contribution of noncoding mutations to autism risk", *Nat. Genet.,* vol. 51, no. 6, pp. 973-980, 2019.
[http://dx.doi.org/10.1038/s41588-019-0420-0] [PMID: 31133750]

[26]   A. Telenti, C. Lippert, P.C. Chang, and M. DePristo, "Deep learning of genomic variation and regulatory network data", *Hum. Mol. Genet.,* vol. 27, no. R1, pp. R63-R71, 2018.
[http://dx.doi.org/10.1093/hmg/ddy115] [PMID: 29648622]

[27]   A. Hosny, C. Parmar, J. Quackenbush, L.H. Schwartz, and H.J.W.L. Aerts, "Artificial intelligence in radiology", *Nat. Rev. Cancer,* vol. 18, no. 8, pp. 500-510, 2018.
[http://dx.doi.org/10.1038/s41568-018-0016-5] [PMID: 29777175]

[28]   A. Krizhevsky, I. Sutskever, and G.E. Hinton, "Imagenet classification with deep convolutional neural networks", *Adv. Neural Inf. Process. Syst.,* p. 25, 2012.

[29]   R.H. Abiyev, and M.K.S. Ma'aitah, "Deep convolutional neural networks for chest diseases detection", *J. Healthc. Eng.,* vol. 2018, p. 4168538, 2018.
[http://dx.doi.org/10.1155/2018/4168538] [PMID: 30154989]

[30]   S. Shinde, S. Prasad, Y. Saboo, R. Kaushick, J. Saini, P.K. Pal, and M. Ingalhalikar, "Predictive markers for Parkinson's disease using deep neural nets on neuromelanin sensitive MRI", *Neuroimage Clin.,* vol. 22, p. 101748, 2019.
[http://dx.doi.org/10.1016/j.nicl.2019.101748] [PMID: 30870733]

[31]   P. Chang, J. Grinband, B.D. Weinberg, M. Bardis, M. Khy, G. Cadena, M.Y. Su, S. Cha, C.G. Filippi, D. Bota, P. Baldi, L.M. Poisson, R. Jain, and D. Chow, "Deep-learning convolutional neural networks accurately classify genetic mutations in gliomas", *AJNR Am. J. Neuroradiol.,* vol. 39, no. 7, pp. 1201-1207, 2018.
[http://dx.doi.org/10.3174/ajnr.A5667] [PMID: 29748206]

[32]   A.K. Jaiswal, "Identifying pneumonia in chest X-rays: A deep learning approach", *Measurement,* vol. 145, pp. 511-518, 2019.
[http://dx.doi.org/10.1016/j.measurement.2019.05.076]

[33]   I.M. Baltruschat, H. Nickisch, M. Grass, T. Knopp, and A. Saalbach, "Comparison of deep learning approaches for multi-label chest x-ray classification", *Sci. Rep.,* vol. 9, no. 1, p. 6381, 2019.
[http://dx.doi.org/10.1038/s41598-019-42294-8] [PMID: 31011155]

[34]   P. Rajpurkar, "Chexnet: Radiologist-level pneumonia detection on chest x-rays with deep learning", *arXiv preprint,* 2017.

[35]   D.R. Aberle, A.M. Adams, C.D. Berg, W.C. Black, J.D. Clapp, R.M. Fagerstrom, I.F. Gareen, C. Gatsonis, P.M. Marcus, and J.D. Sicks, National Lung Screening Trial Research Team, "Reduced lung-cancer mortality with low-dose computed tomographic screening", *N. Engl. J. Med.,* vol. 365, no. 5, pp. 395-409, 2011.
[http://dx.doi.org/10.1056/NEJMoa1102873] [PMID: 21714641]

[36]   D. Ardila, A.P. Kiraly, S. Bharadwaj, B. Choi, J.J. Reicher, L. Peng, D. Tse, M. Etemadi, W. Ye, G. Corrado, D.P. Naidich, and S. Shetty, "Author correction: end-to-end lung cancer screening with three-dimensional deep learning on low-dose chest computed tomography", *Nat. Med.,* vol. 25, no. 8, p. 1319, 2019.
[http://dx.doi.org/10.1038/s41591-019-0536-x] [PMID: 31253948]

[37]   D.N. Louis, A. Perry, G. Reifenberger, A. von Deimling, D. Figarella-Branger, W.K. Cavenee, H. Ohgaki, O.D. Wiestler, P. Kleihues, and D.W. Ellison, "The 2016 world health organization classification of tumors of the central nervous system: a summary", *Acta Neuropathol.,* vol. 131, no. 6, pp. 803-820, 2016.
[http://dx.doi.org/10.1007/s00401-016-1545-1] [PMID: 27157931]

[38]   C. Houillier, X. Wang, G. Kaloshi, K. Mokhtari, R. Guillevin, J. Laffaire, S. Paris, B. Boisselier, A. Idbaih, F. Laigle-Donadey, K. Hoang-Xuan, M. Sanson, and J.Y. Delattre, "IDH1 or IDH2 mutations predict longer survival and response to temozolomide in low-grade gliomas", *Neurology,* vol. 75, no. 17, pp. 1560-1566, 2010.
[http://dx.doi.org/10.1212/WNL.0b013e3181f96282] [PMID: 20975057]

[39]   K. Chang, H.X. Bai, H. Zhou, C. Su, W.L. Bi, E. Agbodza, V.K. Kavouridis, J.T. Senders, A. Boaro, A. Beers, B. Zhang, A. Capellini, W. Liao, Q. Shen, X. Li, B. Xiao, J. Cryan, S. Ramkissoon, L. Ramkissoon, K. Ligon, P.Y. Wen, R.S. Bindra, J. Woo, O. Arnaout, E.R. Gerstner, P.J. Zhang, B.R. Rosen, L. Yang, R.Y. Huang, and J. Kalpathy-Cramer, "Residual convolutional neural network for the

determination of idh status in low- and high-grade gliomas from mr imaging", *Clin. Cancer Res.,* vol. 24, no. 5, pp. 1073-1081, 2018.
[http://dx.doi.org/10.1158/1078-0432.CCR-17-2236] [PMID: 29167275]

[40]   J. Lao, Y. Chen, Z.C. Li, Q. Li, J. Zhang, J. Liu, and G. Zhai, "A deep learning-based radiomics model for prediction of survival in glioblastoma multiforme", *Sci. Rep.,* vol. 7, no. 1, p. 10353, 2017.
[http://dx.doi.org/10.1038/s41598-017-10649-8] [PMID: 28871110]

[41]   A. Ahmad, "Predictive and discriminative localization of IDH genotype in high grade gliomas using deep convolutional neural nets", *2019 IEEE 16th International Symposium on Biomedical Imaging (ISBI 2019),* 2019

[42]   T. Franiel, and M. Röthke, "PI-RADS 2.0 for Prostate MRI", *Radiologe,* vol. 57, no. 8, pp. 665-678, 2017.
[http://dx.doi.org/10.1007/s00117-017-0269-0] [PMID: 28721448]

[43]   J. Ishioka, Y. Matsuoka, S. Uehara, Y. Yasuda, T. Kijima, S. Yoshida, M. Yokoyama, K. Saito, K. Kihara, N. Numao, T. Kimura, K. Kudo, I. Kumazawa, and Y. Fujii, "Computer-aided diagnosis of prostate cancer on magnetic resonance imaging using a convolutional neural network algorithm", *BJU Int.,* vol. 122, no. 3, pp. 411-417, 2018.
[http://dx.doi.org/10.1111/bju.14397] [PMID: 29772101]

[44]   I. Reda, A. Shalaby, M. Elmogy, A.A. Elfotouh, F. Khalifa, M.A. El-Ghar, E. Hosseini-Asl, G. Gimel'farb, N. Werghi, and A. El-Baz, "A comprehensive non-invasive framework for diagnosing prostate cancer", *Comput. Biol. Med.,* vol. 81, pp. 148-158, 2017.
[http://dx.doi.org/10.1016/j.compbiomed.2016.12.010] [PMID: 28063376]

[45]   X. Zhong, R. Cao, S. Shakeri, F. Scalzo, Y. Lee, D.R. Enzmann, H.H. Wu, S.S. Raman, and K. Sung, "Deep transfer learning-based prostate cancer classification using 3 Tesla multi-parametric MRI", *Abdom. Radiol. (N.Y.),* vol. 44, no. 6, pp. 2030-2039, 2019.
[http://dx.doi.org/10.1007/s00261-018-1824-5] [PMID: 30460529]

[46]   P. Peng, K. Lekadir, A. Gooya, L. Shao, S.E. Petersen, and A.F. Frangi, "A review of heart chamber segmentation for structural and functional analysis using cardiac magnetic resonance imaging", *MAGMA,* vol. 29, no. 2, pp. 155-195, 2016.
[http://dx.doi.org/10.1007/s10334-015-0521-4] [PMID: 26811173]

[47]   Y. Zheng, A. Barbu, B. Georgescu, M. Scheuering, and D. Comaniciu, "Four-chamber heart modeling and automatic segmentation for 3-D cardiac CT volumes using marginal space learning and steerable features", *IEEE Trans. Med. Imaging,* vol. 27, no. 11, pp. 1668-1681, 2008.
[http://dx.doi.org/10.1109/TMI.2008.2004421] [PMID: 18955181]

[48]   I. Diaz, P. Boulanger, R. Greiner, and A. Murtha, "A critical review of the effects of de-noising algorithms on MRI brain tumor segmentation", *Annu Int Conf IEEE Eng Med Biol Soc,* vol. 2011, pp. 3934-3937, 2011.
[http://dx.doi.org/10.1109/IEMBS.2011.6090977] [PMID: 22255200]

[49]   A. Wadhwa, A. Bhardwaj, and V. Singh Verma, "A review on brain tumor segmentation of MRI images", *Magn. Reson. Imaging,* vol. 61, pp. 247-259, 2019.
[http://dx.doi.org/10.1016/j.mri.2019.05.043] [PMID: 31200024]

[50]   E.H. Aylward, Q. Li, N.A. Honeycutt, A.C. Warren, M.B. Pulsifer, P.E. Barta, M.D. Chan, P.D. Smith, M. Jerram, and G.D. Pearlson, "MRI volumes of the hippocampus and amygdala in adults with Down's syndrome with and without dementia", *Am. J. Psychiatry,* vol. 156, no. 4, pp. 564-568, 1999.
[PMID: 10200735]

[51]   E. Mak, S. Gabel, L. Su, G.B. Williams, R. Arnold, L. Passamonti, P. Vazquez Rodríguez, A. Surendranathan, W.R. Bevan-Jones, J.B. Rowe, and J.T. O'Brien, "Multi-modal MRI investigation of volumetric and microstructural changes in the hippocampus and its subfields in mild cognitive impairment, Alzheimer's disease, and dementia with Lewy bodies", *Int. Psychogeriatr.,* vol. 29, no. 4, pp. 545-555, 2017.

[http://dx.doi.org/10.1017/S1041610216002143] [PMID: 28088928]

[52]   S. Valverde, M. Cabezas, E. Roura, S. González-Villà, D. Pareto, J.C. Vilanova, L. Ramió-Torrentà, À. Rovira, A. Oliver, and X. Lladó, "Improving automated multiple sclerosis lesion segmentation with a cascaded 3D convolutional neural network approach", *Neuroimage,* vol. 155, pp. 159-168, 2017.
       [http://dx.doi.org/10.1016/j.neuroimage.2017.04.034] [PMID: 28435096]

[53]   D.L. Pham, C. Xu, and J.L. Prince, "Current methods in medical image segmentation", *Annu. Rev. Biomed. Eng.,* vol. 2, pp. 315-337, 2000.
       [http://dx.doi.org/10.1146/annurev.bioeng.2.1.315] [PMID: 11701515]

[54]   J. Kleesiek, G. Urban, A. Hubert, D. Schwarz, K. Maier-Hein, M. Bendszus, and A. Biller, "Deep MRI brain extraction: A 3D convolutional neural network for skull stripping", *Neuroimage,* vol. 129, pp. 460-469, 2016.
       [http://dx.doi.org/10.1016/j.neuroimage.2016.01.024] [PMID: 26808333]

[55]   J. Dolz, X. Xu, J. Rony, J. Yuan, Y. Liu, E. Granger, C. Desrosiers, X. Zhang, I. Ben Ayed, and H. Lu, "Multiregion segmentation of bladder cancer structures in MRI with progressive dilated convolutional networks", *Med. Phys.,* vol. 45, no. 12, pp. 5482-5493, 2018.
       [http://dx.doi.org/10.1002/mp.13240] [PMID: 30328624]

[56]   C. Gros, B. De Leener, A. Badji, J. Maranzano, D. Eden, S.M. Dupont, J. Talbott, R. Zhuoquiong, Y. Liu, T. Granberg, R. Ouellette, Y. Tachibana, M. Hori, K. Kamiya, L. Chougar, L. Stawiarz, J. Hillert, E. Bannier, A. Kerbrat, G. Edan, P. Labauge, V. Callot, J. Pelletier, B. Audoin, H. Rasoanandrianina, J.C. Brisset, P. Valsasina, M.A. Rocca, M. Filippi, R. Bakshi, S. Tauhid, F. Prados, M. Yiannakas, H. Kearney, O. Ciccarelli, S. Smith, C.A. Treaba, C. Mainero, J. Lefeuvre, D.S. Reich, G. Nair, V. Auclair, D.G. McLaren, A.R. Martin, M.G. Fehlings, S. Vahdat, A. Khatibi, J. Doyon, T. Shepherd, E. Charlson, S. Narayanan, and J. Cohen-Adad, "Automatic segmentation of the spinal cord and intramedullary multiple sclerosis lesions with convolutional neural networks", *Neuroimage,* vol. 184, pp. 901-915, 2019.
       [http://dx.doi.org/10.1016/j.neuroimage.2018.09.081] [PMID: 30300751]

[57]   E. Shelhamer, J. Long, and T. Darrell, "Fully convolutional networks for semantic segmentation", *IEEE Trans. Pattern Anal. Mach. Intell.,* vol. 39, no. 4, pp. 640-651, 2017.
       [http://dx.doi.org/10.1109/TPAMI.2016.2572683] [PMID: 27244717]

[58]   O. Ronneberger, P. Fischer, and T. Brox, "U-net: Convolutional networks for biomedical image segmentation", *International Conference on Medical image computing and computer-assisted intervention,* 2015
       [http://dx.doi.org/10.1007/978-3-319-24574-4_28]

[59]   M.Z. Alom, C. Yakopcic, M. Hasan, T.M. Taha, and V.K. Asari, "Recurrent residual U-Net for medical image segmentation", *J. Med. Imaging (Bellingham),* vol. 6, no. 1, p. 014006, 2019.
       [http://dx.doi.org/10.1117/1.JMI.6.1.014006] [PMID: 30944843]

[60]   M.P. Heinrich, O. Oktay, and N. Bouteldja, "OBELISK-Net: Fewer layers to solve 3D multi-organ segmentation with sparse deformable convolutions", *Med. Image Anal.,* vol. 54, pp. 1-9, 2019.
       [http://dx.doi.org/10.1016/j.media.2019.02.006] [PMID: 30807894]

[61]   T. Falk, D. Mai, R. Bensch, Ö. Çiçek, A. Abdulkadir, Y. Marrakchi, A. Böhm, J. Deubner, Z. Jäckel, K. Seiwald, A. Dovzhenko, O. Tietz, C. Dal Bosco, S. Walsh, D. Saltukoglu, T.L. Tay, M. Prinz, K. Palme, M. Simons, I. Diester, T. Brox, and O. Ronneberger, "U-Net: deep learning for cell counting, detection, and morphometry", *Nat. Methods,* vol. 16, no. 1, pp. 67-70, 2019.
       [http://dx.doi.org/10.1038/s41592-018-0261-2] [PMID: 30559429]

[62]   H. Hwang, H.Z.U. Rehman, and S. Lee, "3D u-net for skull stripping in brain mri", *Applied Sciences-Basel,* vol. 9, no. 3, 2019.

[63]   W.K. Huang, and L.K. Hu, "Using a noisy u-net for detecting lung nodule candidates", *IEEE Access,* vol. 7, pp. 67905-67915, 2019.
       [http://dx.doi.org/10.1109/ACCESS.2019.2918224]

[64]   P. Blanc-Durand, A. Van Der Gucht, N. Schaefer, E. Itti, and J.O. Prior, "Automatic lesion detection and segmentation of 18F-FET PET in gliomas: A full 3D U-Net convolutional neural network study", *PLoS One,* vol. 13, no. 4, p. e0195798, 2018.
[http://dx.doi.org/10.1371/journal.pone.0195798] [PMID: 29652908]

[65]   J. Yang, M. Faraji, and A. Basu, "Robust segmentation of arterial walls in intravascular ultrasound images using Dual Path U-Net", *Ultrasonics,* vol. 96, pp. 24-33, 2019.
[http://dx.doi.org/10.1016/j.ultras.2019.03.014] [PMID: 30947071]

[66]   H. Zhu, F. Shi, L. Wang, S.C. Hung, M.H. Chen, S. Wang, W. Lin, and D. Shen, "Dilated dense u-net for infant hippocampus subfield segmentation", *Front. Neuroinform.,* vol. 13, p. 30, 2019.
[http://dx.doi.org/10.3389/fninf.2019.00030] [PMID: 31068797]

[67]   A. Sotiras, C. Davatzikos, and N. Paragios, "Deformable medical image registration: a survey", *IEEE Trans. Med. Imaging,* vol. 32, no. 7, pp. 1153-1190, 2013.
[http://dx.doi.org/10.1109/TMI.2013.2265603] [PMID: 23739795]

[68]   M. Simonovsky, "A deep metric for multimodal registration", *International conference on medical image computing and computer-assisted intervention,* 2016

[69]   Y. Hu, M. Modat, E. Gibson, W. Li, N. Ghavami, E. Bonmati, G. Wang, S. Bandula, C.M. Moore, M. Emberton, S. Ourselin, J.A. Noble, D.C. Barratt, and T. Vercauteren, "Weakly-supervised convolutional neural networks for multimodal image registration", *Med. Image Anal.,* vol. 49, pp. 1-13, 2018.
[http://dx.doi.org/10.1016/j.media.2018.07.002] [PMID: 30007253]

[70]   S. Sun, "Robust multimodal image registration using deep recurrent reinforcement learning", *Asian Conference on Computer Vision,* 2018

[71]   I. Goodfellow, "Generative adversarial nets", *Adv Neural Inf Process Syst.,* 2014.

[72]   H. Emami, M. Dong, S.P. Nejad-Davarani, and C.K. Glide-Hurst, "Generating synthetic CTs from magnetic resonance images using generative adversarial networks", *Med. Phys.,* vol. 45, no. 8, pp. 3627-3636, 2018.
[http://dx.doi.org/10.1002/mp.13047] [PMID: 29901223]

[73]   D. Nie, "Medical image synthesis with context-aware generative adversarial networks", *Med Image Comput Comput Assist Interv,* vol. 10435, pp. 417-425, 2017.

[74]   S.U. Dar, M. Yurt, L. Karacan, A. Erdem, E. Erdem, and T. Cukur, "Image synthesis in multi-contrast mri with conditional generative adversarial networks", *IEEE Trans. Med. Imaging,* vol. 38, no. 10, pp. 2375-2388, 2019.
[http://dx.doi.org/10.1109/TMI.2019.2901750] [PMID: 30835216]

[75]   Y. Chen, "Efficient and accurate MRI super-resolution using a generative adversarial network and 3D multi-level densely connected network", *International Conference on Medical Image Computing and Computer-Assisted Intervention,* 2018

[76]   K. Yan, "Deep lesion graphs in the wild: relationship learning and organization of significant radiology image findings in a diverse large-scale lesion database", *Proceedings of the IEEE Conference on Computer Vision and Pattern Recognition,* 2018

[77]   T.M. Quan, T. Nguyen-Duc, and W.K. Jeong, "Compressed sensing mri reconstruction using a generative adversarial network with a cyclic loss", *IEEE Trans. Med. Imaging,* vol. 37, no. 6, pp. 1488-1497, 2018.
[http://dx.doi.org/10.1109/TMI.2018.2820120] [PMID: 29870376]

[78]   G. Yang, S. Yu, H. Dong, G. Slabaugh, P.L. Dragotti, X. Ye, F. Liu, S. Arridge, J. Keegan, Y. Guo, D. Firmin, J. Keegan, G. Slabaugh, S. Arridge, X. Ye, Y. Guo, S. Yu, F. Liu, D. Firmin, P.L. Dragotti, G. Yang, and H. Dong, "Dagan: deep de-aliasing generative adversarial networks for fast compressed sensing mri reconstruction", *IEEE Trans. Med. Imaging,* vol. 37, no. 6, pp. 1310-1321, 2018.
[http://dx.doi.org/10.1109/TMI.2017.2785879] [PMID: 29870361]

[79] S.J. Esses, X. Lu, T. Zhao, K. Shanbhogue, B. Dane, M. Bruno, and H. Chandarana, "Automated image quality evaluation of T2 -weighted liver MRI utilizing deep learning architecture", *J. Magn. Reson. Imaging,* vol. 47, no. 3, pp. 723-728, 2018.
      [http://dx.doi.org/10.1002/jmri.25779] [PMID: 28577329]

[80] Q. Yang, P. Yan, Y. Zhang, H. Yu, Y. Shi, X. Mou, M.K. Kalra, Y. Zhang, L. Sun, and G. Wang, "Low-dose ct image denoising using a generative adversarial network with wasserstein distance and perceptual loss", *IEEE Trans. Med. Imaging,* vol. 37, no. 6, pp. 1348-1357, 2018.
      [http://dx.doi.org/10.1109/TMI.2018.2827462] [PMID: 29870364]

[81] X. Chen, and E. Konukoglu, "Unsupervised detection of Lesions in brain MRI using constrained adversarial auto-encoders", *arXiv preprint,* 2018.

[82] A. Zhao, "Data augmentation using learned transformations for one-shot medical image segmentation", *Proceedings of the IEEE Conference on Computer Vision and Pattern Recognition,* 2019

CHAPTER 4

AI in Instrumentation Industry

Ajay V. Deshmukh[1,*]

[1] *Phaltan Education Society's College of Engineering Phaltan, India*

Abstract: Artificial intelligence (AI) as the name suggests is a new way of automatically deciding upon the operation and control of real time machines and processes in industry. The advantages of using artificial intelligence in industry are many. First of all the decisions are dynamic and real time without any human intervention. Next, it is not based on any formula which in the past required updating for different process conditions and time. Operational technologies did not deploy complete intelligence systems and there used to be much more complexity in tuning the processes and systems together. Training of the operational people was very much crucial and required periodic updates from time to time as the operational technologies changed. AI can overcome most of these complexities, due to the fact that it obtains a data driven solution in real time. Intelligence could be distributed right from the sensory levels to higher levels of distributed computerized systems. Internet of Things (IoTs) and data analytics can provide dynamic information on the performance of machines and processes. Industries which would benefit from technologies based on Artificial Intelligence (AI), Machine Learning (ML) and Deep learning (DL) are in general any process or manufacturing industries including healthcare, petroleum, power sector, automotive *etc.* In fact this would lead to applicability of Industry 4.0. In this chapter different concepts and applicability of AI in industry have been described. Off course it is possible due to the powerful computational tools, which help not only in doing computations, but also in terms of the capability of communication control, plus data storage, transmission and intelligent decision making.

Keywords: Artificial Intelligence (AI), Industry 4.0., Industry Applications, Machines and Processes, Manufacturing, Process and Healthcare Industries.

INTRODUCTION

Advances in instrument technologies have seen a significant shift as far as the tools and techniques are concerned. Subsequently, it has made and is going to make equally powerful impact on the process and manufacturing industry through Industry 4.0. This is possible with the help of powerful computational tools, communication protocols, for example using wireless communication, as well as

* **Corresponding author Ajay V. Deshmukh:** Phaltan Education Society's College of Engineering Phaltan, India; Tel: +91-7447 4746 52; E-mail: ajay.deshmukh@rediffmail.com

Terje Solsvik Kristensen (Ed.)

much more decision making capacity. This is possible due to the data driven methods and powerful techniques with the help of AI, ML, DL [1 - 3]. Therefore, today almost any complex algorithm could be used for the control of machines and processes. Over and above it has also been IoTs and Data Analytic applications which make decisions on process plants as a whole in real time. This allows monitoring and supervising the performance of process and machines or individual units in a plant. The new top up technologies over the past automation systems do not necessarily require removal or replacement of sensors, transmitters and automation systems however, the data could be made available for the existing data management systems. This would further be sent either over a cloud or there could be edge analytics [4] confined to the boundaries of the process plants. Edge analytics include all the devices like cell phones, camera, except those which are not connected to cloud. Data security and safety are an essential part of the modern instrumentation systems.

It becomes important now to investigate what has changed or changing when AI techniques are applied. Industry 4.0 [5, 6] makes use of cyberphysical systems, so-called smart factories. Important aspect of such systems is that the automation systems are part of physical systems, the cyber layer is going to get added. This requires that there could be a data collection from the existing systems and rest of the things including big data processing [7] and decision making can be done by using AI [8, 9]. This is the first important direction to apply the concept of Industry 4.0 to process or manufacturing industries.

New hope for the future business in this field is to design and deploy AI, ML and DL techniques by applying a slightly top up or higher level electronics and software systems. There is a scope to apply newer and newer communication protocols, reduce the cost of the electronics and software systems, making it more reliable, user friendly and safe, immediate access to operational data, condition monitoring, preventive and predictive maintenance, reduced down times, on line report generation making use of data analytics [5] as applied to a process or manufacturing industry. This is going to help the top management or plant heads to take better decisions like reduced inventories, better supply chain management, and even the plant economy. Business analytics along with plant analytics would survey the whole purpose. In this chapter, sustainable solutions have also been considered in addition to the applicability of the AI to process and manufacturing industries. It would help if a reader can work out Data Analytics and IoT requirements for other industry sector like Health care, Power Sector, Oil and Gas, in order to know the complexities involved in managing such giant industries.

A SYSTEMATIC APPROACH TO APPLIED AI

Industry looks for its own objectives, but responds very quickly to contemporary technologies, as it is going to help in improving the whole business. During Industry 3.0, where only computerization and communication technologies were available, have also seen changes in terms of automation and data management and presentation systems. However, most of those systems landed up with technical data or technical trends and the rest of the economics was not dynamically addressed, due to the complexity of managing big data. In spite of the availability of literature on data analytics and artificial intelligence several years ago, the computational tools and techniques were not capable of handling real time calculations of big data. Neither many experts thought of working on faster algorithms, as it would not serve the purpose to meet the objectives which today AI, ML, and DL methods can fulfill. Uncertainties in building models [11] and even model predictive systems were not sufficient to take care of the whole plants and with respect to time as well. Therefore, there were many unknown parameters, which did not appear. Although the data was available, it was not possible to find out meaningful information quickly for decision making. Most of the data collected even did not contain any meaningful information. Empirical methods did work to a limited capacity but did not provide complete solutions.

Today, in the newer approach, data driven methods making use of AI, ML and DL methods can provide meaningful reports about the process or manufacturing plant, with any complexities and uncertainties.

ARTIFICIAL INTELLIGENCE AND ITS NEED

For better understanding of the need of AI, a simple approach is to consider a chemical industry with processes like distillation column, fermentation units or chemical reactors. The first question such an industry asks is 'what are IoTs? Then how data analytics or AI based systems would overcome the present problems? A clear picture of IoTs and Data analytic systems can provide answers to these questions. Ultimately, one is trying to define AI requirement including other systems like electronics for data collection and processing.

Some of the problems that would be immediately addressed are operation and process control [10, 11] and measurements [12]. This was done earlier and even in many of the present methods in industries with measurement systems, operational technologies, process control and automation including the use of programmable logic controllers, supervisory control and data acquisition systems (SCADA), or using large distributed control systems (DCS). Field bus technologies and variants are normally used for field communication. Modern devices and instruments use wireless communication systems. These industrial communication systems could also take care of powering the field transmitters and allow multidrop connections. Typically Highway Addressable Remote Transducer (HART) protocol is popular and used by many of the modern instruments. The challenges of these systems are how to make them safe, specifically in Hazardous areas [13].

Already a lot of work is done in industries like oil and gas which use electricity and inflammable materials. Standards have been developed and best practices are followed for such sensitive applications. On the other hand, some of the issues like testing, self-diagnosis, calibration, traceability, physical standards [14] have been developed to the expectations of modern industry. Going beyond there are opportunities and challenges to work further on these lines using modern methods based on AI, ML and DL and making use of big data in industries. Process plant safety [15], is again an important problem to be readdressed while deploying these modern methods. Earlier the instrument and safety systems did not allow software usage in emergencies, but today due to reliability and standardization, the software control of safety systems is widely used, however at the cost of potential cyber threats. Therefore, additional protections deploying cybersecurity are needed to overcome such newer problems. As far as control engineering is concerned, there have been a lot of developments. The techniques in these fields have been very well established [16, 17]. These methods allow handling control problems, stability issues and estimation approaches to apply for process control problems. There are many such tools and techniques including those in digital signal processing [18]. Time has come to address the industrial problems in thermodynamics [19] digitally using the modern methods. So topics like thermodynamics and electromagnetics [20] must go hand in hand digitally. For more details a reader may refer to many such reading resources available elsewhere as it is beyond the scope of this chapter. Ultimately there would be lot of changes in addressing the problem of measurement and Process control instrumentation [21]. Now, with the present advancements use of Artificial Intelligence [22] and machine learning techniques, the instrumentation industry is entering into what now is called Industry 4.0.

AI IN CHEMICAL PROCESS INDUSTRY

Chemical process industries, involve unit operations like distillation column, fermentation, evaporations, heat exchangers, boilers, separation processes *etc.* In addition to these there are machines like compressors, pumps, turbines, generators, and many more. First of all, it is necessary to define the role of AI in such applications. Let us consider one example of a process control problem of *pH*, where traditional methods do not lead to any proper control solution to the expectations, even theoretically. There are many such process control problems in industry. As is known, pH is defined as the negative logarithm of hydrogen ion concentration with base 10.

$$p^H = -\log_{10}[H^+] \qquad\qquad (1)$$

pH value ranges from 0 to 14, with 7 being a neutral solution. Below 7 means acidic and above 7 mean alkaline solution. The importance of this problem is so much due to the following reasons:

- A low *pH* of solution causes corrosion of pipes, and pumps, valves and other components.

- Certain applications demand certain pH values.

- Extreme pH values may affect biological activities, specifically in municipal water treatment plants.

- Low pH waste water may dissolve significant quantity of toxic heavy metals.

- Extreme *pH*, may mix with other industrial waste effluents to form toxic products

Safe operation of the units and processes require that those be monitored and controlled. Therefore, operational technologies and automation are essentially required. In this section some of the open challenges have been discussed which are yet to be overcome using the current methods in spite of whatever advancements in automation have been made. Fig. (**1**) shows a schematic of control loops which control the pH of the products. The problem in this application is to control the pH of the process fluid, by adding exact amount of acidic or alkaline reagent, dynamically. This type of pH control is susceptible to temperature changes and is sensitive as well as highly nonlinear. First of all there are rangeability problems which put a significant constraints on pipe sizes and valve sizes. Such problems are more and more difficult to control, in spite of having advanced instrumentation that is deployed today. This is only one example, however almost this kind of degree of difficulty is there in many process control problems. Let us find out the need of AI- and ML- based methods in this particular problem area.

It could be easily observed that the difficulty lies in modeling the process. Next, the type of controllers available today even in software or hardware is not fully able to overcome the problem. Selection of valves, flow meters, reagent controllers and sensors, everything is crucial. Therefore, this would be the best example where AI can help in overcoming some of these problems. The strategies of designing a control system now shall make use of the data that is recorded by the same system as shown in Fig. (**1**). Tuning of loops shall be done with the help of data driven methods. Only the problems related to saturation of valves at extreme positions would be beyond the control. However, for the sake of simplicity let us assume that the process components are such that there is no saturation due to the rangeability of valves. Next, it is assumed that the reagents are available as needed to run the process.

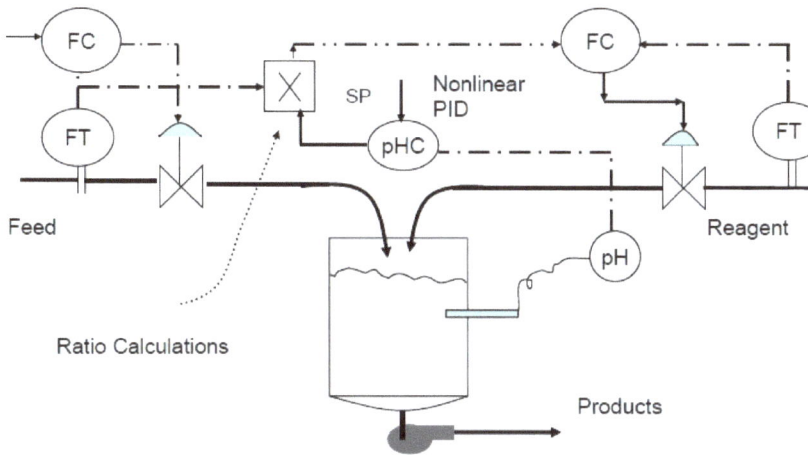

Fig. (1). Example of a pH Control Problem.

Normally it is the ratio of acidic and alkaline reagent that is calculated and based on the desired value of the *pH* (called the set point SP), valves are manipulated using a nonlinear controller. It must be noted that as the process is nonlinear so only nonlinear controllers can solve the problem. Fig. (**2**) shows a schematic of a typical neural network based system to solve the problem.

In Fig. (**2**) x_1, x_2 and x_3 are acid flow, base flow and *pH* value respectively. Whereas the output of the neural network estimates the ratio of these acidic and alkaline reagents. Ultimately, the ratio set point is derived. Normally temperature compensation is done using a separate temperature measurement system and by adding corrections or by maintaining the process temperature constant. There could be variants of the schemes which might substitute the one shown in Fig. (1). However, this can give a good understanding of the process as well as control strategies using AI based method. Again, variants of AI based methods could be deployed. The advantage of using AI based methods is that the data could be processed in real time and there is no need to use any fixed process model.

Furthermore, data analytics would help on the process efficiency, optimization, economic factors, inventory management and material saving.

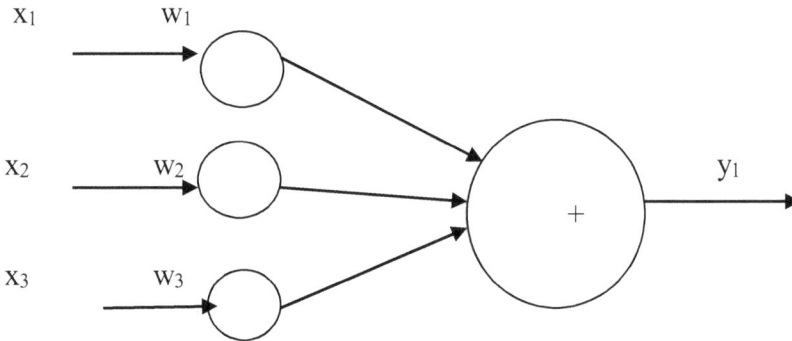

Fig. (2). A neural network model for *pH* control.

AI IN MANUFACTURING PROCESS INDUSTRY

Manufacturing industry involves mechanical operations typically on an assembly line with a lot of automation and instrumentation, testing rigs and quality control systems. Operations like robotic welding and quality testing require intelligent decisions. Industry 4.0 demands use of AI, ML and DL based approaches for such applications leading to a SMART factory or self-optimizing factory or digital factory as termed by different experts in this field. Let us discuss another example from manufacturing industry. Processes like welding are extremely difficult for manual inspections. Some of the past and present efforts include methods based on process supervision, but cannot test the final output quality. Other methods are based on manual inspection or X-ray based testing of welding joints, but all these are time consuming. Sometimes dimensional analysis of the parts is essentially required along with such quality tests so that vision based systems are appearing in manufacturing industries which comprise of a camera. Subsequently, images are digitally processed to verify the dimensions or even for geometry of such parts. As an example of advanced Industry 4.0 approach to do this, consider Fig. (3), which shows a scheme for smart manufacturing process.

To deploy methods making use of data driven approaches, for manufacturing industries the manufacturing process as well as automation forms a physical layer and the cyber layer make a complete digital factory. Therefore, a lot of AI and ML can go into this cyber block to have SMART manufacturing. This can bring augmented reality, digital manufacturing, and digital quality control. Again, the advantages of deploying SMART factories are safe and reliable operation, saving on materials and inventories, reduced cost, digitally controlled supply chain management, better economy of the factory and reduced downtimes with diagnostics and condition monitoring of machines and processes to achieve desired production in time. Some of the methods also save time. Predictive data analytics can bring future predictions about the whole industry business. Some of the problems require AI and ML based methods in order to have better surface finish, accuracies in dimensions, reduced rejection of parts, improved speed of production, and safety in plant, including cyber security. Through some of the visits to automotive manufacturing industries, it was observed that in addition to initial investment, and collaborative working culture, technology advantage is preferred by many operational people. So, AI in an Industry 4.0 system, is going to be a solution to many complex problems which otherwise could not be traced at all.

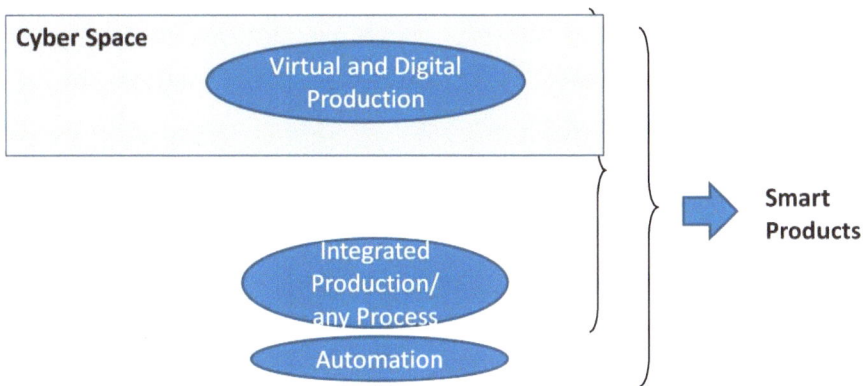

Fig. (3). Industry 4.0 and Smart Manufacturing.

AI for Quality Control

Quality management is essentially required in manufacturing or in any process industry in general. It is not the only output quality, but also at various stages on assembly line of the manufacturing process, it has to be evaluated. At output one may look for dimensions of the parts, distance between two points on a machine object, surface finish, presence of all geometric or morphological aspects, correctness of printed labels on the parts or products. Test jigs for such applications could be based on optical, acoustic, x-ray based, or vision-based systems. As discussed earlier for example welding for automotive chassis could be tested for quality using x-ray based methods and a few other dimension measurements could be done using a vision based system. There are, however quality checks of the input materials and spares, and the process quality management. The processes involve material flows on conveyor belts or through pipelines. This suggest that there is a need of process monitoring not only for operational point of view but also for quality and reliability. Statistical process control is very commonly used in such applications.

AI in Process Monitoring

Data from process input output requires a dynamic monitoring and subsequent corrections in a process plant [11, 23]. In any process there are inputs and outputs. If a process is considered to have M inputs and N outputs then a balance on cost of input and output streams could be attained by equation (2).

$$\sum_{i=1}^{p} a_{ij}x_i = 0 \qquad (2)$$

where $p=M + N$. Variables x could be process variables at the inputs or outputs like flow rate of components, total flow rate, enthalpy for instance. Equation (2) can be written in a matrix form as below,

$$Ax = 0 \qquad (3)$$

Elements of A in general are positive for input variables and negative for output variables. Now x consists of p known variables and unknown variables. Unknown variables are either not accessible or not known at all. This causes a lot of uncertainty. Therefore, accurate process monitoring and control requires managing the unknown variables, where AI and ML based methods are much helpful. Equation (3) is ultimately the energy and mass balance equation. If flow rates of input materials and cost factors are made implicit to the variables, then the cost of materials flowing and energy flowing into a process, could be dynamically evaluated. Therefore, plant economy in terms of material and energy could be obtained as shown in Fig. (**4**).

Process monitoring involves plant health monitoring as well as it must take into account cost involved in the startup and shut down or maintenance cost, specifically the losses in down times. For power systems, effective reactive power management can improve the plant economy, similarly in case of steam driven equipment energy conservation is crucial. Conservation of water and similar resources is a must while reducing the operational costs.

In order to overcome the uncertainty in process measurements, AI tools are essentially required. In presence of noise or uncertainty, based on measurable input and outputs, it can adapt itself to provide the desired performance. This is again due to the data driven methods. There are typical tasks on assembly lines like calculating the volumes and weights of objects moving on conveyor belts, packaging of the products for dispatching. Automation is present in today's systems for such applications. Pattern recognition and AI based approaches find applications here. On-line analyzers are also deployed for quality sorting of products specifically in food, pharmaceutical and chemical industry.

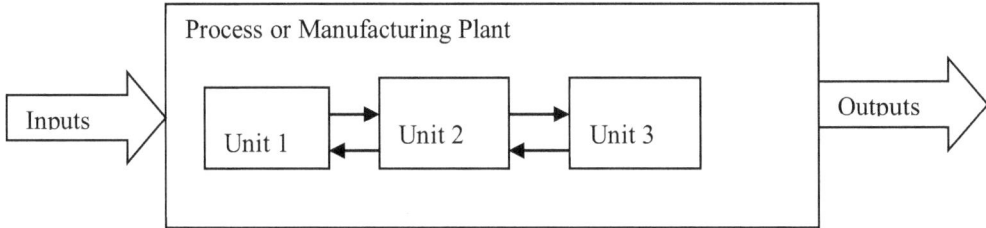

Fig. (4). Process/Manufacturing plant input output cash flows.

AI in Plant Safety

Plant safety is equally important in manufacturing and process industries. Safety of people and safety of machines, safe use of chemicals, electricity, and electrical equipment, fire safety, cybersecurity and safety are considered as far as the safety is concerned. Role of AI in safety [24, 25] is very important. Fault diagnostics and on line analysis requires AI, ML and DL based approaches. A lot of data is normally available in any plant which needs to be filtered and labeled to know the cause of failures because of which safe operations are affected. For example, a simple exothermic reaction or dust or powder accumulating on the parts of rotating machines might cause fire. Heated surface, oxygen and presence of inflammable material are good enough to cause fire. Wearing of machine parts could be understood from vibration monitoring. Failures of sensors could be understood from the data that is recorded. All such applications involve complexity in terms of data processing.

AI safety standards [24] are to be followed while applying AI, ML, DL methods. For instance, AI safety Standards Developing Organization (SDO) is one such nongovernment organization accredited by the American National Standards Institute (ANSI) or (Institute of Electrical and Electronic Engineers) IEEE and (International Society of Automation) ISA guidelines on AI safety are important.

CONCLUSION

Digital world of manufacturing and process control demands AI, ML and DL based methods. Some of the other techniques like Fuzzy logic and expert systems or optimization methods would lead to the expectations of process control managers in terms of overall economics and plant health with real time information. Ultimately, AI is going to decide upon many complex issues in digitalization of manufacturing and process control systems. The discussion in this chapter is towards applicability of AI based systems covering some of the important concepts. It would help in deciding the very first approach towards digital factories and knowing the applicability of AI based methods. It also requires that for the implementation of AI based methods in factories and process industries, a cross disciplinary understanding of manufacturing processes as well as computer and electronics is required.

CONSENT FOR PUBLICATION

Not applicable.

CONFLICT OF INTEREST

The author declares no conflict of interest, financial or otherwise.

ACKNOWLEDGEMENTS

Declared none.

REFERENCES

[1]   F. Amigoni, G. D'Antona, R. Ottboni, and M. Somalvico, "Artificial intelligence in science of measurement: from measurement instruments to perceptive agencies", *IEEE Trans. Instrum. Meas.,* vol. 52, no. 3, pp. 716-723, 2003.
[http://dx.doi.org/10.1109/TIM.2003.814694]

[2]   A. Huang, *The Era of Artificial Intelligence and Big Data Provides Knowledge Services for the Publishing Industry in China.* Publishing Research Quarterly: Springer, US, 2019, pp. 35-164.

[3]   P. Tubaro, and A.A. Casilli, "Artificial intelligence and the automotive industry", *Econ. Polit. Ind.,* vol. 46, no. 3, pp. 333-345, 2019.
[http://dx.doi.org/10.1007/s40812-019-00121-1]

[4]   M. Satyanarayanan, P. Simoens, and Y. Xiao, "Edge analytics in the internet of things", *PERVASIVE computing,* IEEE CS, pp. 24-31, 2015.

[5]   V. Dragan, J. Vešić, and K. Davor, *Industry 4.0: the Future Concepts and New Visions of Factory of the Future Development,* pp. 293-298, 2016.

[6]   S. Zippel, *Process Industry 4.0 : Transforming the process industry with Industry 4.0.,* 2nd EditionInTech Plus, ISA Publication, for Automation and Control Professionals, 2019.

[7]   D.P. Acharjya, and A.P. Kauser, "A survey on big data analytics: challenges, open research issues and tools", *Int. J. of Adv. Comp. Sc and Appl,* vol. 7, no. 2, pp. 511-518, 2016.

[8]   R. Basset, "IoT and industrial AI: Mining intelligence from industrial things", *InTech Magazine,* ISA Publications, 2019.

[9]   G. Shaw, *Future Computed AI & Manufacturing.* Microsoft: USA, 2019.

[10]   W.C. Dunn, *Fundamentals of Instrumentation and Process Control.* Mc-Graw Hill, 2005.

[11]   J. A. Ramagnoli, and A. Palazolu, "Introduction to process control",

[12]   E.O. Doeblin, and N.M. Dhanesh, *Measurement Systems"* 6 e/d. McGraw Hill: Tata, 2007.

[13]   G. Bottrill, and D. Cheyne, *Practical Equipment and Installations in Hazardous Areas.* Elsevier, 2005.

[14]   J.V. Nicholas, and D.R. White, *Traceable Temperatures: An introduction to Measurement and Calibration.* Wiley, 2001.
[http://dx.doi.org/10.1002/0470846151]

[15]   G.L. Wells, *Safety in Process Plant Design.* John Wiley: New York, 1980.

[16]   F.L. Lewis, *Optimal Estimation: With an Introduction to Stochastic Control Theory.* John Wiley, 1986.

[17]   M.S. Fadali, and A. Visioli, *Digital Control Engineering: Analysis and Design.* Academic Press, Elsevier, 2009.

[18]   A.V. Oppenheim, and R. Schafer, *Discrete Time Signal Processing.* Prentice-Hall of India: New Delhi, 2000.

[19]   Cengel Y.A., and Boles M.A., *Thermodynamics: An Engineering Approach"* 8th e/d. McGraw Hill, 2016.

[20]   E.M. Purcell, and D.J. Morin, *Electricity and Magnetism"* 3rd e/d. Cambridge University Press, 2013.
[http://dx.doi.org/10.1017/CBO9781139012973]

[21]   N.A. Anderson, *Instrumentation for Process Measurement and Control"* 3rd e/d. CRC Press, 2005.

[22]   C. Alippi, A. Ferrero, and V. Piuri, "Artificial intelligence for instruments and measurement applications", *IEEE Instrum. Meas. Mag.,* no. June, pp. 9-17, 1998.
[http://dx.doi.org/10.1109/5289.685492]

[23]   A.C. Thomson, "Real-time artificial intelligence for process monitoring and control", *IFAC Proceedings, Science Direct,* vol. 21, 1988no. 13, pp. 67-72. https://www.sciencedirect.com/science/article/pii/S1474667017537015

[24]   S. Ozlati, and R. Yampolskiy, "The formalization of ai risk management and safety standards", *The AAAI-17 Workshop on AI, Ethics, and Society,* p. WS-17-0

[25]   S. Armsrong, and K. Sotala, "The errors, insights and lessons of famous AI predictions and what they mean for the future", *J. Exp. Theor. Artif. Intell.,* vol. 26, no. 3, pp. 317-342, 2014.
[http://dx.doi.org/10.1080/0952813X.2014.895105]

CHAPTER 5

AI in Business and Education

Tarjei Alvær Heggernes[1,*]

¹ Department of Strategy and Entrepreneurship, BI Norwegian Business School, Bergen, Norway

Abstract: In recent years, the interest for artificial intelligence has gone from the computing department to the board room. Business leaders are in a rush to explore the possibilities presented by the abundance of data, processing power and the methods of AI to create business value and business opportunities. In this chapter we will adapt the view of a manager and explore some of technologies used in machine learning. We will also look at how managers should approach artificial intelligence. The chapter will close with a discussion of some cases of usage of the different technologies. One case will come from marketing and discusses the use of reinforcement learning in real-time bidding on an e-commerce platform. The next two cases are from the education industry, one case will discuss reinforcement learning in intelligent tutoring systems, and the final case will discuss neural networks in grading of tests and assignments. There are many exciting use cases for artificial intelligence, it is important for business managers to understand the possibilities, and equally important for programmers to understand how businesses create value.

Keywords: Artificial Intelligence, Deep learning, E-commerce, Education technology, Machine Learning, Neural networks, Real-time bidding, Reinforcement learning, Supervised learning, Unsupervised learning.

INTRODUCTION

There is a lot of talk about artificial intelligence (AI), such as Machine learning and neural networks. These are some of the subsets of AI that have received increased attention from 2016 until today. AI as a concept has been discussed since the 50s, most famously by Turing [1]. The recent years' development in both the cost and capacity for processing of data, as well as for collecting large amounts of data, has made previously theoretical concepts technically feasible and useful.

* **Corresponding author Tarjei Alvær Heggernes:** Department of Strategy and Entrepreneurship, BI Norwegian Business School, Bergen, Norway; Tel: +4793052940; E-mail: tarjei.a.heggernes@bi.no

Science fiction writer Arthur C. Clarke once said that any technology advanced far enough is impossible to distinguish from magic [2]. It is easy to think of artificial intelligence as magic, but it is important to remember that it is software. In each AI project, engineers are working on and improving the set of rules and algorithms needed to make artificial intelligence appear magic.

The same Clarke wrote in Playboy in 1968 that within our lifetime, super-intelligent computers - almost impossible to distinguish from humans - would give us the mixed blessing of a life without work [3]. Now, 50 years later we humans seem to be working more than ever, so that claim is exaggerated. Even so, we can see computers doing more and more tasks that were previously done by humans. A challenge for managers is figuring out which part of a task should be done by machines, and which part is better done by humans.

THE INDUSTRIAL REVOLUTION AND THE LONG ECONOMIC WAVES

With the Industrial Revolution, beginning around 1789, started a global economic process counting five long economic waves, with an average duration of 50-55 years [4]. The technological developments in the different periods have always substituted human power with the power of machines. The first, what we today call the industrial revolution, replaced the organic power of humans and animals with steam power, then came the mass transport period such as the railroad, followed by more power through electricity and manufacturing technology. The fourth economic wave was based on electronics and individual mobility through the proliferation of the automobile. It is during the early part of the fifth economic wave, starting around 1995, that we get the information and communication period. One of the hallmarks of this current period is computer technology, enhancing production technology, robots and the internet.

ARTIFICIAL INTELLIGENCE AND INDUSTRY 4.0

Internet was introduced at the start of the 5th economic wave. As internet became global things started to get linked together, and around 2000 we got The Industrial Internet of Things (iIoT), which is also known as Industry 4.0, when applied to the manufacturing industry. It is a concept of integrating smart manufacturing machinery, AI-powered automation, and advanced analytics to help make every worker and every factory more efficient.

In addition to helping with the heavy lifting, computer technology could also help humans with calculations and remembering. With the advent of I4.0 [5] – the information and communication period, software, computing power, data collection and storage, and data communication made it possible for separate systems to work together in new ways, and to do even more of the heavy mental lifting of mankind by using artificial intelligence.

What can AI do?

What tasks can artificial intelligence perform just as well, or better than humans? In an overview of AI milestones where AI outperforms humans from 1980 until 2015, most of the examples are of computer programs outperform people in all kind of games from chess to advanced computer games. Impressive of course, but in itself not very useful [6]. In 2016, however, an artificial intelligence technique that classifies images in the image database 'Image' managed to classify images with a margin of error of 3%, against the average human error margin of 5%. After this, there have been good improvements in both image recognition and speech recognition, and in 2018, Google developed a deep learning system that could recognize prostate cancer with 70% accuracy, against 61% accuracy in a panel of certified pathologists.

However, it is important not to attach too much weight to these milestones, because so far there are no good ways to transfer artificial intelligence from one application to another. On the other hand, there is a great potential for being able to use AI in business operations, as most tasks performed in a business are neither as complex nor as vital as diagnosing prostate cancer.

Looking at the research that is done in 2018 in the field of artificial intelligence, the main area of research is focused on health and medicine, at least in the western parts of the world. The result of the research will help us stay healthy longer. China has had a tremendous development in AI research in recent years, a lot of the research is applied in the field of agriculture, in other words, to help feed the people efficiently.

During the writing process, a project using sensors to prevent patients in psychiatry from taking suicide is mentioned on the news [7]. The sensors measure sleep rhythm, pulse and presence in the bathroom, and based on the collected data the probability of the patient committing suicide is predicted. In addition to hoping that this can save human life, this case reminds us of two important features of artificial intelligence: The use of data, often from sensors, and the ability of the program to predict probable outcomes in the future. See also [8] on digital suicide prevention.

DEFINITIONS

An overall definition for categorizing this type of software is: IT applications that can sense, understand, act and learn [9, 10]. We return to these properties of the software during the chapter.

We often distinguish between general, broad or strong AI, and specific, or narrow AI [11]. General AI is what we often see in horror scenarios in literature and on film, where an AI becomes conscious of itself, and then finds out that humans are a plague and a nuisance that it will get rid of. A general AI should have the same level of comprehension as human intelligence. We are far from being able to develop this kind of AI [12], it requires both more advanced programming and more powerful processing than what is available today. Still, technology is advancing at an exponential pace, so general AI is a possible scenario for the future.

Narrow AI, however, has a strictly defined field of application with clear rules, and is already in use in several areas. Smart speakers like Alexa and Google Home, self-driving cars, and personal assistants like Siri on iPhone are examples of narrow AI. The development of narrow AI has been driven by a subset of AI called Machine Learning.

Machine Learning

Machine learning can be defined as computational methods using experience to enhance performance or to make accurate predictions [13]. A model is made for predicting a result (B) based on input (A), and a set of data, training data, is used to train the model. Later on, another set of data, test data, is used to test the model [14]. An example often used is input data containing hand-written numbers, and the output a vector with probabilities for which actual number the handwritten number is meant to represent.

We often distinguish between supervised learning, and un-supervised learning and reinforcement learning [14]. In supervised learning, we help in the learning process, while in un-supervised learning, the model teaches itself. In reinforcement learning desirable actions will be reinforced in the model.

The examples in this chapter will address machine learning and deep learning, which is a variant of machine learning. There are also other tools in the field of artificial intelligence that we will not go into detail.

The purpose of a machine learning system is to find output (B) based on input (A). If the input is a recording of a conversation and what we want is a text version of this conversation, our application will be voice recognition. If the input is an image and the desired output is a response to whether the image is of a cat or not, the application will be image recognition. This connection between input and output is key for initiating the use of machine learning in a business.

A mental task that take around a second of the thinking power from a human being can be automated by AI now or in the near future [15]. A human being can quickly determine whether an object is a cat or not. We humans recognize words in our native language instantly, and it takes only a short time to estimate the distance to the car in front of us in traffic and to recognize speed limit signs. Humans learn fast; we do not need much data to recognize objects, nor do we need to see a thousand cats to see the difference between a cat and a dog. Software, on the other hand, needs large amounts of training data to recognize the same things, and make the same assessments as humans.

A human can see the totality of a situation and then make decisions on experience or instinct. Where we see a cat, a computer can only see a digital representation of a cat. It is only able to separate pixels, small dots, in a grid by the value representing different colours. By analysing the individual pixels on many images, the program can be taught to distinguish between different patterns in different types of objects.

Sense, Understand and Act

An AI system requires digital input. If the purpose is to do accounting, some of the input will be digitized versions of invoices. If the invoices are physical, they must be digitized by a scan or photograph and the image file will be input to the system. If the purpose is to drive a car, the input can be pictures of traffic in front and behind the car in addition to digital representations of sounds around the car. If the purpose is to translate text into speech, digital representations of speech will be input to the system. When we say that the system should sense, we mean that it should be able to accept different types of input.

When the system receives an image file with an invoice, it should be able to recognize text that is on the invoice and translate it into system data. Based on data, the system can then recognize the supplier, date, amount *etc.* from the invoice. An image of a car in traffic should be recognized as a car, and based on size, the system can calculate distance to the car in question. From audio files of speech, the system translates speech to text. When we say that the system should understand, we mean that it recognizes the content of the input.

Above we referred to the fact that AI will make decisions on behalf of people. Based on input (A), that is input described above, the system should decide (B). In the example of accounting, we want the system to submit a proposal for an entry into the accounting system where the date, supplier, amount and accounts are filled in automatically. We can choose to approve the proposal before it is entered into the system, or we can choose to have the invoice submitted automatically into the system. The same goes for the example of driving: Either we can get suggestions on how to best manoeuvre the car, or we can let the AI system make all the decisions and carry them out by steering the car. In the case of speech recognition, the translated speech may be input to a new system where the contents of the speech provide commands for the system. An example of this is "Hello Google" that activates the Google Assistant. These are examples of AI system making decisions and performing actions on behalf of the system owner. When we say that the system should *act,* we mean that it should take an action based on the sensing and the understanding of the input.

How Do Systems Learn?

From our previous definition of machine learning, we will now have a closer look at some of the methods for how machines learn. All methods have one common goal: outcome (B) will be determined based on input (A).

Supervised Learning: In the data set that will train the model, it is necessary to manually categorize the input, and then map the input to the correct output. For example, if you want to create a model that reveals junk e-mail, your testing data will consist of lots of e-mails. Attributes such as sender, text content, and links in the e-mail will be categorized. The e-mails with the characteristics of junk e-mail will be mapped to output = junk mail, the rest of the e-mails are mapped to the output = not junk mail. When the model is implemented, it will sort out junk e-mail and for example only display legitimate e-mail to the recipient.

Unsupervised Learning: In this case, the data is not categorized, it is left up to the system to categorize the data, and thus the system itself learns how to put the input (A) into outcome (B) later. Let's say the training data are pictures of ten different breeds of dogs. The system then goes through all the pictures, analyses them, and collects images with the same properties in their own categories, which will hopefully then represent the ten dog breeds. The system itself is of course not aware of the different breeds, or even that the pictures are of dogs, but it is still able to categorize the pictures. When the model is implemented, it will be able to determine which breed a dog belongs to, based on a picture of the dog.

Reinforcement Learning: In this case, the model will be put in an environment with various tools available, and where the model uses the various tools to achieve a goal. Here the environment itself will punish or reward toward achieving the goal. Reinforcement learning is often used for systems to teach themselves to play video games [16, 17]. The goal of the system is to complete the game, the tools available are the virtual buttons that control the game, the punishment from the environment is lose the game. The system reinforces actions that help complete the game and diminishes actions that make it lose the game.

Deep Learning and Neural Networks

Deep learning is a form of machine learning. *"Deep learning allows computational models that are composed of multiple processing layers to learn representations of data with multiple levels of abstraction"* [18]. It differs from other types of machine learning by using so-called neural networks to move from input (A) to output (B). A neural network consists of *neurons*, which represent an information point, and weighted *synapses* that associate the neurons. Deep learning and neural networks are used when the relationship between different types of input (A) and output (B) is complex. An example is value assessment of properties. A simple weighting of for example building year, square meter, number of rooms and neighbourhoods can give an estimate of the price. A model with a fixed weight on building year does not consider more complex contexts. For example, a 1960's building in one neighbourhood will have a reduced the value because it is most likely old and worn, while in another neighbourhood a building from the 1960's will have a higher value due to the construction quality or architectural features. A more complex model will be able to predict the value assessment better by implementing a better weighting structure. It is also possible to develop appraisal models using neural networks based on pictures of the property [19, 20].

A neural network consists of a set of input factors, one set of output, and one or more *hidden layers* performing calculations and filtering data to achieve the most accurate output. As with other types of machine learning, large amounts of data are needed to teach the model and to test the model. If the model does not provide the right value assessment, one can, among other things, change the weight of the synapsis to improve the accuracy of the valuation.

Generative Adversary Networks

A generative adversary networks (GAN) is a method for strengthening the models in neural networks [21]. This method involves putting two neural networks against each other. One network is called the *discriminator network* and should evaluate whether data is real or false. The other network, called the *generator network*, will create false data and mix it with real data, in order to trick the discriminator network into believing that the data is real. The more fake data, for example fake images of cats, the discriminator evaluates, the better it will get at detecting fakes. At the same time, the generator network will get better at generating pictures of fake cats.

AI IN BUSINESS OPERATIONS

An algorithm can be described informally as *"a set of rules that precisely defines a sequence of operations"* [22]. In machine learning, the algorithms are mathematical methods used for calculations in the models we have been talking about. We can compare an algorithm to a recipe: A set of ingredients and a method of combining the ingredients that will result in a dish. The model (in machine learning) is comparable to choosing the right quality and quantity of ingredients and combining them into a meal.

In business operations, there are many tasks that can be compared to an algorithm. Futurist Gerd Leonard has stated that if you can describe your job, it can be automated [23], and it is therefore no surprise that many see potentials in using AI in business operations. Brynjolfsson and McAfee point out that the way to stay relevant in working life in the future is to focus on idea generation and development, look for patterns in the big context, and complex communication. Other tasks will eventually be taken over by machines [24].

AI IN BUSINESS MANAGEMENT

In a survey among leaders all over the world, managers themselves estimate that more than 50% of the jobs they perform consist of coordination and control. These are routine tasks such as planning, budgeting, reporting and follow-up of routines [25]. Furthermore, just under 50% of top executives will rely on decisions made by intelligent systems.

The most successful digitization projects are initiatives from senior management [26], therefore it is an important task for management to understand what AI is and what it can and cannot do.

From an economic perspective, AI has a main function: It lowers the price and increases the accuracy of predictions [27]. This is a good starting point for managers who are going to explore AI. Better predictions lead to better decisions, or at least better input for those making the decisions. When the cost of predictions decreases, the value of predictions will increase, because predictions can be reused in other areas.

Predictions have been used for a long time in business operations, for example for budgeting, but with lower cost, predictions also can solve new kinds of problems. Take self-driving cars, for example, the systems collect data on traffic situation, and can predict both how the traffic situation will develop in the future, and how an average driver would react to the traffic situation. The actual mechanisms for driving the vehicle such as steering, gearing, *etc.* have not changed, but who, or what is steering, have changed.

In order to take advantage of this prediction power, managers can map out business processes, break them down in activities, find out which activities have a significant prediction part, and then calculate how much it costs to make the prediction with AI relative to how much one can save/profit from streamlining the process [28].

One challenge for managers is not only to see what AI can do today, but what it has the potential to do in the future. To envision what might be possible, start with a task that requires prediction, and turn the accuracy of the prediction up far beyond what is possible today. Consider an employment process. Uncertainty is associated with new employees, because it is impossible to know exactly how a person will function both professionally and socially in a workplace. With better prediction tools, we would be able to predict in detail how the person would interact with different colleagues, and what results she would achieve with different clients. The uncertainty surrounding employment would then be reduced.

A task consists not only of predictions. When a task is to be performed, one starts with data as input to the process, and then a prediction is made. After the result of the prediction is known, a decision must be made, which in turn leads to an action which ultimately leads to a result. After the result is known, it is possible to evaluate the various parts of the process: Were the right amount and quality of data collected? Were the right methods for prediction used? Did a person with the right competence make the decision? Was the action well executed? For a leader it is important to see both the prediction and the judgement, better predictions might create a need for better or different judgement skills, or the predictions can make it possible to automate both judgement and action.

Automation is when a computer program can do both the prediction and the judgement. In the years to come, an increasing number of tasks will be performed by machines. For some tasks the judgement cannot be made by software, and therefore human competence is required to make *judgments based on predictions*.

As predictions become better and more accurate, human expertise will become more important in order to run a business well. Agrawal *et al.* [29] outline three judgement areas that might be important in the future. Expertise will be needed for *taking responsible and ethical decisions*, and in *engaging customers and employees*, in other words, competence in relationships and communication; and expertise *in creating, discovering, and making decisions in relation to new business opportunities*, in other words, creativity. The last two types of competences coincide with complex communication and idea generation, as Brynjolfsson and McAfee identified as areas of expertise that cannot be covered by machines and software.

AI IN MARKETING

Use of Reinforcement Learning in Real-Time Auctions for Online Advertising

When a system uses reinforced learning, it is placed in an environment, instruments are available to perform actions, and receive rewards for desired results, and/or punishment for unwanted results. A system that uses reinforced learning is usually set up as a Markov Decision Process [30] where the system is considered an agent, which can act in an environment, and as a consequence of the action, the agent will achieve a new state and will also get a reward or punishment for the action. If the action causes the agent to achieve a better condition than before, the model is reinforced.

Automatic real-time auctions and programmatic advertising purchases are widespread in web marketing [31]. A real-time-bidding strategy can significantly boost an advertiser's revenue, especially in an e-commerce environment [32].

In short, advertisers set a budget and preferences for which customers they want to reach with their ads, the system matches current advertisers with relevant customers, and then an automatic auction will take place based on how much the advertisers want to pay to reach the specified audience. The price paid can be based on different target numbers; the number of impressions, the number of clicks, and the revenue based on the ad that is applicable. The advertiser with the highest bid will get to display the ad to customer.

Chinese technology giant Alibaba owns the e-commerce platform Taobao. A paper [33] discusses a case where programmatic advertising purchase system that uses prediction, reinforcement learning and neural networks is proposed. We will discuss the case at a non-technical level to show opportunities with neural networks and deep learning.

The process is initiated by a customer, for example, by the customer opening the website/app or making a search. Based on customer characteristics, such as usage and preference data, potential ads are matched to the customer based on all ads available. As this is a sales platform, most advertisers are also sellers on the website. For each ad/customer, measures that are critical to the advertiser's willingness to pay are predicted. A real-time prediction engine predicts the click-through rate (pCTR) and conversion rate (pCVR). The bids are normally based on the seller maximizing the revenue from the ad. Once the bids are placed, they are sorted in descending order of eCPM - the estimated cost for an advertiser pr 1000 visitors who see their advertisement on a webpage. (Cost Per Mille). eCPM also represents the platform's income, and the advertiser with the highest bid will achieve the best placement of the ad.

Let's think a little bit business before moving on with the example. For the owner of the trading platform, what will the purpose of this system be? Better accuracy for matching your ads? Higher earnings from sellers? The answer may be both, but the main goal will be increasing the overall revenue on the platform. Both because an increased revenue is a sign that the customers find products they want to buy, and because the earnings model for the platform hosting the sellers' online stores is based mainly on percentages of the sellers' revenue. Hence, increased total revenue will be the goal of using machine learning.

The agents in this example are the advertisers. The action they take is to bid on ad space, the environment is the trading platform, and change in state occurs when they win an auction. The reward is the increased revenue that the ad gives the advertiser. What the article suggests is that reinforcement learning is used to optimize the bid the advertisers provide to maximize revenue. The bid given is initially set by the advertiser, but in addition, the platform is authorized to adjust the bid within certain limits. The machine learning is suggested here to find the optimal adjustment the platform can make on the bids of the individual advertisers to (in the long term) maximize the revenue on the platform.

AI IN EDUCATION

As in other industries, there are many different tasks that meet both students and teachers in both higher and primary education. The students will learn many different subjects. Some subjects have a single right answer to most questions, but many are not as quantifiable. In addition to the subjects learned, the students will, as discussed earlier in this chapter, also be trained in competencies such as communication and interaction with others, making ethical assessments, and being creative and coming up with new ideas. These types of competencies are, at

least for the time being, outside what the machines can achieve, but in many cases AI presents the possibility of augmenting both teachers and students [34].

The teachers have the task of helping students to master the subjects, ideally based on the individual pupil's prerequisites and level of knowledge, in addition to fostering the student's social skills. Seeing each student is an important task for teachers, but in practice, it can be difficult to give all students in a large class attention on an individual level. Assessing the students' efforts on tests and assignments is time-consuming work, and as humans are imperfect and not machines, assignments that objectively have the same quality might get assessed differently.

Systems for Intelligent Tutoring and Adaptive Learning

The idea of systems that support learning is not new. An intelligent tutoring system, a computer program that provides instant and customized feedback to students in a learning process, often without the involvement of a human teacher [35], is already developed. Hypermedia Adaptive Learning Systems is a computer program that creates a model based on knowledge, preferences and goals of each user, and uses this model as the starting point for interaction with the user [36]. Both program and model have in common that they present learning material that are adapted to each user. What distinguishes them is that hypermedia systems have richer contents, such as videos and audio recordings, while the intelligent tutoring system mostly will give written feedback to the user. Basically, the systems are not required to use artificial intelligence to fit the definition, but in practice many of both types of learning systems use artificial intelligence to customize an interactive learning experience.

As in other industries, prediction is an important task for machine learning in an intelligent tutoring system in an educational environment. In the case of learning, it is essential to predict which kind of feedback that will provide the most effective learning based on each individual student.

A prerequisite for being able to use machine learning in education is defining *knowledge points* that the student should be able to achieve, as well as creating a system where knowledge points are ranked to guide the student through a *learning path* that increases the student's level of knowledge. Different learning material should be chosen for different parts of the learning path. The founder of the Chinese company Squirrel AI, Derek Li, exemplifies that secondary school mathematics can have 300 main knowledge points, which in turn can be broken down to a nano level of 30,000 knowledge points [37]. This provides better data on how students learn and where they are positioned in a learning path.

An intelligent tutoring system consists of three models: A student model, a tutoring model and a domain model [38]. The *student model* stores information about the student's condition, or level of knowledge. A counselling agent retrieves information about the student's level of knowledge to the *tutoring model* in order to get a tutoring strategy, and based on the tutoring strategy, learning material is retrieved from the *domain model* and presented to the student.

In order to understand a specific type of knowledge, prior knowledge is often needed. For example, in mathematics a student must understand functions before she can understand derivation. In machine learning a decision tree can represent actions and paths to knowledge, where possible learning paths are represented by tree branches [39]. A student with no prior knowledge of functions will be taken to the part of the learning path explaining functions before being led to learning material explaining derivation.

In the intelligent tutoring system described by Wang [38], if the student asks the system a question such as "What is derivation?" the system will bring up learning materials to explain derivation. In addition, Wang suggests adding reinforcement learning to the system, that is, a model that considers the student's level of knowledge when it fetches the learning material and is reinforced/rewarded when the learning material helps the student to achieve a higher level of knowledge. In this case, the reinforcement learning uses a variant of Markov's Decision Process that we have discussed earlier, as well as a test of the system with and without reinforcement learning. This indicates that the reinforcement learning component contributes to a more efficient system for learning.

Evaluation of Assignments with Neural Networks

Automatic grading of tests, multiple-choice test, correct and partially correct answers will reward the student with a given number of points, and wrong or partially incorrect answers can give zero or negative points. The total number of points a student achieves on a test can then be compared to the number of possible points, and a score can be calculated based on the relationship between the numbers.

But what about answers in text form? Is it possible to correct them? Souza *et al.* [40] describe in an paper how a neural network can evaluate tasks in an introductory course in programming. Basically, code can be evaluated binary: Either the code works, or not. A grading scale could then be that functioning code is pass, and a non-functioning code is fail. Nevertheless, the way the code is written can tell how much the student has understood of the key concepts in the subject, and it is therefore possible to evaluate code on the grading scale. Also, for the most part students will at least check that their code will run before they deliver a programming assignment.

In human assessment of code, different graders can come up with different grades based on personal preferences. Even if most people agree on the properties of a strong and a weak assignment, the individual grader may have strong opinions on the importance of specific parts of the curriculum, or on finer details of how to solve an assignment. The purpose of building a model that predicts probability of an assignment getting a specific grade is to be able to co-ordinate the grading within the human graders.

Input (A) in the proposed model is the code in an exam answer, and the desired output from the model is (B) suggested grade. Training data described in the paper are fully censored exam papers, together with sensor guidelines describing various errors in the various parts of the assignment, and how much the assignments will be penalised for the errors. Hence, the results are largely measured and quantified. The method is an example of supervised learning, where both input and desired output are specified, and then the model finds out the connection between input and output. The purpose of the model is to suggest grades for submitted assignments.

In the paper the grading AI uses a convolutional neural network. Simply explained, this neural network consists of an input layer, which is properties of submitted assignment, an output layer where output is the probability of the assignment receiving each different grade (for example a 12% probability that the assignment will get the grade C, a 68% probability for B and a 20% probability for A), and one or more hidden layers where the information is filtered to get to the right output.

CONCLUSION

We are in a golden age for artificial intelligence due to the abundance of data, processing power and connectivity. Still, the future of AI and its different sub-sets are depending not only on advances in programming techniques and modelling, but also on finding the right use cases and goal for the system. In this way these systems can support and enhance human performance.

CONSENT FOR PUBLICATION

Not applicable.

CONFLICT OF INTEREST

The author declares no conflict of interest, financial or otherwise.

ACKNOWLEDGEMENTS

Declared none.

REFERENCES

[1]   A.M. Turing, "Computing machinery and intelligence", *Mind,* vol. 59, no. 236, pp. 433-460, 1950.
        [http://dx.doi.org/10.1093/mind/LIX.236.433]

[2]   A.C. Clarke, "Hazards of prophecy: The failure of imagination", *Profiles of the Future,* vol. 6, p. 36,
        1962.

[3]   A. C. Clarke, "The mind of the machine", *Playboy,* 1968.

[4]   S. Narkus, N. Kondratieff, Schumpeter, and A. Joseph, *Long-waves Theory: Analysis of Long-cycles
        Theory,* 2012.

[5]   K. Schwab, *The Fourth Industrial Revolution.* Penguin: UK, 2017.

[6]   Y. Shoham, *The AI Index 2018 Annual Report,* ed: Stanford, 2018.

[7]   C. Cantero, S.K. Sællman, and A. Wirsching, "Sensor måler pust – skal forebygge selvmord", *NRK
        Norwegian Brocasting Corporation,* 2019. https://www.nrk.no/sorlandet/denne-sensoren-sk-
        l-forebygge-selvmord-1.14577033

[8]   A. Vahabzadeh, N. Sahin, and A. Kalali, "Digital suicide prevention: can technology become a game-
        changer?", *Innov. Clin. Neurosci.,* vol. 13, no. 5-6, pp. 16-20, 2016.
        [PMID: 27800282]

[9]   V. Kolbjørnsrud, "Kunstig intelligens og lederens nye jobb", *MAGMA,* vol. 20, no. 6, pp. 33-42, 2017.

[10]   H.A. Simon, and A. Newell, "Heuristic problem solving: the next advance in operations research",
        Oper. Res., vol. 6, no. 1, pp. 1-10, 1958.
        [http://dx.doi.org/10.1287/opre.6.1.1]

[11]   R. Kurzweil, *The Singularity is Near: When Humans Transcend Biology* Duckworth: London, 2005.

[12]   B. Goertzel, "Artificial general intelligence", *Scholarpedia,* vol. 10, no. 11, p. 31847, 2015.
        [http://dx.doi.org/10.4249/scholarpedia.31847]

[13]   M. Mohri, "Foundations of machine learning", *Adaptive Computation and Machine Learning Series,*
        2nd edition.The MIT Press: Cambridge, MA, 2018.

[14]   C.M. Bishop, *Pattern Recognition and Machine Learning (Information Science and Statistics).,* New
        York: Springer, 2006.

[15]   A. Ng, *What Artificial Intelligence Can and Can't Do Right Now.* vol. 9. Harvard Business Review,
        2016.

[16]   Y. Zhu, "Target-driven visual navigation in indoor scenes using deep reinforcement learning", In:
        IEEE International Conference on Robotics and Automation (ICRA). IEEE, 2017, pp. 3357-3364.
        [http://dx.doi.org/10.1109/ICRA.2017.7989381]

[17]   M. Kempka, M. Wydmuch, G. Runc, J. Toczek, and W. Jaśkowski, "Vizdoom: A doom-based ai
        research platform for visual reinforcement learning", In: *2016 IEEE Conference on Computational
        Intelligence and Games (CIG)* IEEE, 2016, pp. 1-8.
        [http://dx.doi.org/10.1109/CIG.2016.7860433]

[18]   Y. LeCun, Y. Bengio, and G. Hinton, "Deep learning", *Nature,* vol. 521, no. 7553, pp. 436-444, 2015.
        [http://dx.doi.org/10.1038/nature14539] [PMID: 26017442]

[19]   Q. You, R. Pang, L. Cao, and J. Luo, "Image-based appraisal of real estate properties", *IEEE Trans.
        Multimed.,* vol. 19, no. 12, pp. 2751-2759, 2017.
        [http://dx.doi.org/10.1109/TMM.2017.2710804]

[20]   O. Poursaeed, T. Matera, and S. Belongie, "Vision-based real estate price estimation", *Mach. Vis. Appl.,* vol. 29, no. 4, pp. 667-676, 2018.
[http://dx.doi.org/10.1007/s00138-018-0922-2]

[21]   I. Goodfellow, "Generative adversarial nets", *Advances in Neural Information Processing Systems,* pp. 2672-2680, 2014.

[22]   H.S. Stone, *Introduction to Computer Organization and Data Structures (McGraw-Hill Computer Science Series).* McGraw-Hill: New York, 1972.

[23]   G. Leonhard, *Technology vs. Humanity: The Coming Clash Between Man and Machine.* Future Scapes, 2016.

[24]   E. Brynjolfsson, *The Second Machine Age: Work, Progress, and Prosperity in a Time of Brilliant Technologies.* Norton: New York, 2014.

[25]   V. Kolbjørnsrud, R. Amico, and R.J. Thomas, "How artificial intelligence will redefine management", *Harvard Business Review,* vol. 2, 2016.

[26]   G. Westerman, *LeadinG Digital: Turning Technology into Business Transformation.* Harvard Business Review Press: Boston, Mass, 2014.

[27]   A. Agrawal, J.S. Gans, and A. Goldfarb, "Exploring the impact of artificial Intelligence: Prediction *versus* judgment", *Inf. Econ. Policy,* 2019.
[http://dx.doi.org/10.1016/j.infoecopol.2019.05.001]

[28]   A. Agrawal, and R. Kirkland, "The economics of artificial intelligence", *McKinsey Q.,* 2018.

[29]   A. Agrawal, J. Gans, and A. Goldfarb, "What to expect from artificial intelligence," 2019.

[30]   R.A. Howard, *Dynamic programming and Markov processes.* Technology Press of Massachusetts Institute of Technology: Cambridge, 1960.

[31]   C. Liu, and M. Utreras, *US Ad Spending: eMarketer's Updated Estimates and Forecast for 2015-2020,* 2016.

[32]   J. Zhao, G. Qiu, Z. Guan, W. Zhao, and X. He, "Deep reinforcement learning for sponsored search real-time bidding", In: *Proceedings of the 24th ACM SIGKDD International Conference on Knowledge Discovery & Data Mining* ACM, 2018, pp. 1021-1030.
[http://dx.doi.org/10.1145/3219819.3219918]

[33]   J. Jin, C. Song, H. Li, K. Gai, J. Wang, and W. Zhang, "Real-time bidding with multi-agent reinforcement learning in display advertising", In: *Proceedings of the 27th ACM International Conference on Information and Knowledge Management* ACM, 2018, pp. 2193-2201.
[http://dx.doi.org/10.1145/3269206.3272021]

[34]   S.A.D. Popenici, and S. Kerr, "Exploring the impact of artificial intelligence on teaching and learning in higher education", *Res Pract Technol Enhanc Learn,* vol. 12, no. 1, p. 22, 2017.
[http://dx.doi.org/10.1186/s41039-017-0062-8] [PMID: 30595727]

[35]   J. Psotka, L.D. Massey, and S.A. Mutter, *Intelligent tutoring systems: lessons learned.* Erlbaum Associates: Hillsdale, N.J, 1988.

[36]   P. Brusilovsky, A. Kobsa, and J. Vassileva, *Adaptive Hypertext and Hypermedia*, 1998.
[http://dx.doi.org/10.1007/978-94-017-0617-9]

[37]   S.A. Learning, "Founder of Squirrel AI Learning by Yixue Group Derek Haoyang Li attends Harvard China Education Symposium, interpreting the new trend of AI+ Education",

[38]   F. Wang, Efficient Computing of the Bellman Equation in a POMDP-based Intelligent Tutoring System.*CSEDU*Heraklion, Crete, 2019.
[http://dx.doi.org/10.5220/0007676000150023]

[39]   F. Wang, "A new technique of policy trees for building a pomdp based intelligent tutoring system", In:

Proceedings of the 8th International Conference on Computer Supported Education, 2016, pp. 85-93. [http://dx.doi.org/10.5220/0005796600850093]

[40]   F. Rezende Souza, F. Zampirolli, and G. Kobayashi, "Convolutional neural network applied to code assignment grading", In: *Presented at the CSEDU* Crete: Heraklion, 2019. [http://dx.doi.org/10.5220/0007711000620069]

CHAPTER 6

Extreme Randomized Trees for Real Estate Appraisal with Housing and Crime Data

Junchi Bin[1], Bryan Gardiner[2], Eric Li[3] and Zheng Liu[1,*]

[1] *School of Engineering, Faculty of Applied Science, University of British Columbia, Kelowna, BC, Canada*

[2] *Data Nerds, Kelowna, BC, Canada*

[3] *Faculty of Management, University of British Columbia, Kelowna, BC, Canada*

Abstract: Real estate appraisal plays a vital role in people's daily life. People rely on the estimation of decisions on buying houses. It is well recognized that the criminal activities around the house have significant impacts on house prices. House buyers can make more reasonable decisions if they are aware of the criminal activities around the house. Therefore, a machine learning-based method is proposed by combining house attributes and criminal activities. Specifically, the method firstly infers the intensity of criminal activities from historical crime records.Then, a novel machine learning algorithm, extremely randomized trees (ExtraTrees), is implemented to estimate the house price based on the extracted comprehensive crime intensity and real-world house attributes.The experimental results show that the proposed method outperforms contemporary real estate appraisal methods by achieving higher accuracy and robustness.

Keywords: Ensemble learning, Extremely randomized trees, Machine learning, Real estate appraisal.

INTRODUCTION

For most people in the world, house transaction is one of the most substantial expenses in their life. Buying or investing houses is a high involving a decision. To be more informative, people usually consult real estate agents before making actual transactions. From the real estate agents, house buyers can receive a comprehensive report of house and the estimated market values of the house. Relying on the estimated market values, house buyers can make reasonable decisions during the actual transactions in the housing market. This service is

---

[*] **Corresponding author Zheng Liu:** School of Engineering, Faculty of Applied Science, University of British Columbia, Kelowna, BC, Canada; E-mail: zheng.liu@ubc.ca

Terje Solsvik Kristensen (Ed.)

called real estate appraisal in housing market. To meet with the rapid growing demands from housing market, real estate agents have been developing automated online service of real estate appraisal [1 - 3]. This online service is called automated valuation model (AVM).

Empirical studies concentrate on improving the accuracy of AVM by developing machine learning algorithms such as artificial neural network (ANN) and regression trees [4 - 6]. The implemented data only contains the house attributes like numbers of bedrooms and the size of the house. Beyond the house attributes, academic researchers also regard the demographic and social factors of community as major influential factors in real estate appraisal [5, 7, 8]. For example, the safety of the neighborhood also plays a vital role while people are picking houses. The safety of neighborhoods can be reflected as the reversed values of crime intensity around a house. House buyers always prefer to living in a house with a low risk of being offended as well as well as low crime intensity.

Some studies discovered inappropriate correlation between the crime intensity and house prices [8 - 10]. The evidence indicates that the crime intensity around the house significantly influence house prices. However, none of the previous AVMs investigated the method to extract the crime intensity from raw crime data. Moreover, there is lack of research on suitable computational model for employing both house attributes and the crime intensity in real estate appraisal.

In this study, we employ a novel statistical method to extract comprehensive crime intensity (CCI) in terms of two categories: crime occurrence entropy (COE) and consecutive crime severity (CCS) [11]. First, crime occurrence entropy (COE) represents the spatial severity of crime around a house. Second, consecutive crime severity (CCS) represents the temporal severity of crime around a house. Finally, COE and CCS are combined to represent the comprehensive crime intensity (CCI). On the other hand, a novel machine learning model, extremely randomized trees (ExtraTrees) [12], is proposed to estimate the house prices by combining house attributes and CCI. In summary, our contributions are highlighted as follows:

- A novel statistical crime data analysis method to extract the comprehensive crime intensity (CCI) in terms of different perspectives by exploiting the crime data. The experimental results show that the CCI can increase the accuracy of real estate appraisal.
- A novel machine learning model, extremely randomized trees (ExtraTrees), is proposed to estimate the house price. The experimental results indicate that the proposed model outperforms contemporary methods. To the best of authors' knowledge, this is the first implementation of ExtraTrees in real estate appraisal.

RELATED WORKS

Machine Learning in Real Estate Appraisal

Researchers have researched the problem of real estate appraisal for decades. Linear regression has been used for real estate appraisal since the last century [13]. Assuming house prices have a linear correlation between house attributes, the linear regression model is trained and optimized by the least-square method. After entering the era of big data, linear regression is challenging to fit a massive amount of housing data. Moreover, many research papers revealed the existence of a non-linear correlation between house values and real estate [14 - 17]. Without further techniques to explore the non-linearity, it is difficult to achieve a more accurate and robust estimation by purely using linear regression.

Machine learning is a data-driven solution to automatically discover features and establish a non-linear correlation to complex data and its corresponding target for computer vision and financial techniques. Real estate agents are also aware of the power of machine learning and research its application in real estate appraisal. Currently, machine learning methods are thriving in real estate appraisal. Multilayer perceptron (MLP), is one of the most common techniques in AVM. MLP is famous for its feature learning ability, which allows the model to achieve more accurate performance [18]. On the other hand, the MLP is capable of exploring non-linearity among features by selecting different types of activation functions in neurons [19]. Some studies report their successful application of MLP in AVM [4, 14, 20 - 25].

However, many papers also reveal that MLP is the lack of robustness in real-world applications [16, 17, 21, 22, 26 - 29]. On the other hand, the optimizing problem of MLP also prevents from advanced development in real estate appraisal [6]. To obtain more robust performance, real estate researchers bring the technique of regression tree in real estate appraisal. As described in [5, 30], a single regression tree can achieve outstanding performance in assessing house prices. However, the regression trees are relatively easy to overfit, which prevents its application in property value assessment [5]. Random forest (RF) and boosted regression trees (BRT) are the ensemble methods to combine many weak regression trees for the robust and accurate performance of assessment [5, 31, 32]. In the empirical studies presented in [5, 21, 22, 24, 26, 28, 30], the BRT and RF are applied to house attributes and achieve state-of-the-art predictive results. To enhance the robustness of tree induction algorithms, extremely randomized trees (ExtraTrees) are developed to reduce the variance of model outputs by explicit randomization of the split-point of trees [12]. Moreover, the randomization scheme of ExtraTrees also improves its computational efficiency. Although it has engineering applications widely [12], the application of real estate appraisal is a lack of investigation.

Real Estate Appraisal beyond House Attributes

With continuously accumulating various data in cities, many researchers have been researching incorporating various types of data for real estate appraisal [11, 23, 33 - 36]. Many papers indicate the house images may improve the accuracy of real estate appraisal [24, 25, 36]. On the other hand, some empirical statistical researches indicate that the community condition greatly influences its house prices [11, 33]. A case study incorporates open urban data like check-point and criminal activities on the problem of recommending houses by ranking algorithms [11]. However, none of them incorporate crime data to estimate house prices.

METHODOLOGY

Overall Architecture of Proposed Method

This section describes the overall architecture of the proposed method. Specifically, the proposed approach consists of two steps: (1) comprehensive crime intensity (CCI) extraction around the house, and (2) the estimation of the house prices based on ExtraTrees with CCI and house attributes. The first step presents the details of statistical method to extract CCI from raw crime records around a house (within 1 Kilometer). Then, the second step provide the general information of proposed ExtraTrees for ultimate appraisal. The overall architecture is shown in Fig. (1).

Fig. (1). The illustration of overall architecture of proposed method.

Data Collection and Description

House Attributes

In this study, the housing data is collected from the City of Philadelphia and provided by Estated [3]. There are around 15815 houses in Philadelphia. In the housing data, each house contains several numerical attributes to describe the houses comprehensively. All the house attributes that we are used in this study are shown in Table **1**.

Table 1. Description of house attributes.

Attributes	Description
Longitude, latitude	Location of houses
Depth	The distance between house and main street
Frontage	Width of the lot
Interior	The overall condition of interior
Baths	Number of bathrooms
Beds	Number of bedrooms
Rooms	Number of rooms
Story	Number of stories
Size	The total area of the house
Livable area	The total livable area of the house
Year built	The year of completion of construction

Comprehensive Crime Intensity

The raw crime dataset contains numerous records of criminal activities recorded by police officers, which are published on Open Data Philly (https://www.opendataphilly.org/). The raw crime data is formatted by *<coordinates, types, time>*. *Coordinates* represent the longitude, latitude, and zip codes of the criminal events. *Types* indicate the types of crimes like sex offending and assault, while *time* indicates the occurring time of the crime. A novel statistical method is implemented to extract the crime intensity from the raw crime data [18]. Two statistical factors are calculated to extract the comprehensive crime intensity (CCI) from raw data: crime occurrence entropy (COE) and consecutive crime severity (CCS), in terms of spatial severity and temporal severity of criminal activities. The criminal records are aggregated within 1 Kilometers of a house. Here, only fatal and property-related crimes are aggregated. Then, the crime records are aggregated into 48 time slots, *i.e.*, 24 hours for weekdays and weekends. Assuming *t* denotes each time slot, $C_{t,j}$ is the set of crime records occurred in *t* time slot for *i*th house. The COE is defined as Equation (1)

$$COE_i = -\sum_{i:P_{k,i}\neq 0} P_{k,i} log P_{k,i}$$ (1)

Where $P\_(t, i)=|C\_(t,i)|/|c\_t|$ is the probability of crime occurrence in th house.

According to Z. Yao *et al.* [11], the returning criminal prefers to conducting crimes in the same area within period. Therefore, the area of higher serial crime records also implies a lower safety level around the house [8, 9, 11]. From the point of view, it is also valuable to know the consecutive crime severity (CCS). In this study, if numbers of consecutive crimes occur within 7 days, these crimes will be collected as a sequence {C1,C2,...,Cn} for th house. The CCS is defined as below:

$$E(S) = \max_{2\leq n\leq N}\{7 - D(C_{n-1}, C_n) + 1\}$$ (2)

$$CCS_i = \sum E(S)$$ (3)

Where returns the time difference of crime events. After both crime occurrence entropy (COE) and consecutive crime severity (CCS), the comprehensive crime intensity (CCI) for th house is calculated as shown in Equation 4.

$$CCI_i = COE_i + CCS_i$$ (4)

Fig. (2) illustrates the spatial distribution of CCI and house prices. It is obvious that the CCI has a strong inappropriate correlation with house prices in the City of Philadelphia, especially for highlighted areas.

Extremely Randomized Trees

The ultimate objective of the proposed method aims to estimate house prices. Linear regression is a global model to predict the house prices based on the entire feature space. A linear regression model can be defined as follows:

$$Y = \beta_0 + \beta^T X + \gamma X X^T + \epsilon$$ (5)

Where and are the learnable coefficient. However, the linear regression model is impossible to fit a large dataset due to its small capacity of the model. For shrinking the feature space, decision trees are used to divide the whole space into splits for linear regression model. Then, recursively replicating the manipulation until having models. Finally, combining all the linear regression models for robust results [12].

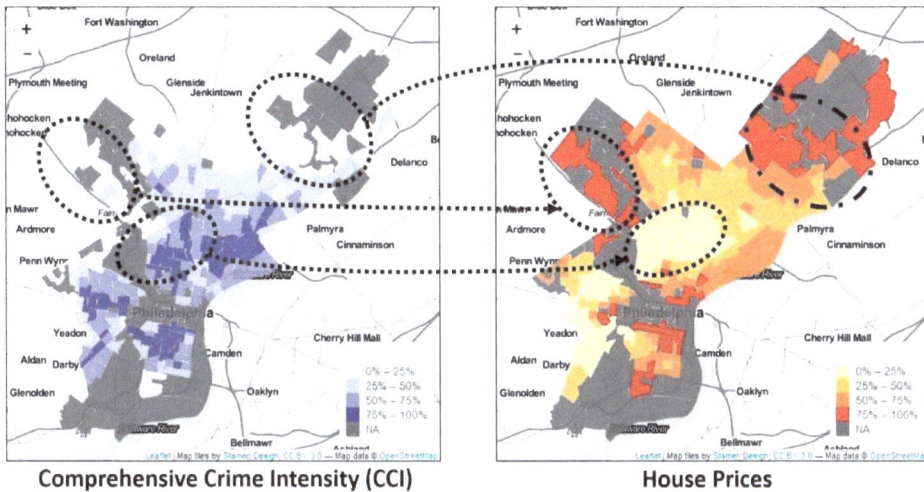

Comprehensive Crime Intensity (CCI)   **House Prices**

Fig. (2). The illustration of distribution of comprehensive crime intensity (CCI) and house prices.

The extremely randomized trees (ExtraTrees) is an ensemble learning method to integrate multiple regression trees according to classical tree-based hierocracy procedure [12]. According to [12], ExtraTrees strongly randomly samples both inputs and split nodes while splitting a tree. Due to the strong randomization mechanism, the ExtraTrees can avoid the overfitting and has better accuracy and robustness. On the other hand, ExtraTrees averages all the outputs from numerous regression trees to reduce the variance of outputs. In this study, the ExtraTrees is the implemented to estimate the house price based on house attribtues and comprehensive crime intensity I. The procedure of constructing ExtraTree is shown in Algorithm **1**.

In Algorithm 1, the house attributes and comprehensive crime intensity are firstly concatenated to be the input for the ExtraTree. Then, the ExtraTrees generates regression trees for ensemblc. For each tree, it randomly selects attributes from , and generate splits. Scores are evalutated between splits and to reduce the variance among splits.

The calculation of the score is defined as

$$Score(s_i, X) = \frac{var(y|X) - \frac{|y_l|}{|X|} var(y_l|X) - \frac{|y_r|}{|X|} var(y_r|X)}{var(y|X)} \qquad (6)$$

Where is the variance of output in; and are the two subsets from randomly samples of according to [12, 37]. Then, the model selects the best split based on corresponding scores and construct the regression tree. Finally, the proposed model calculates the final house price by averaging outputs from regression trees. The details of ExtraTrees can be found in [12].

Algorithm 1: Extremely randomized trees for real estate appraisal.

Input: house attributes , comprehensive crime intensity I. **Output: estimated house prices.**

Main()
.
.
For
    - Select randomly attributes {} from.
    - Generate splits {} according to the confidence level of attributes from , where domSplit,   - Select a split.
    - Build a linear regression model based on and Eq. (5).
    - .**End**
Obtain by averaging the outputs from .**RandomSplit**(S,A) [12]
    - Let d denote the mamixmum and minimum values of the in
    - Draw a random cut-point uniformly in.
    - Return the splits if

Main()
.
.
For
    - Select randomly attributes {} from.
    - Generate splits {} according to the confidence level of attributes from , where domSplit,   - Select a split.
    - Build a linear regression model based on and Eq. (5).
    - .**End**
Obtain by averaging the outputs from .**RandomSplit**(S,A) [12]
    - Let d denote the mamixmum and minimum values of the in
    - Draw a random cut-point uniformly in.
    - Return the splits if

EXPERIMENTS

Experimental Setup

The whole data is shuffled and split into training (80%) and testing set (20%). The maximum number of trees is 1000, which is determined by grid search. The ExtraTrees is implemented under Scikit-Learn in Python as well as other baseline models. To prevent training from overfitting, we used 5-fold cross-validation to determine if the overfitting occurs. Only the best evaluation results are presented in this section without overfitting. The model is trained on a computer with Intel I5 CPU and a single NVIDIA 950M GPU.

Evaluation Metrics

For evaluating the performance of the proposed method, two evaluation metrics are used: mean absolute error (MAE) and R-squared. MAE is a measure of the difference between two continuous variables. The lower values of MAE mean higher accuracy in these studies. On the other hand, R-squared can measure the variance between two continuous variables. The lower values of R-squared represents the higher robustness of the model. They are formulated as:

$$\mathbf{MAE} = \frac{1}{n}\sum_{i=1}^{n} |y_i - y_i'| \tag{7}$$

$$\mathbf{R}\text{-squared} = 1 - \frac{\sum(y_i - y_i')}{\sum(y_i' - y_i^-)} \tag{8}$$

Where is the real house price; is the estimated house price, and is the average real house price of the whole data.

Performance Comparison

Several baseline models in real estate appraisal are compared to validate the effectiveness of the proposed method:

• Linear regression (LR), which is optimized by the least square method [31].

• Multi-layer perceptron (MLP), which employs a neural network of multiple layers for estimating house price [31]. In this study, an MLP consists of two layers of 128 and 64 units respectively.

- K-nearest neighbors (KNN), which is classical a non-parametric regression method in real estate appraisal [5, 29]. The number of neighbors is set as 6 in this study.

- Regression tree (RT), which only contains a single regression tree to estimate the house price [5, 38].

- Random forest (RF), which combines numerous of regression trees to improve predictive results [5, 17, 30]. The number of estimators is set as 1000.

- Gradient boosting machine (GBM), which is a variance of tree-based ensemble learning method optimized by boosting algorithm [5, 17, 30, 39]. The number of estimators is set as 1000 as well as random forest and ExtraTrees.

Table **2** shows the experimental results of baselines and proposed ExtraTrees. Compared with model performance between with and without comprehensive crime intensity (CCI), it is evident that the additional information can improve the models' performance. This phenomenon can validate the effectiveness of including CCI extracted from raw crime data in real estate appraisal. On the other hand, it is obvious that the machine learning method significantly outperforms the classical linear regression (LR). The ability to capture non-linearity does improve the performance of real estate appraisal. Among the baseline models, all the tree-based ensemble models (GBM, RF and ExtraTrees) significantly outperform the other baseline models in terms of lower MAE and higher R-Squared. However, by comparing ExtraTrees with GBM and RF, the ExtraTrees has the lowest value of MAE and the highest value of R-Squared. Without CCI, the MAE of ExtraTrees is decreased by approximately 1.8% and the R-squared is only increased by 0.1% compared with the RF. However, with CCI, the MAE of ExtraTrees is decreased by 2.8%, and R-Squared is increased by 0.5% compared with the RF. By analyzing the experimental results from different perspectives, it can be concluded that the proposed ExtraTrees is more effective for real estate appraisal in terms of accuracy and robustness. On the other hand, combining CCI and house attributes can achieve better performance in real estate appraisal. For better illustration, the experimental results are also presented in Fig. (**3**).

Table 2. Experimental results for each algorithm with and without crime data.

Methods	Without CCI		With CCI	
	MAE	R-Squared	MAE	R-Squared
LR	28096	27.2	26088	35.2

(Table 2) contd.....

	Without CCI		With CCI	
MLP	19807	40.5	18831	45.5
KNN	12985	73.3	12085	75.0
RT	13217	63.4	12306	66.7
GBM	12066	81.1	11047	82.0
RF	9681	82.3	9593	83.4
ExtraTrees	9506	82.4	9313	83.9

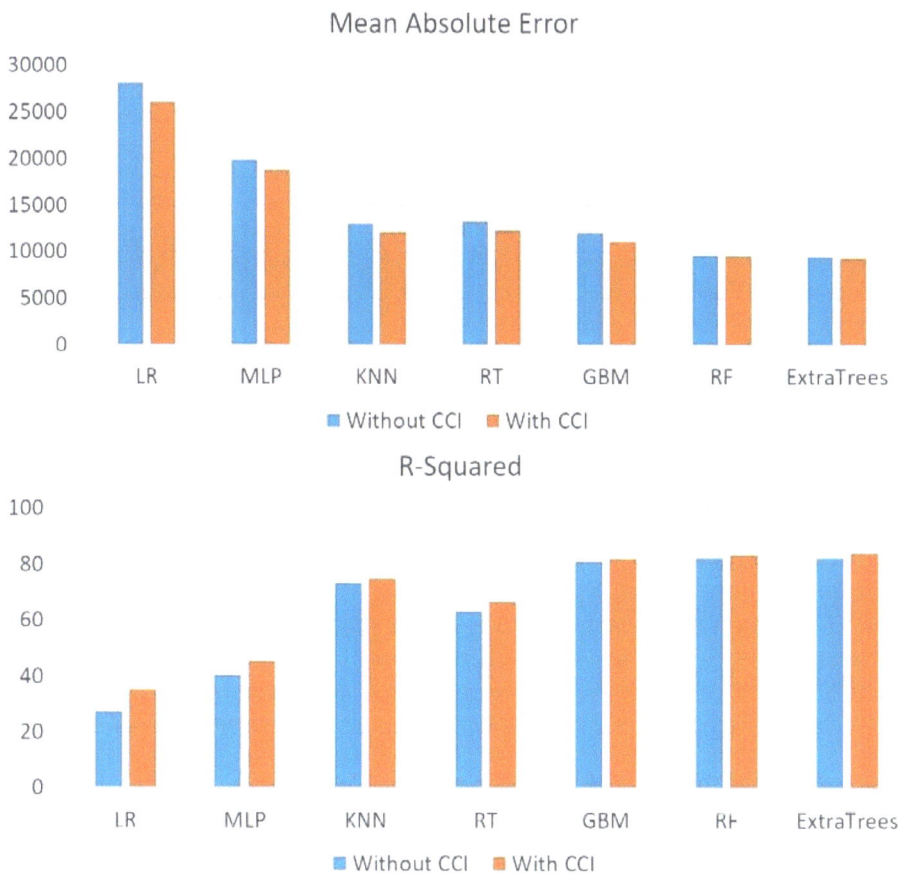

Fig. (3). The illustrate of mean absolute error (MAE) and R-squared comparison.

CONCLUSIONS

In this study, we develop a new tree-based ensemble learning model, *i.e.*, extremely randomized trees (ExtraTrees), to estimate the house price. The model takes advantage of combing house attributes and crime data to have an accurate and robust estimation. The proposed approach implements a powerful random sampling method to enhance performance while splitting the regression trees. The experimental results demonstrate its effectiveness. Moreover, with extracted comprehensive crime intensity (CCI), the ExtraTrees have better performance in terms of accuracy and robustness as well as baseline models. The phenomenon demonstrates the usefulness of additional information in real estate appraisal. In future research, we will investigate various data (demography, point of interest, *etc.*) to see if they are suitable for improving real estate appraisal. Moreover, using advanced data fusion and machine learning methods to enhance the estimation.

CONSENT FOR PUBLICATION

Not applicable.

CONFLICT OF INTEREST

The author declares no conflict of interest, financial or otherwise.

ACKNOWLEDGEMENTS

This study was supported by Mitacs Accelerate Program (IT10011) through collaboration between Data Nerds and the University of British Columbia – Okanagan Campus. The authors present appreciation to Fang Shi (QHR Technologies), Shuo Liu (Two Hat Security), Dr. Huan Liu (China University of Geosciences) and Kaiqi Zhang (AECOM New York) for the precious discussion when the work was carried out.

REFERENCES

[1]   *Home for sales,* Zillow, 2018.https://www.zillow.com/

[2]   RF/MAX, *Home estimates,* 2018.https://www.remax.ca/

[3]   *Property reports,* Estated, 2018.https://estated.com/

[4]   H. Selim, "Determinants of house prices in Turkey: Hedonic regression versus artificial neural network", *Expert Syst. Appl.,* vol. 36, no. 2, pp. 2843-2852, 2009.
       [http://dx.doi.org/10.1016/j.eswa.2008.01.044]

[5]   B. Park, and J.K. Bae, "Using machine learning algorithms for housing price prediction: the case of Fairfax County, Virginia housing data", *Expert Syst. Appl.,* vol. 42, no. 6, pp. 2928-2934, 2015.
       [http://dx.doi.org/10.1016/j.eswa.2014.11.040]

[6]   N. Vo, "A new conceptual automated property valuation model for residential housing market",

[7]   F.T. Wang, and P.M. Zorn, "Estimating house price growth with repeat sales data: What's the aim of the game?", *J. Hous. Econ.,* vol. 6, no. 2, pp. 93-118, 1997.
       [http://dx.doi.org/10.1006/jhec.1997.0209]

[8]   S. Gibbons, "The costs of urban property Crime", *Econ. J. (Lond.),* vol. 114, no. 499, pp. F441-F463, 2004.
       [http://dx.doi.org/10.1111/j.1468-0297.2004.00254.x]

[9]   B.L. Linden, and J.E. Rockoff, "Estimates of the impact of crime risk on property values from Megan's laws", *Am. Econ. Rev.,* vol. 98, no. 3, pp. 1103-1127, 2008.
       [http://dx.doi.org/10.1257/aer.98.3.1103]

[10]   J.C. Pope, "Fear of crime and housing prices : Household reactions to sex offender registries", *J. Urban Econ.,* vol. 64, no. 3, pp. 601-614, 2008.
       [http://dx.doi.org/10.1016/j.jue.2008.07.001]

[11]   Z. Yao, Y. Fu, B. Liu, and H. Xiong, "The impact of community safety on house ranking", *Proceedings of the 2016 SIAM International Conference on Data Mining,* 2016pp. 459-467
       [http://dx.doi.org/10.1137/1.9781611974348.52]

[12]   P. Geurts, D. Ernst, and L. Wehenkel, "Extremely randomized trees", *Mach. Learn.,* vol. 63, no. 1, pp. 3-42, 2006.
       [http://dx.doi.org/10.1007/s10994-006-6226-1]

[13]   S. Sheppard, Hedonic analysis of housing markets.*Handbook of Regional and Urban Economics.* Elsevier, 1999, pp. 1595-1635.

[14]   E. Worzala, M. Lenk, and A. Silva, "An exploration of neural networks and its application to real estate valuation", *J. Real Estate Res.,* vol. 10, no. 2, pp. 185-201, 1995.

[15]   G-Z. Fan, S.E. Ong, and H.C. Koh, "Determinants of house price: a decision tree approach", *Urban Stud.,* vol. 43, no. 12, pp. 2301-2315, 2006.
       [http://dx.doi.org/10.1080/00420980600990928]

[16]   S. Chopra, T. Thampy, J. Leahy, A. Caplin, and Y. LeCun, "Discovering the hidden structure of house prices with a non-parametric latent manifold model", *KDD '07 Proceedings of the 13th ACM SIGKDD international conference on knowledge discovery and data mining - KDD'07,* 2007
       [http://dx.doi.org/10.1145/1281192.1281214]

[17]   M. Graczyk, T. Lasota, B. Trawiński, and K. Trawiński, "Comparison of bagging, boosting and stacking ensembles applied to real estate appraisal", *Proceedings of the Second International Conference on Intelligent Information and Database Systems: Part II,* 2010pp. 340-350
       [http://dx.doi.org/10.1007/978-3-642-12101-2_35]

[18]   I. Goodfellow, Y. Bengio, and A. Courville, *Deep learning.* MIT Press: Cambridge, 2016.

[19]   Y. LeCun, Y. Bengio, and G. Hinton, "Deep learning", *Nature,* vol. 521, no. 7553, pp. 436-444, 2015.
       [http://dx.doi.org/10.1038/nature14539] [PMID: 26017442]

[20]   I.D. Wilson, S.D. Paris, J.A. Ware, and D.H. Jenkins, "Residential property price time series forecasting with neural networks", *Knowl. Base. Syst.,* vol. 15, no. 5, pp. 335-341, 2002.
       [http://dx.doi.org/10.1016/S0950-7051(01)00169-1]

[21]   M. Graczyk, T. Lasota, and B. Trawiński, "Comparative analysis of premises valuation models using KEEL, RapidMiner, and WEKA", *First International Conference,* 2009pp. 800-812
       [http://dx.doi.org/10.1007/978-3-642-04441-0_70]

[22]   T. Lasota, P. Sachnowski, and B. Trawiński, "Comparative analysis of regression tree models for premises valuation using statistical data miner", *Computational Collective Intelligence. Semantic Web, Social Networks and Multiagent Systems,* Springer: Berlin Heidelberg, pp. 776-787, 2009.

[23] K. Vrijdag, *Auction Price Prediction: An Instance-Transfer Learning approach.* Eindhoven University of Technology: Eindhoven, Netherlands, 2016.

[24] A.J. Bency, S. Rallapalli, R.K. Ganti, M. Srivatsa, and B.S. Manjunath, "Beyond spatial auto-regressive models: Predicting housing prices with satellite imagery", *2017 IEEE Winter Conference on Applications of Computer Vision (WACV),* 2017pp. 320-329
[http://dx.doi.org/10.1109/WACV.2017.42]

[25] X. Liu, Q. Xu, J. Yang, J. Thalman, S. Yan, and J. Luo, "Learning multi-instance deep ranking and regression network for visual house appraisal", *IEEE Trans. Knowl. Data Eng.,* vol. 30, no. 8, pp. 1496-1506, 2018.
[http://dx.doi.org/10.1109/TKDE.2018.2791611]

[26] T. Lasota, Z. Telec, B. Trawiński, and K. Trawiński, "A multi-agent system to assist with real estate appraisals using bagging ensembles", *Computational Collective Intelligence. Semantic Web, Social Networks and Multiagent Systems,* Springer: Berlin Heidelberg, pp. 813-824, 2009.
[http://dx.doi.org/10.1007/978-3-642-04441-0_71]

[27] B. Sirmaçek, and C. Ünsalan, "Using local features to measure land development in urban regions", *Pattern Recognit. Lett.,* vol. 31, no. 10, pp. 1155-1159, 2010.
[http://dx.doi.org/10.1016/j.patrec.2009.09.018]

[28] V. Kontrimas, and A. Verikas, "The mass appraisal of the real estate by computational intelligence", *Appl. Soft Comput.,* vol. 11, no. 1, pp. 443-448, 2011.
[http://dx.doi.org/10.1016/j.asoc.2009.12.003]

[29] W. Zhao, C. Sun, and J. Wang, "The research on price prediction of second-hand houses based on KNN and stimulated annealing algorithm", *Int. J. Smart Home,* vol. 8, no. 2, pp. 191-200, 2014.
[http://dx.doi.org/10.14257/ijsh.2014.8.2.19]

[30] E.A. Antipov, and E.B. Pokryshevskaya, "Mass appraisal of residential apartments: an application of Random forest for valuation and a CART-based approach for model diagnostics", *Expert Syst. Appl.,* vol. 39, no. 2, pp. 1772-1778, 2012.
[http://dx.doi.org/10.1016/j.eswa.2011.08.077]

[31] K. Johnson, and M. Kuhn, *Applied predictive modeling.* Springer, 2013.

[32] V.N. Vapnik, *Statistical learning theory.* Wiley-Interscience, 1998.

[33] H. Crosby, P. Davis, and S.A. Jarvis, "Exploring new data sources to improve UK land parcel valuation", *Proceedings of the 1st International ACM SIGSPATIAL Workshop on Smart Cities and Urban Analytics - UrbanGIS'15,* 2015pp. 32-35
[http://dx.doi.org/10.1145/2835022.2835028]

[34] D. Demetriou, ""A spatially based artificial neural network mass valuation model for land consolidation," Environ. Plan. B Urban Anal", *City Sci.,* vol. 44, no. 5, pp. 864-883, 2016.

[35] Y. Fu, H. Xiong, Y. Ge, Z. Yao, Y. Zheng, and Z-H. Zhou, "Exploiting geographic dependencies for real estate appraisal: A mutual perspective of ranking and clustering", *KDD '14 Proceedings of the 20th ACM SIGKDD International Conference on Knowledge Discovery and Data Mining,* 2014pp. 1047-1056
[http://dx.doi.org/10.1145/2623330.2623675]

[36] Z. Bessinger, and N. Jacobs, "Quantifying curb appeal", *2016 IEEE International Conference on Image Processing (ICIP),* 2016pp. 4388-4392
[http://dx.doi.org/10.1109/ICIP.2016.7533189]

[37] F. Zhang, J. Bai, X. Li, C. Pei, and V. Havyarimana, "An ensemble cascading extremely randomized trees framework for short-term traffic flow prediction", *KSII Trans. Internet Inf. Syst,* vol. 13, no. 4, 2019.

[38] A. Bellotti, "Reliable region predictions for automated valuation models", *Ann. Math. Artif. Intell.,* vol.

81, no. 1, pp. 71-84, 2017.
[http://dx.doi.org/10.1007/s10472-016-9534-6]

[39]   T. Chen, and C. Guestrin, "XGBoost: A scalable tree boosting system", *Proceedings of the 22nd ACM SIGKDD International Conference on Knowledge Discovery and Data Mining - KDD'16,* 2016pp. 785-794
[http://dx.doi.org/10.1145/2939672.2939785]

CHAPTER 7

The Knowledge-based Firm and AI

Ove Rustung Hjelmervik[1] and **Terje Solsvik Kristensen**[1,2,*]

[1] *Biotech Innovation Center Bergen AS, Bergen, Norway*

[2] *Department of Computing, Mathematics and Physics, Western Norway University of Applied Sciences, Bergen, Norway*

Abstract: Radical innovation is disruptive. It is a change that sweeps away much of a firm's, or an entire industry's, existing investment in technological assets, skills, and knowledge. Such innovation has occurred throughout history and wealth has been accumulated in its wake. Companies have flourished because of such ingenuity, yet there is no evidence in the literature that radical innovation is a result of senior management's decision, rather it takes place through learning. To understand what drives a knowledge-based organization, one must look at the inside of the firm where implemented structures and tools are supporting employees' empowerment to unleash their creativity. What the firm knows is stored in the employees' head and in the firm's procedural structure, and the firm learns in two ways - by its employees and through hiring new employees. Thus, development of radical innovation, such as artificial intelligence (AI), will either be learned by the firm's employees and/or through hiring experts. Whenever management prevents new methods from being applied, or employees refuse to acknowledge and learn new techniques, productivity suffers, resulting in firm and industry obsolescence. This is exactly what is happening in the case of AI. Almost eighty years after Alan Turing introduced AI theory, we see a world flabbergasted by its potential impact on productivity. Our case study is based on interviews of a dozen or so R&D managers in private and public sectors. Although our observations are not a guarantee to lead to a consistent agreement or interpretation, valid knowledge that can lead to better performance and organizational survival, may nevertheless provide useful learning for relevant readers.

Keywords: Bounded rationality, Creative destruction, Gödel's incompleteness theorem, Organizational learning, Radical innovation, The knowledge-based firm, The resource-based view of the firm, Turing groundbreaking technology, Turing machine, Turing test.

---

* **Corresponding author Terje Solsvik Kristensen:** Department of Computing, Mathematics and Physics, Western Norway University of Applied Sciences, Bergen, Norway; E-mail: Terje.Kristensen@hvl.no

Terje Solsvik Kristensen (Ed.)
All rights reserved-© 2021 Bentham Science Publishers

INTRODUCTION

Artificial Intelligence (AI) is a disruptive and radical innovation, which, until a few years ago, most business and organizational leaders were unacquainted with. Why is this a problem, you may ask? In 2017 Kliner Perkins [1] reported that there had been a dramatic shift in the top ten global firms, ranked by capitalization (value), during the last five years. Among the top ten global firms in 2012 there were three technology firms using AI technology in their business model: Apple, Microsoft, and IBM. In 2017, the number has grown to seven: Apple, Google/Alphabeth, Microsoft, Amazon, Facebook, Tencent and Alibaba. While in 2012 all three were US-based, in 2017 five were US-based while the last two were China-based. Furthermore, IBM, the global technology flagship, with its Watson AI technologies, were relegated from the seventh place in 2012 to out of the top 20 list for 2017.

In 1879 George Eastman succeeded in developing a photosensitive celluloid film and thus disrupted a complete industry having made its living from photography for more than 50 years. But, on January 19th, 2011, after 132 years with the 'Kodak moment' and due to the electronics development, Eastman Kodak came to a grinding halt as they filed for chapter 11 [2]. General Motors, once the world's largest automaker, established in 1908, files for chapter 11 on June 1st, 2009 [3]. Both companies had failed to develop technology which could compete in the new marketplace. Thus, IBM could well have followed into the mire where industry giants such as Eastman Kodak (failed to digitize photography) and General Motors (failed to produce more fuel-efficient vehicles) already had gone.

Norway is, by some standards, seen as a digitalized nation. However, during the last year or so researchers and economists are concerned about Norway's cavalier attitude to digitalization, and specific "Big Data" technology. According to a leading economist at the Norwegian School of Economics and Business Administration [4] these changes will be disruptive, and "we are not prepared". Furthermore, "it is difficult to get management teams to ram up enthusiasm for the digitalization process". A participant in an IBM Norway seminar in 2018, where the manager of its Norwegian office gave a talk on digitalization, reported that "the participants were skeptical about his message on Big Data" [5]. Today's leading industries, making a living from obsolete technologies, do not necessarily adapt well to the business environment created by new technologies, as these corporations are more concerned with the quarterly earnings than the technological development [6].

In our contact with leaders of R&D companies and institutions in the city of Bergen, we found little interest for them to apply AI in their businesses. In 2016 we started interviewing [7] what they knew about AI, and what they did in relation to AI technology.

1. We contacted several firms, primarily within the processing industry and strong on R&D, from small businesses to global leaders. They all said the same thing: we apply current technology, as for instance conventional statistical analysis. We see no reason to change such methods, and we do not know if others do it either. We are not interested in applying AI[1].

2. We contacted academic and research leaders. We asked whether they would be willing to change conventional statistical analysis methods to AI- methods. Although conventional statistical methods were the accepted norm[2], they had no plans to change methodology, neither at the unit level, nor at the organizational level, even though we pointed out a possible productivity gain, *i.e.* finishing a research project faster, with a possibly more reliable result, or higher degree of reproducibility [8]. One leader of a large institution asked specifically about what AI was, and one scientist was thinking of using Phyton at the TRL[3] [9] level 1 and 2.

All the interviewed organizations are knowledge-based [10], that is, their resources are people, processes, and stored knowledge representations. Summarizing our experience from the many interviews, we found a clear tendency:

• Unfamiliarity with AI/Machine learning, and possible productivity implication.
• Neither groups could see any benefits from applying such technology.
• No need to acquire such knowledge.

Our observations are in line with an online questionnaire[4] carried out by McKinsey & al [11] saying in their 2017 study that only 20 percent of the respondents say their companies have embedded at least one AI capability in their business processes. Furthermore, only a few companies have the foundational building blocks that enable AI to generate value at scale. The biggest challenges, and barrier, to adopting and implementing AI, according to McKinsey's study, is a lack of clear AI strategy followed by a lack of appropriate talent, functional silos that constrain end-to-end AI solutions, and a lack of leaders who demonstrate ownership of and commitment to AI. We believe that the information age, started in the early 1990s by promising greater productivity leaps, never materialized in a magnitude fashion because industry leaders never understood Alan Turing's contribution to computer science. This is an AI paradox.

AI - A CREATIVE DESTRUCTION TECHNOLOGY

Technology drives society's advancement. However, there is no accounting for a lack of preparedness for the disasters that have yet to come - or even, in some cases, the precautions that prevented worse outcomes. In this section we will look at how new technology destroys established routines while striving for recognition.

Schumpeter's Disruptive Technology and Radical Innovation

According to Joseph Schumpeter [12], the "gale of creative destruction" describes the "process of industrial mutation that incessantly revolutionizes the economic structure from within, incessantly destroying the old one, incessantly creating a new one". Creative destruction is a result of long-run economic waves, such as the Kondratieff wave[5], and refers to the continuing product and process innovation mechanism as an 'essential fact about capitalism'. The process of Schumpeterian creative destruction permeates major aspects of macroeconomic performance during its long-run economic fluctuations[6]. The dynamic forces behind these economic waves are technological inventions followed by radical innovation[7] [13] which may lead to technology diffusion.

In 1975 Gerhard Mensch [14] supported Schumpeter's theory on creative destruction, arguing that economic stagnation occurs due to lack of basic innovation. Basic or radical innovation is innovation which changes a business model within an industry, for instance from horse and buggy to cars or from Kodak to electronics. Basic innovation creates totally new products and processes, and industries that expand current markets into more specialized niches, resulting in attracting consumption away from older industries, for instance from printed to electronic media. Newly developed industries transform existing consumption practice and change money streams. In fact, successful radical innovation is normally a source of temporary market power[8], eroding the profits and positions of old firms, yet ultimately succumbing to the pressure of new inventions commercialized by competing entrants [15].

Creative destruction is a powerful economic concept because it can explain many of the dynamics, or its causes of industrial change: the transition from a competitive to a monopolistic market, and back again [16]. In 1957 Robert Solow[9] [17] developed a growth model which states that permanent growth is achievable only through technological progress, and according to Paul Romer[10] [18] it is technology which drives growth and that a monopolistic situation arises because technology "is a nonrival, partially excludable good". Furthermore, this technology is endogenous at the firm, industry, and national level [19]. That is, radical innovation at the firm level is a partial excludable good, creating monopolistic gain.

IT and The Productivity Paradox

Productivity consists of two elements: efficiency and effectiveness. While efficiency relates to doing things right, effectiveness concerns doing the right thing. Thus, effectiveness first, followed by doing it in the most efficient manner. Any improvement represents productivity. In the current hype about AI, we seem to have forgotten the previous hype – the information technology (IT) and its productivity paradox. For years we heard that the only people profiting by the installation of computers in firms, were the consultants recommending the technology and the equipment vendors installing it, or as concisely stated by Robert Solow [20] "we see the computer age everywhere except in the productivity statistics". Attempting to measure the productivity of IT, the fundamental economic measure of a technology's contribution, Brynjolfsson [21] run a comparative analysis of various empirical studies into the issue of productivity and IT, both in the manufacturing and service industries. The result was mixed. He called it a paradox, as he did not have "a definitive answer to the question of whether the productivity impact of IT has actually been unusually low", but hoped "that there is something wrong with the measurement techniques".

In 1998, yet another study was completed by Brynjolfsson and Hitt [22]. They concluded that "productivity growth comes from working smarter. Thus, computers are pulling their weight". That is, the benefits of computers come from investments in organizational structures and business processes. "Once these investments are made, these companies will be positioned to reap the benefits of continued technological progress in the computer industry, while others may be left further and further behind".

In an effort to explain the difference in the output between those with a good IT infrastructure and those without, Brynjolfsson and Hitt's analysis alludes the ongoing inside the firm. "About half of the IT value is due to unique characteristics of firms, and what goes on inside the 'black box' of the firm has a substantial influence on the productivity of IT investments. The long-term benefits were substantially larger than the short- term, from two to eight times as much as short-term benefits" [22]. Decentralized structures, self-directing teams, empowerment of methods, processes and tempo, increased training and incentive systems are all elements supporting IT productivities. Not only are they more productive, but the productivity gap will have an accumulating effect. The authors are offering two arguments as to why there is an inertia to change costs and ingrained habits. While some firms eventually were successful in managing this change, "the unmistakable lesson was that purchasing computerized equipment was the smallest part of the overall cost of creating a new manufacturing system. The biggest costs were changing the organization".

ALAN TURING'S DISRUPTIVE RESEARCH AND INNOVATION

Alan Turing [23, 24] is mostly known for his groundbreaking test (Turing test) and his work on the Enigma machine, which was used to crack the German code in World War II. On the other hand, his disruptive development in mathematics is seldom mentioned because of its theoretical nature. However, he laid the foundations for the modern computer. Probably you have heard about the *Imitation Game*, but not heard about his contribution to mathematics which has had great consequences for how modern computers are designed. The theoretical computer he defined was first named the *alfa-machine* and later called the '*Turing machine*' [25]. Today this is no longer a 'new' invention, but at that time (1930) it was a great, disruptive, research and innovation step [26].

Turing Machine

A Turing machine needs an input, a set of states to be in and a program that tells the machine what to do with this input. Even for a small problem, the set of states may be large, and the program tells how the computer may switch between the given states to compute the response of the input. This led Turing to a new theoretical concept, which is to decide what can or cannot be computed by a computer [26, 27]. It is a theoretical model of computation that defines an abstract machine. The machine prints its outputs on an infinite memory tape.

Turing's next step was to define what is now known as a *Universal Turing Machine*. This machine is programmable, and the input also includes a complex program. In addition, it may simulate any other Turing machine. A Turing machine is therefore equivalent to the concept of an algorithm.

Turing then launched the '*Halting problem*'. Suppose you have a program consisting of some code lines. You may then ask the computer to run it. Will the program finish after one minute, an hour, a year, or ever? This problem is *undecidable*.

So, what does it mean to be undecidable? A set S of elements is consistent when no contradiction is provable from the set S. S is complete if every sentence A is decided by S: if either S proves A or S proves not A. If neither A nor not A is provable in S, A is said to be undecidable by S and S is said to be incomplete [28].

The Halting problem has also been solved by Alonzo Church. His invention, *the lambda calculus* [29], is more difficult to understand because of its abstract mathematical nature. However, a Turing machine is a more intuitive concept. In [29] a formal proof is given that shows the equivalence between a Turing machine and Church's lambda calculus that allows computability functions to be replaced by λ-definitions.

Turing's radical ideas and inventions were a huge step towards understanding what computing is about. This also has created much innovation, as people now was able to ask deep questions about computers and what a computer is able to do or compute. Following Schumpeter, the Turing machine is thus a creative destruction, but difficult to spot.

Turing Test

In 1950, Alan Turing published a famous paper *Computing Machinery and Intelligence* [30]. In this paper he introduced a test to decide if a computer is intelligent or not. By using this test, it may be possible in theory to decide if a computer is intelligent or not. The experiment consists of a computer and a person both communicating with a 'judger' behind a wall. The conversation would be blind. Based on the conversation the judger should be able to identify which answers came from the computer and which from the person. If the judger is not able to decide which answers came from the machine and which from the person, the judger will consider the machine as intelligent.

The computer has passed the Turing test when a human being, after communicating in written form, is not able to discern between a human and a machine. Such a computer to be able to emulate a human being must have several properties, as for instance:

- Recognize and generate natural language expressions and be able to communicate with a human being.
- Save and represent information or knowledge in the memory.
- Do reasoning and making new conclusions based on this knowledge.
- Be able to learn to adapt to new circumstances and extract patterns.

To be an intelligent physical system the computer must also have a computer-vision system to see objects in the environment and be able to manipulate and move them.

Problem Solving

What does Alan Turing teach us about problem solving in general? First, he gives us a lesson in 'design thinking'. In the movie '*Imitation Game*' Alan Turing makes a remarkable progress in the problem-solving process and gives us a lesson in how to solve a problem and design a solution. Creative solutions do not happen in a command structure. You cannot command persons to do research and obtain innovations. Organizational people are thinking they can instruct a person to do so. However, this is a great misunderstanding. You may stimulate people to do research or innovation activities, but not command people to do so. This also means that as a leader of an innovation project you need to tolerate people that seem to be somewhat eccentric, as for instance Alan Turing himself, as a mathematician, a thinker, and a great researcher. People like Alan Turing are creative people and often come up with a solution not thought of in the beginning of the process. They do not always follow a rational model but are often taking great unexpected steps during the solution process.

The second lesson he teaches us is that the solution of a problem needs teamwork. He pointed this out for the military personnel by simply saying to them 'I think you need me more than I need you'. We also need diversity in the project team, and this may also be realized for instance by letting women be included in projects. Women are often thinking differently than men, so it is good for a project to include them. In the history of IT only two women have been mentioned, Ada Lovelace and Grace Hopper [31]. They both contributed greatly in different areas.

Ada Lovelace was one that understood The Analytical Engine of Charles Babbage. She was very interested in his ideas and inventions and was also working with him to develop programs for his machine. Her contribution to the development of the computer cannot be overestimated. She encouraged Babbage to continue, and further developed his ideas. In addition, she published his ideas in journals so that other scientists could get access to them. Ada Lovelace is considered as the world's first programmer. The programming language ADA is bearing her name. It is a bit strange that the first programmer was a woman when you see how men dominate the IT field today.

Grace Hopper may be known as the world's first debugger. Every data program contains some bugs. Much work is often needed to debug the program. She was one of the persons behind the COBOL language, a preferred program in the banking and assurance industry, but which now is being faded out. She worked during her whole life for the US Marine and got many awards. She was also taking part in the development of the Mark I and Univac I computers that are considered as the first modern computers.

The third lesson Turing teaches us is that competition is a good design property in a project. In the *Imitation game* there was a competition between Germany and Britain and a race between coders and code breakers using old and new methods. All these different kinds of competition were good for the project since, if used in the right way, they can be motivating and stimulating to find quick solutions.

Turing's Connectionism

Few people, even people in computer science, know that Turing also anticipated the neural network computers. Connectionism is about doing computing with networks of artificial neurons. A training algorithm is running that adjusts the connection between the neurons. Frank Rosenblatt who published the first of many papers in 1957, has been considered as the founder of this type of computing [31]. However, very few know that Alan Turing already had investigated a connectionist network as early as in 1948 in his small 'Intelligent Machinery' paper [23]. This paper, characterized by Sir Charles Darwin as a 'schoolboy essay', was the first manifestation in the field of Artificial Intelligence. The paper was unpublished until 1968, 14 years after Turing's death. The British mathematician not only defined the field of connectionism, but also introduced many of the concepts that today are central to AI. So, his thinking was far beyond his time, even in this field. It was not until 1954, the year of Turing's death, that two scientists at MIT were able to run the first computer simulation of a small neural network. In 1954 Turing was found dead in his bedroom with a pile of handwritten notes about neural networks that even today, decades later, are not fully understood.

Gødel and AI

Alan Turning lay the foundation of AI almost 80 years ago. However, in 1931 the Austrian mathematician, Kurt Gødel, published a paper that made great impact on the science society and forced the mathematicians to change their view on what mathematics is about. The paper is known as *Gødel's Incompleteness Theorem*, or just *Gødel's Theorem* [32] and is one of the most important theorems ever proved, ranking alongside with Einstein's Theory of Relativity, Heisenberg's Uncertainty Principle and Maxwell's equations. Astonishingly, few people know about this theorem and the consequences it implies for the relationship between AI and mind.

Kurt Gødel was at Princeton when Alan Turing arrived there in December 1938. Albert Einstein had already arrived in 1931 to get away from the Nazis. Alonso Church, Alan Turing's PhD mentor, was there also. So, we believe they must have had a lot of discussions around AI that Turing had introduced, and the consequences it may have for understanding the structure of the human mind.

What is this theorem about? David Hilbert, one of the most famous mathematicians ever, believed that a proof in mathematics always can be realized in an automated way by using an axiomatic system. However, Gødel demonstrated by his theorem the impossibility of this assumption. He was able to translate a formal system into numbers. He then formulated a statement, for instance, 'This formula is unprovable in the system's arithmetic'. He was also able to formulate the negation of the sentence in arithmetic. If the truth value of the statement could be calculated, the truth value of the negation could also be calculated which causes a contradiction. So, we may always find a Gødel sentence like the one above which makes the truth value undeterminable.

Turing described his abstract machine, called a Turing machine, as being able to calculate any kind of algorithmic problem. However, he also demonstrated that the Halting problem is computationally insoluble and would run indefinitely because of Gødel incompleteness theorem. What Gødel's theorem has shown us is that all mathematical understanding cannot be reduced to plain computation and any mathematical understanding cannot be reduced to a set of computational rules. The best example of this is the Halting problem of Alan Turing. According to Penrose [33, 34] there must exist something more beyond computation in the human mind. According to Gødel's theorem there will always be a statement in an AI system that is not provable, and thus will limit the reasoning process of an AI system. Gødel's theorem applies only for *deductive* systems. However, human beings may not be reduced to making only deductive inferences.

Today's most important AI systems are connectionistic. So, how is the relation between Gødel's Theorem and the Connectionism including Deep Learning [35]? This may be a challenge to the reader to ponder more about.

THE KNOWLEDGE-BASED ORGANIZATION

Organizational learning and creativity, stimulated by its management, are success-factors embedded in a knowledge-based organization, and may lead to Schumpeterian innovation giving it sustained competitive advantage.

The Resource-Based View of The Firm

The resource-based view (RBV) of the firm [10, 36 - 43], as a strategic theory, brings into focus the internal resources and their abilities to support sustained competitive advantage. In the RBV knowledge is assumed to be valuable, rear, inimitable and non-substitutable. Furthermore, by combining the knowledge resource, as it relates to the firm's operative activities, with an ICT[11] resource, this combination can be said to be part of the RBV theory. It is further assumed that linking resources, such as knowledge and knowledge development, with ICT, can result in developing radical innovation and thus create sustained competitive advantage for the firm [44]. For a firm to benefit from the RBV, their employees, management and otherwise, "should accept the responsibility of creating, nurturing, and exploiting resources and capabilities that can generate competitive advantage for the firm" [45].

Whenever the industrial conditions are changing, such as introduction of AI, or new entrants, Core Competencies [38] and Dynamic Capabilities[12] [37] are relevant concepts. For both concepts, the commonality for earning above normal profit (Ricardian rent) [15] lies in the ability of the firm to apply their valuable, rear, and costly-to-imitate resources in a new business model. For both Core Competencies and Dynamic Capabilities, organizational learning and the application of a common knowledge base that can be reconfigured in a dynamic market [36], are central to success. Furthermore, new knowledge creation plays a prominent role in innovation intensive, high-velocity markets [40], as you may find in Silicon Valley. By applying simple routines, organizations should be capable of rapidly restructuring experiments, adapting to changing conditions, and bringing learning from knowledge developer to implementation within the organization.

Organizational Learning

What the firm knows is stored in the employees' head and in the firm's procedural structure. The firm learns in two ways a) by the learning of its employees or b) by hiring people from outside the organization who have knowledge the organization didn't previously have [46]. While the watershed in the field of Organizational Learning (OL) took place with the special issue of Organization Science, February 1991, the source of organizational learning is based on the writings as far back as to John Dewey [47]. He wrote about experiential learning and the need for social interaction among internal resources of the firm and "the dominant role that increasing knowledge plays in economic processes" [8], tacit knowledge [48] and situated knowledge [49]. Due to the fast development of OL theory, authors have taken different tacks, different terminologies, and variation of definitions, resulting in fragmentation and confusion of the field [50 - 53]. However, let us look at three descriptive theories within OL dealing with learning, economics, and management:

- *Organizational learning* is concerned with how organizations learn [54 - 59].
- *Organizational knowledge* is related to economics and focuses on the importance of knowledge as a firm resource [10, 44], of 'tacit' knowledge and routine-learning in operations [60, 61], and of organizational knowledge and empowerment [62].
- *Knowledge Management* is concerned with how organizations should manage its stock of knowledge in a most effective and efficient way.

The process of organizational learning occurs when any of its members acquires knowledge that may be related to the organization [57]. The more knowledge about the subject an organization possesses, the more of the message it will understand [63]. An organization that applies the learned knowledge faster, will have an advantage in the marketplace [64], which means its capability to adapt to its environment and learn from its experience [53]. The firm's capacity to learn faster through disseminating knowledge throughout the organization and applying it for enhanced value creation, depends on its organizational learning process instigated by its management. Such processes require motivational power related to empowerment. This implies implementing organizational processes capable of converting new knowledge into routines for diffusion in the organization. Thus, "organizational learning is a consequence of an organization that learns through accumulating experience, articulating such experience through transfer, codifies it into new knowledge, and diffuses the new knowledge to its members" [44]. Therefore, in the information age ICT is part of the learning process, both a real and a virtual process, capable of supporting advanced organizations' learning achievements.

Bounded Rationality

Organizations learn in two ways, by their employees and through hiring new employees. Furthermore, organizations learn through data codified and stored *e.g.* in ICT and made available for members of the organization for further learning [44]. The process of developing knowledge, such as new technology, or routines to operate new technology, is the result of an organization's ability to learn and accumulate knowledge. Routines seem to play an important role in sustaining a firm's competitive advantage. "Our general term for all regular and predictable behavioral patterns of firms is 'routine' " [60].

Once an expert has achieved success on a previous occasion applying a particular method, or routine, this expert will try to use the same type of method to solve a similar task [65]. In doing so, an organization can be reassured to repeat experiments in the same way as previously. However, let us suppose that the complexity of a new task renders the method sub-optimal. Then, according to March and Simon [65] the organization, or an individual expert, will continue to use such a method as long as the method gives a "satisfactory alternative". Only in exceptional cases is it concerned with the discovery and selection of an optimal alternative. Finding the optimal alternative is a radical different problem from finding a satisfactory alternative. To optimize it require processing several orders of magnitude more complex than those required to satisfy. In the language of productivity, 'satisfactory' implies doing things more efficient, while 'optimizing' require management to identify and implement a more effective process, including bringing on entirely new technologies.

March and Simon [65] argue that human capacity is limited to deal with complex problems. To take rational decisions, either as an individual or an organization, the decision model must be simplified, or bounded, without representing all its complexities. It is the search for a relative stable structure "insofar as there are boundaries of rationality that must be or are in fact taken as given ... If there were no boundaries of rationality, or if the boundaries varied in a rapid and unpredictable manner, there could be no stable organizational structures" [65]. Implementing, through learning, radical innovation in the organization requires processes that are several orders of magnitude more complex than just doing current operations more efficient.

DISCUSSION

Radical innovation both create and destroy industries, exemplified by the demise of Eastman Kodak and General Motors, and the emergence of Apple and Tesla. There are countless examples of catastrophes that, in retrospect, could have been less disastrous if only industries had heeded what they had known, ahead of time. That is, identifying, learning, and implementing right technology and applying right process.

Alan Turing's algorithmic theory has radical implications and has laid the foundation for the current surge in AI technology, almost 80 years later. We recall Robert Solow's [17] argument of the missing productivity gain, promised by the computer industry. We ask if Turing's theory may be the "missing link" of the productivity leap Brynjolfsson [21] inquired about. In meeting with R&D managers and employees in non- and for-profit organizations we found it difficult to lead a meaningful dialogue around AI due to the participants' lacking the conceptual understanding related to AI-technology.

According to Thomas S. Kuhn [66], radicalness relates to shift in the trajectory development of technology. It is not enough to continue to develop along the same trajectory, which means being more efficient in the old technology, when newcomers in the field have moved their curve upward to the right, which means implemented new and more effective technologies. Kuhn called this a paradigm shift [66].

It is this ability to understand that one's own technology, or the one you rely on in your business model, is approaching its discontinuity, and shift your organization to the next level, which signifies a true knowledge-based organization. Thus, possessing relevant knowledge to be a leader of today's paradigm may not be enough, even to be a participant in the new one. Unfortunately, as both Eastman Kodak and General Motors so blatantly demonstrated, ignorance and invincibility is part of the scenario. It can all be referred to Simon's [59] bounded rationality and selecting the right thing.

New knowledge can only be developed through experience, or in communication with others holding such knowledge, and that this experience being communicated to its organizational members. Such processes require motivational power related to empowerment. But, if a member does not have a foundation to understand new information, or that management does not possess meaning and purpose for stimulating members of the organization to acquire new information for the purpose of innovation, an organization's rationality is bounded.

In the case of AI, few have, as McKinsey [11] pointed out, applied it to business, and few have therefore a reference to understand its implications. It is the role of management to identify and encourage the development of new knowledge. As long as they do not possess a foundation for understanding such new knowledge, they will not recognize the knowledge as new and disruptive, and therefore will fail to acquire such knowledge.

For the Eastman Kodaks of the world who wants to participate in the new paradigm, this means investing in restructuring your organization to become a true knowledge-based company. First then your organization may be capable of performing radical innovation.

CONCLUSION

Radical innovation disrupts current industry structures and upheave ingrained practices, leading to industry and business failures. However, management investing in a firm's ability to develop new knowledge, leading to radical innovative processes, may give the firm long-term benefits.

In this chapter we are proposing that the missing link of productivity gain in AI is an organization's lack in the understanding of Turing's theoretical concepts. To be more specific, whenever management is lacking knowledge of, and insight into Turing's radical ideas, one is incapable of implementing such ideas into their business.

NOTES

[1] They may of course have changed their mind after we interviewed them.

[2] We should point out that current methods were approved by the medical authorities which were financing some of these R&D projects.

[3] According to the Technology Readiness Level (TRL) definitions, science and technology (and technical) maturity increases as system capabilities are successfully demonstrated at higher levels of integration. TRL consists of 9 levels, where 1 is basic research and 9 is commercialization.

[4] Online survey from February 6 to February 16, 2018, and garnered responses from 2,135 participants representing the full range of regions, industries, company sizes, functional specialities, and tenures.

[5] The Austrian born Harvard professor Joseph Schumpeter named the ´55-year´ long waves after its discoverer, the Russian economist Nikolas Kondratieff.

[6] Schumpeter identified four stages in the K-wave: Prosperity, recession, depression, and recovery.

[7] James M. Utterback, professor at MIT, defined radical innovation as "change that sweeps away much of a firm's existing investment in technical skills and knowledge, design, production technique, plant, and equipment".

[8] A firm is able to obtain a Ricardian rent, *i.e.* above normal profit, as a result of "an inherent scarcity of resource supply".

[9] Robert Solow was in 1987 awarded the Nobel Prize in Economics for his work.

[10] Paul M. Romer received in 2018 Nobel Prize in Economics "for integrating technological innovations into long-run macroeconomic analysis" according to The Sveriges Riksbank.

[11] Information and Communication Technology.

[12] David J. Teece refers to his 1997 article where he coined this phrase.

CONSENT FOR PUBLICATION

Not applicable.

CONFLICT OF INTEREST

The author declares no conflict of interest, financial or otherwise.

ACKNOWLEDGEMENTS

Declared none.

REFERENCES

[1]   M. Meeker, *Capital Marked Report,* Kliner Perkins, 2017.

[2]   M.J. de la Merced, *Eastman Kodak Files for Bankruptcy,* The New York Times, 2012. January https://dealbook.nytimes.com/2012/01/19/eastman-kodak-files-for-bankruptcy/

[3]   D.E. Sange, J. Zeleny, and B. Vlasicmay, "G.M. to seek bankruptcy and a new start", *The New York Times,* in front of 2009. https://www.nytimes.com/2009/06/01/business/01auto.html

[4]   https://www.nhh.no

[5]   J.M. Moberg, Teknisk Ukeblad, Oslo, Norway, 2018, 29\018 (In Norwegian).

[6]   J.M. Utterback, *Mastering the Dynamics of Innovation.* HBS Press: Boston, MA, 1994, p. 30.

[7]   O.R. Hjelmervik, and T.S. Kristensen, Unpublished, *Interviews with a dozen small, medium and large firms and organizations, in period 2016-2018,* 2018. December 2018.

[8]   M. R. Munafò, "A manifesto for reproducible science", *NATURE HUMAN BEHAVIOUR,* vol. 1, Macmillan Publishers Limited, part of Springer Nature, p. 0021, 2017. [http://dx.doi.org/10.1038/s41562-016-0021]

[9]   *Defense Acquisition Guidebook.* Department of Defence: USA, 2008.

[10]   E.T. Penrose, *The theory of the growth of the firm.* Wiley: New York, NY, 1995. [http://dx.doi.org/10.1093/0198289774.001.0001]

[11]   "Notes from the AI frontier: AI adoption advances, but foundational barriers remain", *McKinsey Analytics,* McKinsey & Company, 2018.

[12]   J.A. Schumpeter, "Capitalism, socialism and democracy", *Introduction by Richard Swedberg, Stockholm University,* 5th edGeorge Allen & Unwin (Publishers) Ltd: London: Routledge, pp. 82-83, 1942.

[13]   J.M. Utterback, *Mastering the Dynamics of Innovation.* HBS Press: Boston, MA, 1994, p. 200.

[14]   G. Mensch, and R. Schnopp, "Historische konjunkturforschung", *Stalment in Technology,* Stuttgart: Germany: Klett-Cotta, 1980.

[15]   M.A. Peteraf, "The cornerstones of competitive advantage: A resource-based view", *Strateg. Manage. J.,* vol. 14, pp. 179-191, 1993. [http://dx.doi.org/10.1002/smj.4250140303]

[16]   J.G. Sidak, and D.J. Teece, "Dynamic competition in antitrust law", *J. Compet. Law Econ.,* vol. 5, no. 4, pp. 581-631, 2009. [http://dx.doi.org/10.1093/joclec/nhp024]

[17]   R.M. Solow, "Technical change and the aggregate production function", *Rev. Econ. Stat.,* vol. 39, no. 3, pp. 312-320, 1957. [http://dx.doi.org/10.2307/1926047]

[18]   P.M. Romer, "Endogenous technological change", *J. Polit. Econ.,* vol. 98, no. 5, 1990. [http://dx.doi.org/10.1086/261725]

[19]   P.M. Romer, The origins of endogenous growth.*Journal of Economic Perspectives,* vol. 8, no. 1, pp. 3-22, 1994. [http://dx.doi.org/10.1257/jep.8.1.3]

[20]   R. Solow, "We'd better watch out", *New York Times Book Review,* p. 36, 1987.

[21]   E. Brynjofsson, "The productivity paradox of information technology", *Communication of the ACM,* vol. 36, Cambridge, MA: MIT Sloan School of Management, no. 12, 1993.

[22]   E. Brynjolfsson, and L.M. Hitt, "Beyond the productivity paradox: computers are the catalyst for bigger changes", *Communication of the ACM,* 1998. August http://ccs.mit.edu/erik/

[23]   S. Naser, *A Beautiful Mind.* Simon & Schuster: New York, NY, 1998.

[24]   H.R. Lewis, and C.H. Popadimitrow, *Elements of the Theory of Computation,* Prentice-Hall International Editions, Inc: London, UK, 1981.

[25]   A.M. Turing, "On computable numbers, with an application to the Entscheidungs problem", *Proc. Lond. Math. Soc.,* vol. 42, pp. 230-265, 1936.

[26]   A.M. Turing, "Computability and λ-definability", *J. Symb. Log.,* vol. 2, pp. 153-163, 1937. [http://dx.doi.org/10.2307/2268280]

[27]   A.M. Turing, "Computing machinery and intelligence", *Mind,* vol. LIX, no. 236, pp. 433-460, 1950. [http://dx.doi.org/10.1093/mind/LIX.236.433]

[28]   M. Davis, *The Undecidable, Basic papers and Undecidable propositions, Unsolvable problems and computable Functions* Raven Press: New York, 1965.

[29]   H.P. Barendregt, "The lambda calculus: its syntax and semantics", *Studies in Logic 103, second,* revised editionNorth-Holland: Amsterdam, 1984.

[30]   T. Kristensen, *Information, Communication and Technology,*   2nd edition. Cappelen Academic Publisher: Oslo, Norway, (in Norwegian), 2001.

[31]   T. Kristensen, *Neural Networks, Fuzzy Logic and Genetic Algorithms.* Cappelen Academic Publisher: Oslo, Norway, 1997.

[32]   M. Davis, "The Imcompleteness Theorem", *Not. Am. Math. Soc.,* vol. 53, no. 4, pp. 414-418, 2006.

[33]   R. Penrose, *The Emperor's New Mind.* Oxford University Press: New York, NY, 1989. [http://dx.doi.org/10.1093/oso/9780198519737.001.0001]

[34]   R. Penrose, *Shadows of the Mind.* Oxford University Press: New York, NY, 1994.

[35]   I. Goodfellow, Y. Bengio, and A. Courville, *Deep Learning.* MIT Press: London, England, 2016.

[36]   J. Barney, "Firm Resources and Sustained Competitive Advantage", *J. Manage.,* vol. 17, no. 1, pp. 99-120, 1991. [http://dx.doi.org/10.1177/014920639101700108]

[37]   D.J. Teece, *Managing Intellectual Capital.* Oxford University Press: Oxford, UK, 2000.

[38]   C.K. Prahalad, and G. Hamel, "The core competence of the corporation", *Harv. Bus. Rev.,* 1990.

[39]   R.M. Grant, "Toward a knowledge-based theory of the firm", *Strategic Management Journal,* vol. 17, no. Winter Special Issue, pp. 109-122, 1996. [http://dx.doi.org/10.1002/smj.4250171110]

[40]   R.C. Andreu, and C. Ciborra, "Organisational learning and core capabilities development", *J. Strateg. Inf. Syst.,* vol. 5, no. 2, pp. 111-127, 1996. [http://dx.doi.org/10.1016/S0963-8687(96)80039-4]

[41]   K.M. Eisenhardt, and J.A. Martin, "Dynamic Capabilities: what are they?", *Strateg. Manage. J.,* vol. 21, pp. 1105-1121, 2000. [http://dx.doi.org/10.1002/1097-0266(200010/11)21:10/11<1105::AID-SMJ133>3.0.CO;2-E]

[42]   B. Wernerfelt, "A resource-based view of the firm", *Strateg. Manage. J.,* vol. 5, pp. 171-180, 1984. [http://dx.doi.org/10.1002/smj.4250050207]

[43]   H.A. Haverman, "Follow the leader: Mimic isomorphism and entry into new markets", *Adm. Sci. Q.,* vol. 38, pp. 593-627, 1993.

[http://dx.doi.org/10.2307/2393338]

[44] O.R. Hjelmervik, "Knowledge-driven value creation", In: *PhD monograph*NTNU, Tapir print, Trondheim, Norway, 2/2007, 2007.

[45] J.B. Barney, *Gaining and Sustaining Competitive Advantage.,* 2nd Edition Upper Saddle River, NJ: Prentice Hall, 2002.

[46] B. Levitt, and J.G. March, "Organizational Learning", *Annu. Rev. Sociol.,* vol. 14, pp. 319-340, 1988. [http://dx.doi.org/10.1146/annurev.so.14.080188.001535]

[47] J. Dewey, "Democracy and Education: An introduction to the philosophy of education", London, UK: Collier-Macmillan, 1916.

[48] M. Polany, *Personal knowledge: toward a post-critical philosophy.* Chicago University Press: Chicago, Illinois, 1962.

[49] F.A. Hayek, "The use of knowledge in society", In: *The American economic review, 1945, in Individualism and Economic Order.* University of Chicago Press: Chicago, Illinois, 1948.

[50] M. Easterby-Smith, and M.A. Lyle, "Introduction: Watersheds of organizational learning and knowledge management", In: *The Blackwell handbook of Organizational learning and Knowledge management* Blackwell publishing Ltd: London, UK, 2003.

[51] D. Vera, and M. Crossan, "Organizational learning and knowledge management: Toward an integrated framework", In: *The Blackwell Handbook of Organizational Learning and Knowledge Management.* Blackwell Publishing Ltd: London, UK, 2003.

[52] E.W.K. Tsang, "Orgaizational learning and the learning organization: a dichotomy between descriptive and prescriptive research", *Hum. Relat.,* vol. 50, no. 1, pp. 73-89, 1997. [http://dx.doi.org/10.1177/001872679705000104]

[53] M. Easterby-Smith, "Disciplines of organizational learning: contributions and critiques", *Hum. Relat.,* vol. 50, no. 9, pp. 1085-1113, 1997. [http://dx.doi.org/10.1177/001872679705000903]

[54] R.M. Cyert, and J.G. March, *A behaviour theory of the firm.* Blackwell Publishers: Cambridge, MA, 1992.

[55] V.E. Changelosi, and W.R. Dill, "Organizational learning: Observations toward a theory", *Adm. Sci. Q.,* vol. 10, no. 2, pp. 175-203, 1965. [http://dx.doi.org/10.2307/2391412]

[56] C. Argyris, and D.A. Schön, "What is an organization that it may learn?", In: *Organizational Learning II.* Addison Wesley: Reading, MA, 1996.

[57] J.G. March, "Exploration and Exploitation in Organizational learning", *Organ. Sci.,* vol. 2, no. 1, pp. 71-87, 1991. [http://dx.doi.org/10.1287/orsc.2.1.71]

[58] G.H. Huber, "Organizational Learning: the contribution processes and the literatures", *Organ. Sci.,* vol. 2, no. 1, pp. 88-115, 1991. [http://dx.doi.org/10.1287/orsc.2.1.88]

[59] H. Simon, "Bounded Rationality and Organizational Learning", *Organ. Sci.,* vol. 2, no. 1, pp. 125-134, 1991. [http://dx.doi.org/10.1287/orsc.2.1.125]

[60] R. Nelson, and S. Winter, *An Evolutionary Theory of Economic Change.* Harvard University Press: Cambridge, MA, 1982.

[61] I. Nonaka, and H. Takeuchi, *The Knowledge Creating Company* Oxford University Press: New York, NY, 1995.

[62] J-C. Spender, "Making knowledge the basis of a dynamic theory of the firm", *Strategic Manag. J.,* vol.

17, no. Winter special issue, pp. 45-62, 1996.
[http://dx.doi.org/10.1002/smj.4250171106]

[63]   W.M. Cohen, and D.A. Levinthal, "Absorptive Capacity: A New Perspective on Learning and Innovation", *Adm. Sci. Q.,* vol. 35, pp. 128-152, 1990.
[http://dx.doi.org/10.2307/2393553]

[64]   A.P. De Geus, "Planning and learning", *Harv. Bus. Rev.,* vol. 66, no. 2, pp. 70-74, 1988.

[65]   J.G. March, and H.A. Simon, *Organizations, New York.* John Wiley & son, Inc.: NY, 1958.

[66]   T.S. Kuhn, *The Structure of Scientific Revolutions* 2nd Ed. The University of Chicago: Chicago, Illinois, 1962.

CHAPTER 8

A Mathematical Description of Artificial Neural Networks

Hans Birger Drange[1,*]

[1] Western Norway University of Applied Sciences (HVL), Faculty of Engineering and Science, Bergen Norway

Abstract: After a short introduction to neural networks generally, a more detailed presentation of the structure of a feed forward neural network is done, using mathematical language, functions, matrices and vectors.

Further, emphasis has been made on perceptrons and linear regression done by using ANN. Central concepts like learning, including weight updates, error minimization with gradient descent are introduced and studied using these simple networks.

Finally, multilayer perceptrons are defined with their error functions and finally backpropagation are described precisely using composite functions and the concept of error signals.

Keywords: Backpropagation, Chain rule, Composite functions, Computing neurons, Feedforward, Matrices, Multiple perceptron, Neural network, Perceptron, Transfer function, Vectors.

INTRODUCTION

The main intention with the chapter is to define the concepts and the mathematics used in Neural Networks in a precise way.

Neural Networks is a special case of Machine Learning. This latter term again means that you use a computer to obtain information from large data sets where you do not try to analyze these data sets in detail, the way you do in traditional programming. Instead mathematics is used more directly to extract the information you want.

---

[*] **Corresponding author Hans Birger Drange:** Western Norway University of Applied Sciences (HVL), Faculty of Engineering and Science, Bergen, Norway; E-mail: xansbd@gmail.com

Terje Solsvik Kristensen (Ed.)

The reason that you do not use traditional programming methods is that this would be practically impossible because of the kind of information you intend to draw out.

Consider for example a firm that wants to get information about what customers would prefer in connection with specific issues. Would they prefer to buy cheap cars or cars that would last for long? The firm has collected a lot of data about the customers that are relevant for this purpose.

But how could they get the information they want from all these data clustering?

Another example, a bit different, is the problem of having a computer read handwritten characters. A natural way to attack this problem might be to try and find rules that characterize the different characters. This has been tried, but has turned out to be too difficult. There are too many situations to cover.

Instead the problem has been solved by the use of a mathematical model inspired by the way the human brain is working, that is by using Neural Networks.

Exactly how we do this is the theme of this writing, so we return to this shortly.

Now suffice it to say that the way one talks about these things is by saying for instance that we learn from data. This is achieved by establishing a learning algorithm that provides us with the knowledge we want.

Next, to realize this learning algorithm one uses a computer, that is a machine, hence the term machine learning makes sense. But this seems to be normally understood to mean that the machine is learning and not you.

Finally, we should emphasize that in addition to the word learning, the word training is also used here. Both of these words suggest that the algorithm we use to get knowledge is akin to the method humans use to get knowledge generally.

ARTIFICIAL NEURAL NETWORKS, ANN

We suggested above that to solve for instance the problem of recognizing handwritten characters, we can use a mathematical model inspired by how the brain is working.

Neurons in the Brain

We give here a short simplified explanation of how the brain works. It consists of *neurons*, specialized nerve cells, that are interconnected and which are sending nerve signals to other neurons as well as receiving signals themselves.

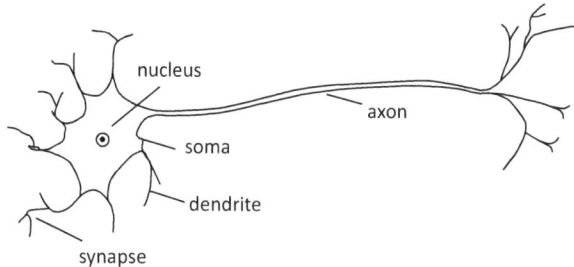

Fig. (1). The biological neuron.

The way this sending and receiving of signals is organized is as follows. Each neuron has dendrites, by which they receive signals from other neurons, a cell body where a signal received is processed, and an axon along which the processed signal is transmitted to one or more dendrites of receiving neurons.

The connection between the axon of a sending neuron and a dendrite of a receiving neuron is called a *synapse* and is a very important part of this system. A signal arriving at the synapse may be reinforced or weakened, or perhaps totally inhibited.

A Mathematical Model

We can model this mathematically in the following way. *The cell body*, also called the *soma*, is modelled by a *function*. Let us call this function F. We return later to the question of what it may look like. The function F is meant to simulate that the signal arriving at the soma is processed in some way.

The signal itself *arriving* at the cell body is modelled by a *number S* and the signal *leaving* the cell body and propagating down the axon, is represented by the value of the function F, that is $F(S)$,.. Let us name the value that this function takes by y. Then we have, $y = F(S)$, and the function itself is called *the transfer function*.

The Synapse

This is very important and is modelled by a number w, and the effect that the synapse has on the signal x arriving there from another neuron is simply obtained by the product $w{\cdot}x$. The number w is called the strength of the synapse and $w{\cdot}x$ is the signal entering the cell body.

Before leaving this point about the mathematical model of a neuron we should note that a neuron normally receives signals from many neurons, in keeping with the fact that a neuron has many dendrites, and that we denoted the signal entering a neuron by the letter S. This letter is chosen because we consider S to be the *sum* of all the signals entering a cell body from the dendrites belonging to it.

Thus we have the following expression for S (a linear combination of x_j):

$$S = \sum_{j=1}^{n} w_j x_j \qquad\qquad (1)$$

Where n is the number of dendrites entering the cell body. Here we have indexed the signals sent *from* other neurons in the layer below to the one we consider by x_j. And likewise we have indexed the strengths of the synapses from the neurons in the layer below, w_j.

Here we used the word layer. Just like the neurons of the brain are arranged in layers, locally at least, we adopt the same structure for our system of artificial neurons. That is, every neuron in our system belongs to a layer and only to one layer, and we consider the layers to constitute a sequence. That is, we have a first layer, a second and so on, and finally the last layer. It is also possible to have only two layers.

Letting S denote the signal *entering* a cell body $y = F(S)$, the signal *leaving* the cell body is $y = F(S)$ like we said earlier. We repeat this here because we want to stress another fact, namely that this signal y leaving, is the same signal that we denoted by x above, only then we looked at it as the signal sent to a neuron in the next layer. That is, as long as there is a next layer, which is the case of course if the layer of the sending neuron is not the last layer.

A Mathematical Structure

Before we continue we now revise our language since we no longer consider ourselves to be making a mathematical model, but to be building a mathematical structure. We detach this structure from the formal model we described. So we shall no longer talk about dendrites, axons and synapses, but connections between the neurons, and the strengths of synapses we shall call weights. And finally, the connection between two neurons has a direction, so we talk about the connection from one neuron to another neuron.

However we shall still talk about signals from one neuron to another. But the term neuron is frequently replaced by the words node or unit. The word unit is sometimes referred to as a computing unit, the reason for this should be obvious from then relation mentioned above.

But there is an exception. The role of the units in the first layer is not to compute, but just to hand on the signal it gets from the outside world. So the first unit does not compute anything.

Next, if for any given connection between two neurons the direction is from a neuron in one layer to a neuron in the next layer, the network is called a feed forward network. If some connections also go from neurons in one layer to neurons in an earlier layer, the network is called a recurrent network.

A feed forward network is the simplest one, and also the oldest. In this chapter we shall only talk about feed forward networks. If sometimes it should happen that we say something about a recurrent network, we shall explicitly make that clear.

So we shall need to talk about the connections between the neurons in one layer and the neurons in the next one. And we shall identify the neurons in a layer by numbering them. To get an expression for the signal entering a neuron i in a layer from neurons in the layer below, we use the expression in (1):

$$S_i = \sum_j w_{ij} \cdot x_j \tag{2}$$

Where the summation index j runs over all the neurons in a layer that send signals to neuron i in the next layer. Note the meaning of thesubscripts in the notation . w_{ij} By w_{ij} we mean the weight of the connection *to* neuron i *from* neuron j.

Now, there is more to be said about the structure of a neural network. First, from any layer except the last one, there is for every neuron in that layer a connection to one or more neurons in the layer above. And for every layer except the first one, there are connections to all the neurons in this layer from neurons in the layer below.

Having said this much, there is still a large freedom concerning which neurons are connected to which neurons, and also the number of neurons in the layers may vary. Usually the layers do not contain the same number of neurons.

And finally, there is a special name for the first layer and last layer. The first layer is called the *input layer*, the last one is called the *output layer*, and the layers in between are called *hidden layers*.

The two first names suggest to a certain degree how a neural network is used. We have some input data introduced to the input layer and get the result from the output layer. However, this is a pretty rough description and it has to be made much more precise.

For instance consider the problem of reading written characters. What sort of data do you put into the input layer, and how do you get hold of it? And what sort of data do you get out and what does this tell you?

To get right to the point as quickly as possible. What you put into the input layer are numbers, one number into each neuron. And the final result you get are also numbers one number from each neuron in the output layer.

The Network as a Function

You may also express this by saying that you start out with a *n-tuple* of numbers and end up with a n-tuple of numbers. These n-tuples may also conveniently be called *vectors*, n-vectors.

Suppose that there are 4 neurons in the input layer og 2 neurons in the output layer. You then put in (x_1, x_2, x_3, x_4) and get out (y_1, y_2). So actually for this network you have a function, mapping 4-tuples of numbers into 2-tuples of numbers. This tells us that *a neural network actually defines a function*.

If you denote by f the function defined by the network mentioned above, you may therefore write:

$$f(\boldsymbol{x}) = \boldsymbol{y}, \quad \text{where} \quad x = (x_1, x_3, x_3, x_4) \text{ and } \boldsymbol{y} = (y_1, y_2) \tag{3}$$

Here the numbers x_1, y_1 may be real numbers or integers depending on the application, and we have used bold face letters to designate the n-vectors. We return to this later when we study more concrete examples.

When we pointed to the fact above that a neural network actually defines a function, we only referred to the input and output layers. But by the explanation we gave there it is clear that no matter how many hidden layers there are in the network, the same thing can be said. For we did not refer to any hidden layers in that explanation. But if we also take the hidden layers into consideration, we can give a more detailed description of the function. It can be written as a composition of functions, one function for each hidden layer, but we do not elaborate on this now.

Description of the Weights

Instead we shall talk a little about the role of the weights and take up the functions attached to the layers later. For the question of the weights is a more fundamental theme. The function defined by the network is dependent on all the weights of the network. If we change one weight, the function is also changed, so that $f(x)$ after the change is different from $f(x)$ before.

The weights thus are parameters of the function. And since the weights of the connections from the neurons in one layer to the neurons in the next layer can be presented as elements in matrices, we can use these matrices as part of the total notation for the function with its parameters.

How do the weights appear in the matrices? We get a hint if we study the expression in equation (2). It has the form of a matrix row multiplied by a column matrix. Here are examples of two such matrices:

$$W = \begin{bmatrix} w_{11} & w_{12} & w_{13} \\ w_{21} & w_{22} & w_{23} \\ w_{31} & w_{32} & w_{33} \end{bmatrix} \quad W = \begin{bmatrix} w_{11} & w_{12} & w_{13} \\ w_{21} & w_{22} & w_{23} \end{bmatrix} \tag{4}$$

Using this to exhibit the parameters in the function we get:

$$f(\boldsymbol{x}, W^1, W^2, \cdots, W^h) \quad \text{where } h-1 \text{ are the number of hidden layers} \tag{5}$$

Note that a row of the matrix contains the weights of the connections to a neuron in a layer from all the neurons in the layer below. So the first matrix in (4) represents the connections *to* a layer of 3 neurons *from* the previous layer of 3 neurons. And the second matrix displays the weights to a layer of 2 neurons from the previous layer of 3 neurons so that each neuron i in the second layer has 3 connections, $w_{i1}w_{i2}w_{i3}$ $i = 1, 2$ from the first layer. (Fig. **1**).

Also if there is no connection between two neurons, the corresponding element in the matrix is set to zero. So we define a weight in this case also, only it is zero. Consequently we can let the summation index in formula (2) run over *all* the neurons in the layer below.

Turning to the Matrices Themselves

The superscripts (k) of the matrices in equation (5) correspond to a numbering of the layers in the network, where $W^{(1)}$ contains the weights for the connections from the first layer, (which is the input layer) to the second layer. Thus W^k contains the weights from layer number k to layer number k - 1 .

Let us now look at a specific example, from the point of view of the number of layers. If there are 5 layers in our network, there are 3 hidden layers and 4 weight matrices. The last matrix $W^{(4)}$ contains the weights from layer 4, the last hidden layer, to layer 5, the output layer. Referring to the superscripts of the matrices in equation (5), we here have $h = 4$.

The Functions of the Network

As to the description of a neural network, let us finally complete the details by describing the functions appearing in the network. We mentioned above that a neural network defines a function in the following way.

When you use a neural net, you introduce an n-tuple of numbers to the input layer, given that it consists of n neurons. And at the output layer you collect the result which is an m-tuple of numbers, where m is the number of neurons in the output layer. So we are entitled to say that a neural net behaves as a function f, in that it maps n-tuples of numbers, $x = (x_1, x_2, \dots x_n)$ to m-tuples of numbers, $y = (y_1, y_2, \dots y_m)$ that is $y = f(x)$.

This is all there is to it if the neural net does not have hidden layers. Else the function can be written as a composition of functions like we said earlier, one function for each hidden layer and one for the output layer. The first one of these functions, let us call it f_1 , is transforming the vectors that are input to layer 1, (that is input to the network as a whole), into the vectors that are output from layer 2, which is the first hidden layer.

So there seems to be no output from layer 1? At least we did not say anything about it. However there is an output from layer 1. But it is equal to the input. The input to layer 1, is just passing through and continues as the input to layer 2, where it is transformed by the f_1.

The next function f_2 transforms this output from layer 2, which is the input to the next layer 3, into the output from layer 3. If there is only one hidden layer, the output of this function is the output from the whole network. We can then write this out in detail to get:

$$\text{(i)} \quad y = f(x) = f_2\big(f_1(x)\big) \quad \text{or} \quad \text{(ii)} \quad f = f_2 \circ f_1 \qquad \textbf{(6)}$$

Here f is the function for the whole network and x is the input vector tor the network.

As to equation (6), the expression in (ii) tells us the same as the expression in (i), only that the expression in (ii) does not involve the argument x and function value y. It is the standard way of writing that f is a composite function that you get from first applying f_1 and then f_2 on what results from f_1 .

Likewise, if there are more than one hidden layer, there are of course also *more functions*. If we let *h* stand for the number of computing layers, there are in all *h* functions. The first *h* - 1 of which transforms the *input* to a hidden layer into the *output* from this layer, and the last function transforms the output from the last hidden layer into the output from the network itself. Finally it should be appropriate to repeat here that the first layer is not a computing layer, so no function is associated to it. As a result there is a total number of *h* + 1 layers and the function *f* of the network can be written thus, (see (6), where *h* = 2 .

$$f = f_h \circ f_{h-1} \circ \cdots \circ f_2 \circ f_1 \tag{7}$$

Also note that the numbering we used for the functions associated to the layers follows the numbering of the weight matrices. If you look further up, you will see that the matrix denoted by W^k contains the weights for the connections *from* layer *k to* layer *k* + 1 and f_k denotes the function taking the output *from* layer *k* as input and *returns* the output from layer *k* + 1 .

The Details of what the Functions f_k do to their Arguments

We then get this:

$$\boldsymbol{y} = f_k(\boldsymbol{x}, W^k) \text{ where } \boldsymbol{y} = (y_1, \dots, y_m), \ \boldsymbol{x} = (x_1, \dots, x_n) \tag{8}$$

W^k is a *m* x *n* matrix where the rows consist of the weights of the connections to layer *k* + 1 from layer *k* and $y_i = F\left(\sum_{j=1}^n w_{ij}^k x_j\right)$

So y_i is the output from *neuron i* in layer *k* + 1 whereas the vector $\boldsymbol{y}$ is the output from the *whole layer k* + 1 .

The summation expression in the argument of the function *F* is exactly what we denoted by S_i, see (2). Let us call it the activation[1]. We next see that this expression appears naturally in the matrix multiplication where the column matrix *X* is defined to have its elements equal to the components of the vector $\boldsymbol{x}$. If we likewise denote the *column matrix* having its elements equal to S_i by S_2, we can write *S* = *W**X.

Finally, we construct a generalized transfer function that we also denote by *F*. It is defined to be acting on the column matrix *S* and give us the column matrix whose elements are $F(S_i)$ as function values. Then we can write the relation $\boldsymbol{y} = f_k(\boldsymbol{x}, W^k)$ compactly as *Y* = *F*(*S*), where the column vector *Y* originates from $\boldsymbol{y}$ in the same way that X comes from x.

In the next equation we give the exact definitions of the quantities X, Y, S, mentioned above as well as the definition of the new function F.

$$X = [x_1 \ x_2 \ \cdots \ x_n]^T, Y = [y_1 \ y_2 \ \cdots y_m]^T, S = [S_1 \ S_2 \ \cdots S_m]^T$$

$$F(S) = F([S_1 \ S_2 \ \cdots \ S_m]^T) = [F(S_1) \ F(S_2) \ \cdots \ F(S_m)]^T$$

(9)

Here the superscript T of a matrix means transposition, as is usual practice.

Study of the Function f of the whole Network

We choose a concrete example of 4 layers with the input layer having 5 neurons, the second layer 3 neurons, the third 4 and the output layer 3 neurons. That is we have

$$f = f_3 \circ f_2 \circ f_1 \quad \text{or equivalently this} \quad f(x) = f_3(f_2(f_1(x)))$$

(10)

Where x is a 5-tuple,), $x = (x_1, x_2, x_3, x_4, x_5)$ the input vector to the network.

We shall analyze the computation in (10) and infer all the relevant details. In so doing we shall make use of the relations in (8). We first consider $y = f_k(x, W^k)$ and note that we shall need to index y, to keep the different outputs apart. This we do by using upper indices.

Next, as to the function f_k , its argument x is the output from layer k and its function value is the output from layer $k + 1$.

Finally we remember that the components of y^{k+1}, that is y_i^{k+1} are defined to be equal to the value of the transfer function with the activation of neuron i in layer k as argument, see (8). This activation must also be indexed, the index of which is set equal to k. To summarize this we can write

$$y^{k+1} = f_k(x, W^k) \text{ where } x = y^k \text{ and } y_i^{k+1} = F(S_i^k) \ S_i^k = \sum_{j=1}^n w_{ij}^k x_j$$

(11)

$$k = 1, 2, 3$$

We then start out to present (10) in detail and start with the innermost computation, $f_1(x)$. To find this we need the argument x, which is equal to y^1, as we see from by setting $k = 1$. It is the output from layer 1.

But what is the output from layer 1? The behavior of layer 1 is an exception from the behavior of all the other layers, in that the output is equal to the input. So $y^1 = x$ where x is the input to the whole network.

Starting with x, and using the notation in (11) we then get successively from the bottom up, remembering that the number of neurons in our example is 5, 3, 4, 3 for the layers 1 to 4.

$$y^4 = f_3(y^3, W^3) \text{ from layer 4 with } y_i^4 = F(S_i^3) \text{ and } S_i^3 = \sum_{j=1}^{4} w_{ij}^3 \cdot y_j^3 \; i = 1 \cdots 3$$

$$y^3 = f_2(y^2, W^2) \text{ from layer 3 with } y_i^3 = F(S_i^2) \text{ and } S_i^2 = \sum_{j=1}^{3} w_{ij}^2 \cdot y_j^2 \; i = 1 \cdots 4$$

$$y^2 = f_1(y^1, W^1) \text{ from layer 2 with } y_i^2 = F(S_i^1) \text{ and } S_i^1 = \sum_{j=1}^{5} w_{ij}^1 \cdot y_j^1 \; i = 1 \cdots 3 \tag{12}$$

$$y^1 = x \text{ is output from layer 1 } y_i^1 = x_i \; i = 1 \cdots 5$$

Just don't forget that the input to a layer from layer 2 onwards is equal to the output from the previous layer, and that the weight matrices W^k have the dimensions 3 x 5, 4 x 3 and 3 x 4. From the dimensions of these matrices for $k = 1,2,3$ we see that the numbers of elements in the rows are 5, 3 and 4. These numbers appear as the upper limits of the summation index j in the sum expressions for $S_i^k k = 1,2,3$.

This should be properly understood.

What we now have done is to follow what happens in our example network, when you introduce a 5–tuple to it and finally receive a 3–tuple as result. We then talk about this process as a *forward propagation*. What is propagated is the n–tuples or n–vectors.

However let us also remind ourselves of the fact that we can use matrix computations to work out the details of the function evaluation in $y = f_k(x, W^k)$, see (8) and the explanations following this equation up to and including the next equation (9). We then get, in turn,

$$Y^{k+1} = F(S^k) \;\; S^k = W^k X \;\; X = Y^k \quad k = 1, 2, 3. \tag{13}$$

Where F and S have generalized meanings as matrix objects, see (9).

To get to the next point we see that in the function definitions of all the functions $f_p p = 1,2,3$ in (12) the weight matrices occur as parameters.

Determination of the Correct Weight Matrices

To do this is the decisive point of our whole theory of supervised neural networks, namely how to determine the weights so that they are correct.

But when are they correct? They are correct when we can compute the wanted function values associated with the arguments.

But in order to compute these function values we need to know the weights, and we do not know the weights. So we are stuck somehow. But if we can get to know some pairs of arguments and function values without basing this on the knowledge of the weights, then we can get underway.

And this is precisely what can be done. The next task then is to adjust the weights so that the function values computed when you use these weights coincide as well as possible with the wanted function values known from elsewhere.

This is done as a successive approximation scheme. And the process of carrying through this is called learning. We talk about a learning network.

We return to this idea in a concrete way for three different classes of examples in the three chapters to follow.

But still there is one important question that we have not tried to expose yet.

The Actual Mathematical Objects that we Manipulate

These objects are n-tuples and the way this done is crucial if you want to be successful with your supervised neural net application. We shall not delve into this in any way. But we shall give an idea of how to do it.

Imagine that you want to construct a neural network that can read handwritten characters. You intend to base it on a lot of examples of each character and you make pictures/photographs of these that all are turned into pictures with the same number of *pixels* horizontally and vertically.

Then you can make a number sequence of these pixels done in the same way for all the pictures. If it takes N pixels in all to cover a picture, you can define a N-vector $\boldsymbol{x} = (x_1, x_2, ..., x_N)$ where $x_i . i = 1 ... N$ are the color values of the pixels in some way.

Thus we have got our N-vectors that we need to do our calculations.

PERCEPTRON

The perceptron is the simplest neural network that you could conceive of. It is also the oldest, dating from 1943 and generalized around 1960 *. It consists of an input layer and one layer above it, which is the output layer. However the output layer very often or perhaps more often than not has only one neuron.

The word perceptron itself was coined by Rosenblatt and bears relation to the human vision, inspired by the word perception.

However we shall study logical functions in order to have a simple example, and try to understand two of these with the help of a perceptron. We first study the OR function and next the XOR function.

We then have to deal with the logical values "true" and "false". But these are not numbers, so therefore we represent "true" and "false" by the numbers 1 and 0. This is a standard choice for applications where logical values occur. To be precise we consider an input layer with two neurons and an output layer with one neuron.

As to the OR function, calling it h, we then get the function values as follows:

$$h(1,1) = 1, \ h(0,0) = 0, \ h(0,1) = 1, \ h(1,0) = 1 \qquad \textbf{(14)}$$

This is perhaps an issue somewhat contrary to the natural use of neural nets, given that we merely wanted to show that a *known* function can be realized by a neural net. Because usually you start out the other way around, namely to find a function that you *do not know*, but of which you know *something*, namely the function values for a certain set of arguments. This stuff can be found in reference [1], chap. 2.

And this we shall do here too in order to give a very simple demonstration that a learning network is functioning as it should. But first we present the transfer function that we are going to use.

Where b is called a threshold. **(15)**

$$F(x) = \begin{cases} 1, x > b \\ 0, x \le b, \end{cases} \quad \text{where } b \text{ is called a threshold.} \qquad \textbf{(15)}$$

Next, following the notation in the previous chapter, we get from equation (11) that

$$\boldsymbol{y}^2 = f_1(\boldsymbol{x}, W^1) \text{ where } \boldsymbol{x} = \boldsymbol{y}^1 \text{ and } y_i^2 = F(S_i^1) \ \ S_i^1 = \textstyle\sum_{j=1}^2 w_{ij}^1 x_j \tag{16}$$

Here we have used $k = 1$ in (11). Further the subscript i is equal to 1 when we have only one neuron in the output layer, and that is what we have here. And the vector $\boldsymbol{y}^2$ is 1-dimensional, since it has only one component. That is, it is a mere number. And $\boldsymbol{x} = \boldsymbol{y}^1$ is a 2-vector and S_1^1 a mere number.

Further the dimension of the weight matrix is 1 x 2, so it is a row matrix with two elements, $W^1 = [w_{11}^1 w_{12}^1]$. We repeat in words what they mean: w_{11}^1 is the weight of the connection from neuron 1 in layer 1, (the input layer), to neuron 1 in the next layer, (the output layer), and w_{12}^1 is the weight of the connection from neuron 2 in layer 1 to neuron 1 in the next layer.

Instead of using n-vectors or n-tuples, we could also use matrices, which is more effective when we make calculations, be it by hand or using a computer. Using $k = 1$ in (13) we then get

$$Y^2 = F(S^1), \ \ S^1 = W^1 X, \ X = Y^1 \tag{17}$$

Here Y^2 is a 1 x 1 matrix, that is a number[1], Y^1 is 2 x 1 matrix, that is a column matrix, and S^1 is also a mere number, being the product of a 1 x 2 matrix with a 2 x 1 matrix.

A Special Notation for Two Layers and an Output Layer of only One Neuron

We make the following definitions:

$$S = S^1, \ w_{11} = \ w_{11}^1 \text{ and } w_{12} = w_{12}^1, W = W^1, y = Y^2 \text{ and } X = Y^1 \tag{18}$$

The point is that we don't use superscripts because we don't need them to avoid ambiguities. The motivation for the notation y is that Y^2 is just a number, it is the function value of the transfer function F, so we can write in a natural way that $y = F(S)$. We also set $f = f_1$. Remember that we used f as a name for the network function and in our case f_1 is equal to the network function.

Training of the Network

We remember that training the network is just another word for having the network learn. And what it means is to get the weights set right.

We then first figure out what we know about the function we want the network to learn, and pretend that we only know the function values for the arguments and, see (14), and shall use this information to find the weights that (hopefully) will secure us that the function f is equal to h.

We start by choosing a value $W_\circ$ for the weight matrix and compute $y = f(x, W_\circ)$ for the argument $x = (1,1)$. Next we consider the error that we get, doing this. We talk about an error because this function value y probably will not be equal to the correct function value d^2 of f.

If they are not equal, that is, if the error $d - y$ is not equal to zero, we make a correction to the weight matrix.

To get started, let us choose $W_\circ = [0\ 0]$. Then we compute $y = f(x, W_\circ)$, next the error $d - y$ and finally use the following rule, called the *delta rule*, to update W.

$$\Delta W = \eta\,(d - y)\,X^T, \quad \eta \text{ a small positive number called the learning rate} \qquad \textbf{(19)}$$

Having computed ΔW we set $W_\circ + \Delta W$ for the corrected weight matrix.

What is the motivation for this formula (19)? We return to this further down in this section.

About the Threshold b

The threshold b is an unknown parameter of the function F. So we cannot compute y if b is unknown. This is because $y = f(x, W) = F(S)$ and to find the value of F, we need to know b. See (15) above for the function F.

But this is remedied by determining b as we go along. We follow a standard way of attacking this problem and reformulate by adding a new neuron to the input layer. We denote the weight of this neuron by $w_\circ$ and the input by $x_\circ$.

To see how this works, note that to apply the function F on a number x we check the function definition, see (15), to see which inequality is satisfied, this one $x > b$ or the other one $x \le b$. In our case $x = S$, since we want to calculate $F(S)$, and therefore we check the inequality

$$S = WX = [w_1\ w_2]\begin{bmatrix} w_1 \\ w_2 \end{bmatrix} = w_1 x_1 + w_2 x_2 > b \qquad \textbf{(20a)}$$

which is equivalent to

$$-b \cdot 1 + w_1 x_1 + w_2 x_2 > 0 \qquad \textbf{(20b)}$$

Having added a neuron to the input layer, we of course get a new W, X and S:

$$W = [w_0\ w_1\ w_2],\ X = \begin{bmatrix} 1 \\ x_1 \\ x_2 \end{bmatrix}\ \text{and}\ S = WX$$

Here we have set $w_o = -b$. and $x_o = 1$, where x_o is the input to the added neuron. The left hand side of inequality (20b) is therefore equal to the new S and we see that the transfer function (15) for the expanded network has a threshold equal to 0.

We now update the weights again the way we did in the lines before and after equation (19).

The general procedure is that we take one input X at a time and update the weights using (19) for this input. So in all we get an iteration scheme.

To begin with we have no weights at all, so to get started we need to choose a weight matrix,, to have something to work on for the first update. Later we keep track of the iterations by $W(n)$ letting stand for iteration number n.

$$W(n + 1) = W(n) + \Delta W,\ n = 0, 1, 2, \cdots,\ \Delta W = (d - y)\ X^T,\ \eta = 1^{20}$$

Before we continue, remember that now we have 3 neurons in the input layer. So when we originally had an input $x = (x_1, x_2)$, we now have $x = (1, x_1, x_2)$, see (14). But it is only the last two components that have a significance for our application. The first component is equal to 1 all the time.

We choose $W(0) = [0\ 0\ 0]$ as start value and let $x = (1,1,1)$ be our first input vector so that $d = 1$ see (14). Then the scheme goes like this:

$$W = W(0) = [0\ 0\ 0],\ X = [1\ 1\ 1]^T,\ d = 1$$

$$y = F(S) = F(WX) = F([0\ 0\ 0][1\ 1\ 1]^T) = F(0) = 0$$

(21a)

That $F(0) = 0$ we see from (15) with $b = 0$. We now can update W.

$$\Delta W = (d - y)\ X^T = (1 - 0)[1\ 1\ 1]\ =\ [1\ 1\ 1]$$

$$W(1) = W(0) + [1\ 1\ 1] = [0\ 0\ 0] + [1\ 1\ 1] = [1\ 1\ 1]$$

(21b)

Now we update the weights again, this time we use the input $x = (1,0,0)$,

Repeating (21) for this case, we get

$$W = W(1) = [1\ 1\ 1],\ X = [1\ 0\ 0]^T,\ d = 0$$

$$y = F(S) = F(WX) = F([1\ 1\ 1][1\ 0\ 0]^T) = F(1) = 1$$

(22a)

$$\Delta W = (d - y)\, X^T = (0 - 1)[1\ 0\ 0] = [-1\ 0\ 0]$$

$$W(2) = W(1) + [-1\ 0\ 0] = [1\ 1\ 1] + [-1\ 0\ 0] = [0\ 1\ 1]$$

(22b)

What we have done so far is to update the start weights [0 0 0] so that the network possibly can reproduce the correct function values of OR for the two arguments x = (1,1) and x = (0,0), in turn. We first updated the weight matrix [0 0 0] to [1 1 1] hoping to get a correct value for x = (1, 1) and next we updated [1 1 1] to [0 1 1] in order to get a correct value for x = (0, 0) . But can we be sure that the last update will preserve the first value for x = (1,1)? And can we be sure in the first place that the first update will give you the correct value for x = (1, 1) .

Let us compute the function value for x = (1,1,1) and x = (1,0,0) using the new weight matrix W = [0 1 1] , , to see if we get y = $f(x, W)$ = 1 and y = $f(x, W)$ = 0 respectively.

$$f(x,W) = F(S) = F(WX) = F([0\ 1\ 1][1\ 1\ 1]^T) = F(2) = 1$$

$$f(x,W) = (S) = F(WX) = F([0\ 1\ 1][1\ 0\ 0]^T) = F(0) = 0$$

and we did. In fact the weight W = [0 1 1] also secures the correct function value for x = (1, 1, 0) and x = (1, 0, 1)

Now it is time to say something about the error correction formula (19) that we used to update the weights.

When $d - y = 0$, there is nothing to do, because in this case there is no error, that is the network function f gives the correct value and we leave the weight matrix intact.

Otherwise, we note that $y = F(S)$ where $S - \sum_{i=0}^{2} w_j x_j$ so we could influence the value of S and therefore the value of y, by changing some or all of w_j . Increasing w_j will increase S and therefore y^5. So if we had $d - y > 0$, the error would tend to be less for the same input with the new weights.

This is just an interpretation of formula (19) and no proof of it. But what we find makes sense.

However, using the perceptron convergence proof, we can see that the formula

(19) will lead to a correct network function, see [3].

The formula (19) will also appear from the use of the least mean square. But then we need a differentiable transfer function. We return to this in the next section where we write about regression.

Not all Logic Functions can be defined by a Simple Perceptron

One example is the XOR function. It is defined like this:

$$h(1,1) = 0, \ h(0,0) = 0, \ h(0,1) = 1, \ h(1,0) = 1 \qquad \textbf{(23)}$$

We study it the same way that we did for the OR function, by adding a third neuron with weight and a constant input $x_0 = 1$. We then try to find a weight matrix such that $y = f(x, W)$ gives us the values in (23) only that now we have $x = (1,1,1)$, $x = (1,0,0)$, $x = (1,0,1)$ and $x = (1,1,0)$ in the same order. Like we had for OR, it is the last two components that has direct relevance for our application.

Now we compute $y = f(x, W)$ where $W = [w_0, w_1, w_2]$ and get four inequalities for $S = WX$ resulting from the fact that $Y = F(S)$ and that the threshold of now is equal to 0. Therefore we get $F(S) = 1 \leftrightarrow S < 0$ and $F(S) = 0 \leftrightarrow S \leq 0$. In all:

$$w_0 + w_1 + w_2 \leq 0, w_0 \leq 0, w_0 + w_2 > 0, w_0 + w_1 > 0$$

These inequalities have no solution. For adding the last two gives $w_0 + w_1 + w_2 > - w_0$. But $- w_0 \geq 0$. Therefore $w_0 + w_1 + w_2 > 0$. But this contradicts the first inequality.

The fact that the simple perceptron cannot realize the XOR function is not just an accidental fact. It is the consequence of a fundamental property of the simple perceptron. But before engaging in this problem, (see the section **A geometric criterion** further down) we first present a more general problem to use ANN networks to solve. Trying to define the OR and XOR functions is just a simple example of such a problem.

Solving Pattern Classification with a Simple Perceptron

In this section so far, we used the perceptron to study the OR and XOR function. Both of these were binary logical functions. But you can view them otherwise, looking upon their arguments as patterns that we want to classify.

We then have two classes, one that we shall denote by 1 and the other by 0. As to the OR function, the patterns belonging to the class denoted by 1 were (1.1), (1, 0) and (0,1) and the class denoted by 0, only contained one pattern, namely (0,0).

So by the word *pattern* we here mean a *n-vector*. As to classification in general, these n-vectors could for example result as measurements or at any rate be established by some relations to items that we want to classify.

Now suppose we have two sets of patterns, P_1 and P_2 in R^n, and we want to use a *perceptron* to decide to which of the two sets a given pattern in $P_1 \cup P_2$ belongs.

Let us call this *the classification problem*.

Solving the classification problem therefore means that when we have a given n-vector x as input to the perceptron, we can find a weight matrix W such that the output $f(x, w)$ is equal to 1 if x is a pattern in P_1 and equal to 0 if x belongs to P_2.

Further, as we know, the value $f(x,w)$ of the network function is defined to be equal to $F(S)$ where F is the transfer function of the output neuron and $s=WX$. But WX can be written as a scalar product between a n-vector w whose *components* are the *elements* in the 1 x n matrix w and the n-vector x. Thus $S = w \cdot x$. In this way we can reason directly with geometrical quantities.

A Geometric Criterion for the Solution of the Classification Problem

To obtain this we see from (15) that a necessary and sufficient condition for the perceptron to classify a pattern in $P_1 \cup P_2$ to belong to P_1 or P_2, is that there exists a weight vector w such that

$$x \in P_1 \leftrightarrow w \cdot x > b \text{ and } x \in P_2 \leftrightarrow w \cdot x \le b \qquad (24)$$

But $w \cdot x = b$ is the equation of a hyperplan in R^n. A hyperplan divides the whole space R^n in two halves. Let us call the half space defined by $w \cdot x > b$ the positive half space and the complement defined by $w \cdot x \le b$ the corresponding negative half space.

The conclusion then is that a perceptron solves the classification problem if and only if the sets P_1 and P_2 can be separated by a hyperplan with equation $w \cdot x = b$ so that the set P_1 lies in the positive half space and P_2 in the negative. (Here b is the threshold of the transfer function and w is the weight vector of the perceptron.)

We have already two examples of classification from R^2, the OR function and the XOR function. For the OR function we let $P_1 = \{(1,1),(1,0),(0,1\}$ and $P_2 = \{(0,0)\}$. And the line[6] with equation $x_1+x_2 = 0$ can be seen to separate the sets P_1 and P_2. Therefore we can say that the OR function solves the classification problem when we let P_1 be the subset of the plane where OR takes the value 1 og P_2 the set where OR takes the value 0.

But the XOR function does not solve the classification problem. This can be seen from a picture of R^2 where you plot the the two points of XOR where it takes the values 1 and the two points of value 0. Then we see that it is impossible to separate these pair of points by a straight line.

Using this technique of drawing lines for the AND function, we see that the point where AND has value 1 and the two points of value 0 can be separated by the line $x_1 + x_2 = 3/2$. This is consistant with the fact that the AND function can be realized by a perceptron with two input neurons, both having weigths 1 and a transfer function with threshold equal to 3/2. But how can we compute this weight vector?

The perceptron convergence theorem tells us that we can find a correct weight in a finite number of steps where we update the weights according to (19) using input vectors from P_1 and P_2. See [3].

This computation is done *after* we have added a new neuron with weight equal to minus the threshold and a constant input equal to 1, like we did when finding the network function for OR using the computations in (21) and (22).

REGRESSION AS A NEURAL NETWORK

In the previous section we used the perceptron to study functions that had natural numbers as values. In this section we will use the perceptron to study functions with real numbers as function values as well as having arguments that are real numbers.

As an example, let us think of buying pigs and raising them to sell later.

It is reasonable to think that the cost to raise a pig will depend on how much a pig weighs when you buy it, and how much you feed them underway. Suppose you have two sorts of food. Then we have a function, that maps a vector x in to a number y. The vector x has three components, where we can let each component express mass in kg. Let us also express y, the total cost to raise a pig, in dollars.

Solving by Standard Linear Regression

That is we seek a function h of the form

$$h(\boldsymbol{w}, \boldsymbol{x}) = w_0 + w_1 x_1 + w_2 x_2 + w_3 x_3 \tag{25}$$

Where $w = (w_0, w_1, w_2, w_3)$, $x = (x_0, x_1, x_2, x_3)$ and w_i $i = 0 \cdots 3$, are parameters that are real numbers.

This function h is not the function that solves our problem of finding the cost y to raise a pig based on the feature vector $x = (x_1, x_2, x_3)$ *exactly*. It is an affine[6] function that we construct to be an *approximation* of the real function.

No matter what we do, we shall have to use hard facts about raising a pig. So we build our method on the knowledge of some pairs of (argument, function value) of the function that we seek.

Assume that we know the pairs $(x_1, y_1), (x_2, y_2), \ldots , (x_N, Y_N)$.

To determine the parameters of the function h according to linear regression we set up the error function E, where

$$E(w) = \frac{1}{2} \sum_{k=1}^{N} \left(y_k - h(w, x_k) \right)^2 \tag{26}$$

Note that the expression raised to 2 under the sum sign is the *vertical* distance from the point (x_k, y_k) to the hyperplan that is the graph of h. It tells us by how much the function value $h(w, x_k)$ misses the correct value y_k.

Our goal further is to choose the parameters that minimize the error function. This can be done by setting the gradient of equal to zero and solve for w. That is we solve the eqauations.

$$\partial E / \partial w_i = 0 \quad i = 0 \cdots 3 \tag{27}$$

with respect to w_i.

But we would not do that. There is a better way when we want numeric results, namely to use gradient descent. This we carry through next, but in the context of the perceptron, because the idea of minimizing the error function in (26) will turn up there too.

Solving by Using the Perceptron

We use a perceptron with one output neuron and 4 input neurons. In addition to defining these two numbers, we also need to define the transfer function. This is taken to be the linear function:

$$F(x) = x \tag{28}$$

Next we aim at obtaining the *network function*

$$f(x, W), \quad \text{where } x \in R^4 \text{ and } W \text{ is a } 1 \times 4 \text{ matrix} \tag{29}$$

that we can use to *predict* the cost of raising the pigs. But to achieve this, the network must learn to do so. So we build upon a series of measurements of the start weight of a pig, the weight of food1 and food2 and the corresponding cost price to raise it.

We assume that we know a number of pairs (x_1, y_1), (x_2, y_2), ..., (x_N, y_N) upon which we build our results like we did when we used linear regression, and try to learn from this data. Then again we consider an error function

$$E(W) = \frac{1}{2} \sum_{k=1}^{N} \left(y_k - f(x_k, W) \right)^2 \tag{30}$$

However, the vectors x_i this time belong to R^4 while to give the start weight and weight of food1 and food2 it only takes three numbers, that is a vector in R^3, so how do we choose the numbers for the first components of the vectors x_i?

Since we are aiming at reconstructing the function h in (25) we choose the first component in every x_i to be equal to 1, because then the right hand side of (25) can be written $w_0 \cdot 1 + w_1 x_1 + w_2 x_2 + w_3 x_3$, the scalar product of w and any of the new x_i vectors.

Next, inspecting (30), we see that when the weight matrix W is such that $y_k = f(x_k, W_k)$, $k = 1 \dots N$, then $E(W = 0)$ else it is positive. So when the squared quantities under the sum sign is zero, which is equivalent to the $E(W)$ itself being zero, the network function renders the cost of every one of the N measured weights of the pigs *without errors*.

But instead of working with the weight matrix $W = [W_0 W_1 W_2 W_3]$ *directly* we shall use the weight $w = (W_0, W_1, W_2, W_3)$ *vector* since the computations that we shall do is tightly connected to geometry.

And we shall find this weight vector by using a method that is called *Gradient Descent*.

That is, we shall not solve the equations you get when you set equal to zero. Instead we choose one weight at random for a start and then find a better weight by using the information in the gradient. Next we repeat this with the new weight as the next start.

And we shall do this generally without thinking about the pairs (x_1,y_1), (x_2, y_2), ... , (x_N, y_N) to represent pig data. However we do it for a network with 4 input neurons. Restricting ourselves to four input neurons instead of working with an arbitrary number of neurons, will not disguise the principles that we shall present.

To get underway we then need to compute the gradient of with respect to W,

$$\nabla E = (\partial E/\partial w_0, \partial E/\partial w_1, \partial E/\partial w_2, \partial E/\partial w_3). \tag{31}$$

This is a vector in R^4 pointing in the direction of increasing E and the norm or length of this vector is equal to the greatest rate of increase of E as you change the value of w^8. Accordingly $-\nabla E$ has the direction of the largest *decrease* of and the norm or length of it is equal to this rate of decrease.

So to find a weight vector w that makes $E(w)$ as small as possible, we start with a weight vector w_0 chosen at random and use $-\nabla E$ to lead us in the direction of a place in R^4 with a smaller E. But what distance should we go, the whole length of $-\nabla E$? That is not a good idea. The solution that has been chosen is to introduce a parameter called the *learning rate*. Let us denote it by η.

The use of the learning rate is to adjust the length we move in the direction of minus the gradient. This distance is obtained by multiplying $-\nabla E$ by the learning rate η, that is, it is equal to $\eta (-\nabla E)$. So therefore η must be a positive number.

So imagine that you stand at the point w_0 in R_4. From there we go to the new weight vector w following this formula:

$$w = w_0 + \Delta w, \text{ where } \Delta w = -\eta \nabla E \tag{32}$$

We now compute the gradient ∇E that is the partial derivatives $\delta E/\delta w_i$. Expressing the network function in terms of the transfer function, $f(x,w) = F(w \cdot x)$, and using the weight vector w to write $WX = w \cdot x$ we can write

$$E(w) = \frac{1}{2} \sum_{k=1}^{N} \left(y_k - F(w \cdot x_k) \right)^2, \ F(x) = x \tag{33}$$

and get (34) by using the chain rule twice.

$$\partial E/\partial w_i = \partial/\partial w_i \left\{ \frac{1}{2} \sum_{k=1}^{N} \left(y_k - F(w \cdot x_k) \right)^2 \right\} =$$

$$\sum_{k=1}^{N} -\left(y_k - F(w \cdot x_k) \right) F'(w \cdot x_k) \, \partial/\partial w_i \, (w \cdot x_k) \tag{34}$$

Next, letting x_{ki} be the components of $\boldsymbol{x}_k$ so that $\boldsymbol{x}_k = (x_{ko}, x_{k1}, x_{k2}, x_{k3})$, then $\delta/\delta w_i$ $(\boldsymbol{w}$. $\boldsymbol{x}_k) = \delta/\delta w_i(w_o x_{ko} + w_1 x_{k1} + w_{2o} x_{k2} + w_3 x_{k3}) = x_{ki}$

And consequently from (34) and the simple fact that $F'(x) = 1$:

$$\partial E / \partial w_i = \sum_{k=1}^{N} -\left(y_k - F(\boldsymbol{w} \cdot \boldsymbol{x}_k)\right) x_{ki}$$

We finally keep this result in the form of a formula for, Δw_i see (32) and (34):

$$\Delta w_i = \eta \left\{ \sum_{k=1}^{N} \left(y_k - F(\boldsymbol{w} \cdot \boldsymbol{x}_k)\right) x_{ki} \right\} \qquad \textbf{(35)}$$

This formula is called the ***delta rule***. Note that although it looks a bit different from (19), it is actually identical to it, because (19) has a training set consisting of only one pair while (35) has a training set consisting of pairs.

A Little More about the Learning Rate and Finding the Minimum

In order to study the descent from a starting weight $\boldsymbol{w}_o$ to a weight $\boldsymbol{w}$ where the error function has a minimum, it is advantageous to be aware of the level sets of E.

Given any function value c of E, the level set c of E is simply the set of all points in R^4 where E takes on the value of c. A level set will normally be a hypersurface in R^4. That is, it has a dimension of 4-1, one less than the dimension of the whole space R^4. We should also note that in the vicinity of a minimum point the level sets are closed surfaces[9].

It is also a characteristic of the gradient at a point that it is perpendicular to the level set through that point.

Now suppose we have a weight vector $\boldsymbol{w}_o$ or point $\boldsymbol{w}_o{}^9$ lying on a given level set E_o and use the formula (32) to find the next weight vector $\boldsymbol{w}$ by multiplying - ∇E by η. Then we shall end up at a level set $E < E_o$ if everything is working all right.

If it is not working all right, we might end up at a weight vector lying on a level set $E \geq E_0$ so that we have not got any closer to the minimum point. The reason for this is that the learning rate is too big so that we end up on the other side of minimum point.

The remedy is to choose a smaller learning rate. But choosing a learning rate that is too small is a bad thing too because it will take the algorithm, doing the calculations, too long to reach the minimum point.

So choosing the right learning rate is a very crucial point which we shall not pursue any further. But there is one more problem about gradient descent.

It is correct to think that if you have a minimum point, then ∇E is zero. But if ∇E is zero, you do not necessarily have a minimum point, it might be a saddle point, and there might also be several minimum points. How do we know that we have found the one with the smallest value, which is what we want to find.

We shall not try to find out of this dilemma. You can read about it here [4]. But how do we know that the weights we have found are correct?

This is an important question and generally it is difficult to give a short answer. But one thing is sure, we cannot find a mathematical formula that can tell us what we want to know, we have to rely on numerical computations and we must return to what we know for a fact.

That is, we return to the pairs of input vectors and output vectors that we used to have the network learn the weights:

$$(x_1, y_1), (x_2, y_2), \cdots, (x_N, y_N) \tag{36}$$

See the discussion before and after equation (30).

But of course, we cannot use this set of pairs to test whether the weights are correct, since we used them to find the weights. So what we do is to split these pairs into two sets of pairs and use the first set to have the network learn and use the second and last set to test if the weights we found are correct.

Let us put $N = N_1 + N_2$ letting the number of pairs in the learning set be N_1.

So, letting W be the weight matrix that we found using the first set of pairs, we compute $f(x_k, W)$ $k = N_1 + 1 \dots N$ to see for what percentage of N_2 we get the answer y_k to a satisfactory accuracy.

If we feel satisfied, we can start to use the network to predict values for other input vectors than the ones we have in (36). This last part of the whole theory of neural networks where we *use the network to predict*, goes by the name of *generalization*.

MULTILAYER PERCEPTRONS, MLP

In the previous chapter we used a perceptron to realize linear regression. We then described how we can make this network learn by using gradient descent and ended up with the delta rule in (35).

Further, a perceptron is not very important in the modern development of neural networks. To have a neural network achieve interesting results and really solve problems, we must include hidden layers of neurons.

Such a network is called a *multilayer perceptron or a multilayer network*.

But even if a perceptron is extremely simple, there are concepts and ways of solving problems that are common to both perceptrons an MLP. Such methods were presented in the previous chapter on linear regression and includes *learning, testing* and *generalization*.

However like we just said, to solve real and important problems, we have to include hidden layers, but in so doing we have to pay a prize, for new problems then arise so that old issues become harder to deal with.

The most noticeable such problem is the learning problem, on how to update the weights. We treat this in the next chapter which is the last one. The way it is done goes by the name of backpropagation. We finally look quickly into one more problem related to testing.

It concerns a minor problem called *overfitting*. This may occur during the learning process and may lead to a poor or useless generalization.

It may happen because the network learns too well. The reason it may learn too well is that there are so many degrees of freedom, so many weights that they adapt too easily to the data we want to match, so that when you apply the network later, the new facts will not be caught by the network. It is not easy to explain this from scratch with the background we presuppose, but you can read about it here [4].

BACKPROPAGATION

If you look up this word on the internet, you are likely to get the impression that this is a very obscure or difficult theme. The reason is that it is mathematically demanding.

We shall also do it mathematically, but we do it slowly and rigorously following an idea from the book [2]. The backpropagation algorithm was worked out in the 1980's, years after the perceptron was established.

We consider an example where we have 4 neurons in the output layer, a hidden layer of 3 neurons below the output and a layer of 4 neurons below the layer with 3 neurons. This last mentioned layer of 4 neurons could be the input layer or another hidden layer.

These numbers that we chose have no importance in themselves. We chose them to be able to make drawings of the network that match the number of neurons in the layer, (Figs. **2** and **3**). Backpropagation is about taking derivatives.

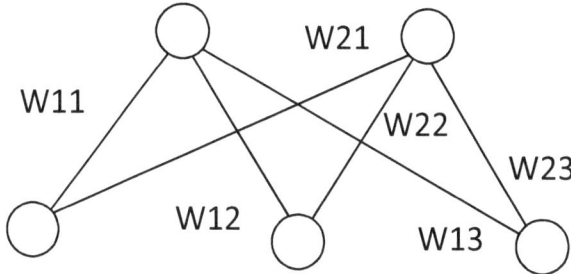

Fig. (2). The weight matrix between the different layers of a neural network.

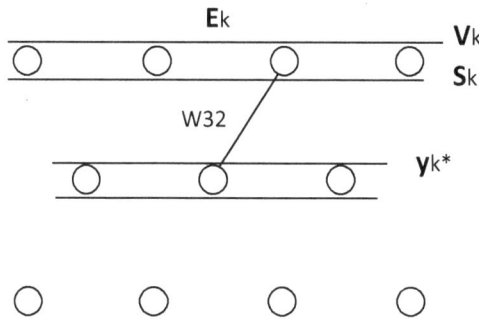

Fig. (3). Updating the first layer of weights.

To be specific we are going to evaluate $\delta E/\delta w_{ij}$ where w_{ij} is the weight of the connection to a neuron i in one layer from a neuron j in the layer below. This is used to update the weights of the network.

In the previous chapter we updated the weights of a *linear* perceptron and ended up with the formula (35). For a perceptron which has a transfer function that is *not linear*, there is a correction factor due to the derivative $F'(w \cdot x_k)$ of the transfer function which is no longer equal to 1. So that instead of (35) we get:

$$\Delta w_i = \eta \left\{ \sum_{k=1}^{N} (y_k - F(\boldsymbol{w} \cdot \boldsymbol{x_k}))F'(\boldsymbol{w} \cdot \boldsymbol{x_k}) x_{ki} \right\} \tag{37}$$

We now write this with a different notation, the one we shall use from now on:

$$\Delta w_i = \eta \left\{ \sum_{k=1}^{N} (d_k - y_k)F'(S) x_{ki} \right\} \tag{38}$$

The difference is that here we use d_k for the desired or wanted output for input x_k, while y_k is the actual output, $y_k = f(\boldsymbol{x_k}, W) = F(S)$. $S = \boldsymbol{w} \cdot \boldsymbol{x_k}$

The starting point to get formula (37) or the revised one (38) is

$$\Delta w_i = -\eta\, \partial E / \partial w_i \tag{39a}$$

(or rather we started out with the gradient of E, $\Delta w = \nabla E$) while the starting point for the MLP network will be

$$\Delta w_{ij} = -\eta\, \partial E / \partial w_{ij} \tag{39b}$$

If you look at (39a) and (39b) there is a difference in the notation of the weights, because updating the weights of the MLP using backpropagation we must work with *matrices* of weights, but when updating the perceptron we only have to deal with a *simple vector* of weights[10].

But there is one more difference between the backpropagation update method and the update method of the perceptron, a more important difference. It concerns the *error function* that we use for backpropagation.

The error function for MLP is constructed in a way similar to the perceptron, although there is an important difference. For the perceptron it goes like this:

$$E(\boldsymbol{w}) = \tfrac{1}{2}\sum_{k=1}^{N}(d_k - y_k)^2 \text{ where } y_k = f(\boldsymbol{x}_k, \boldsymbol{w}) = F(S) \tag{40}$$

and $\boldsymbol{x}_k$ is the input vector number k

using the notation introduced in (38). Then $d_k - y_k$ is the error (or *algebraic* error) for a *single input* and $(d_k - y_k)^2$ is the corresponding squared error and *the sum of all these is called the total error.*

The total error is the one we minimized to update the weights using (35) and the slightly more general formula (37).

For a MLP network, the error for *a single input vector* $\boldsymbol{x}_k$ involves *several neurons* because there are several neurons in the output layer. So for *each input vector* x_k we get a *sum* of squared errors:

$$E_k = \tfrac{1}{2}\sum_{i=1}^{m}(d_{ki} - y_{ki})^2 \tag{41}$$

This is contrasting the simple perceptron which has only one output neuron for each input vector, so that we have only one term $(d_k - y_k)^2$. Summing E_K further gives us the total error for the MLP network:

$$E(W) = \sum_{k=1}^{N} E_k = \sum_{k=1}^{N} \left\{ \frac{1}{2} \sum_{i=1}^{m} (d_{ki} - y_{ki})^2 \right\} \tag{42}$$

However for the MLP network we shall not minimize the total error (42) directly but the error for a single input vector (41). So let us start with E_k and compute

$$\partial E_k / \partial w_{ij} \tag{43}$$

Computation of the Weight Updates

Before we start, we mention that we shall refer to the connections from one layer to the next as *a layer of connections* or a layer of weights Also it is convenient to start counting layers from the top, the output layer being layer 1,[11] since we shall work our way backwards.

Another thing to note is that the symbol E_K in (41) is a symbol for a number, but we shall use it for a function symbol too, as a matter of fact different functions whose values are the same, namely the error, given by the sum E_k . So we shall let E_k stand for both a function and the function value of this function. This is a common practice.

For instance the function E_k might be the one determining the error E_k from, y_{ki} where y_{ki} is the output of neuron i in the output layer caused by the input vector x_k. This function value we write $E_k (y_{ki})$ in the usual way, and it is a $R \rightarrow R$ function.

But we shall also meet $R^n \rightarrow R$ functions with vectors as arguments, such as $E_k(y_k)$ as well as $R \rightarrow R^n$ functions, with vectors as function values, such as $S_k(y^*_{k2})$.

These functions will all be composite functions so when we compute derivatives we shall have to use the chain rule.

Updates for the Weights in the First Layer of Connections

Let w_{rs} be the weight of the connection to neuron r in layer 1, (output layer) from neuron s in layer 2, (counting backwards). To update this weight we calculate $\delta E_k / \delta w_{rs}$, but carry out the calculation for the special choice $rs=32$, to have a concrete example, since it will be obvious how to generalize to un unspecified rs.

When we take this derivative, only w_{32} in the first layer of weights is varied so only the component S_{k3} of S_k and y_{k3} of y_k are influenced, (Fig. 3).

Therefore we can compute $\delta E_k / \delta w_{32}$ by using the composite function defined in

(44a) below:

$$E_k = E_k(y_{k3}), \quad y_{k3} = F(S_{k3}), \quad S_{k3} = S_{k3}(y_{k2}^*) \quad \text{with}$$
$$S_{k3} = \sum_{j=1}^{3} w_{3j} y_{kj}^* \,{}^{29} \tag{44a}$$

From (41) with $m = 4$, and the sum expression in (44a)[12] we get (44b) and then (45)

which is the derivative that we seek:

$$\partial E_k/\partial y_{k3} = -(d_{k3} - y_{k3}), \quad \partial y_{k3}/\partial S_{k3} = F'(S_{k3}), \quad \partial S_{k3}/\partial w_{32} = y_k^* \tag{44b}$$

$$\partial E_k/\partial w_{32} = (\partial E_k/\partial y_{k3})(\partial y_{k3}/\partial S_{k3})(\partial S_{k3}/\partial w_{32})$$

$$\partial E_k/\partial w_{32} = -\{(d_{k3} - y_{k3})\,F'(S_{k3})\}\,y_{k2}^* \tag{45}$$

Before we go on, it should be noted that the quantity in braces in (45) is called the *local error signal* of neuron 3 and is denoted by δ_{k3}.

Using this, the update of the weight w_{32} can therefore be written compactly:

$$\Delta w_{32} = -\eta\,\partial E_k/\partial w_{32} = \eta(d_{k3} - y_{k3})\,F'(S_{k3})y_{k2}^* = \eta\,\delta_{k3}y_{k2}^*$$

And finally, generalizing from sub index 32 to sub index *rs* we finally get for the update of the weights *in the first layer of connections*.

$$\Delta w_{rs} = \eta\delta_{kr}y_{ks}^* \tag{46}$$

Definition of the Local Error Signals

For later reference we note here the definition of δ_{kr}, the local error signal of neuron *r* in *the first layer* as well as the relationship between δ_{kr} and $\delta E_k/\delta S_{kr}$

$$\delta_{kr} = (d_{kr} - y_{kr})\,F'(S_{kr}) \tag{47a}$$

$$\delta_{kr} = -\partial E_k/\partial S_{kr} \tag{47b}$$

Where (47b) follows from (44):

$$\partial E_k/\partial S_{k3} = (\partial E_k/\partial y_{k3})(\partial y_{k3}/\partial S_{k3}) = -(d_{k3} - y_{k3})\,F'(S_{k3}) = -\delta_{k3}$$

And finally, for *any layer p* and a neuron *r* in this layer *p* we *define* the local error signal by generalising formula (47b)

$$\delta_r^p = -\partial E/S_r^p \ {}^{30}$$
(48)

In the final section we shall see that this is meaningful. In the above we used the notation δ_r for δ_r^1 and δ_r^* for δ_r^2. Below we shall mostly use the * notation.

Updates of the Weights in the Second Layer of Connections

Let w_{rs} be the weight of the connection to neuron r in layer 2 from neuron s in layer 3. We seek the derivative $\delta E_k/\delta w_{12}$, but we work it out for a concrete example, like we did for the first weight layer, see (Fig. **3**).

When we take this derivative, all the weights but w_12 are constant and therefore the only nonzero component of s_k^* is s_k^{*1}, and the only nonzero component of y_{kk}^* is k, (Fig. **3**).

So we see now that E_k can be written as the composition of the five functions presented here:

$$E_k = E_k(\boldsymbol{y}_k) \quad \boldsymbol{y}_k = \boldsymbol{F}(\boldsymbol{S}_k) \quad \boldsymbol{S}_k = \boldsymbol{S}_k(y_{k1}^*) \quad S_{ki} = \\ \sum_{j=1}^3 w_{ij}\, y_{kj}^* \ \ i = 1 \cdots 4$$
(49)

Composing the three first functions gives us $E_k = E_K(y_{k1}^*)$ so that we get

$$\partial E_k/w_{12} = \{(\partial E_k/\partial y_{k1}^*)(\partial y_{k1}^*/\partial S_{k1}^*)\}(\partial S_{k1}^*/\partial w_{12})$$
(50)

For the last of these derivatives we have $\delta S_{k1}^*/\delta w_{12} = y_{k2}^*$, which we see from the sum expression for S_{kl}^*. The middle one is straightforward being equal to $F'(S_{k1}^*)$, but to compute the first one needs a bit of work. The result is:

$$\partial E_k/\partial y_{k1}^* = \sum_{j=1}^4 (\partial E_k/\partial S_{kj})(S_{kj}/\partial y_{k1}^*) \ {}^{31}$$
(51a)

$$= \sum_{j=1}^4 (-\delta_{kj})\, w_{j1}$$
(51b)

To see that the first part of (51) is correct, we compose the first two functions in (49) and get $E_k = E_k(\boldsymbol{S}_k)$ and then compose this with $\boldsymbol{S}_k = \boldsymbol{S}_k (y_{k1}^*)$ to get $E_k = E_k(y_{k1}^*)$. Then we use the chain rule on $E_k = E_k(y_{k1}^*)$ and note that $\delta E_k/\delta \boldsymbol{S}_k$ is a *gradient* and $\delta \boldsymbol{S}_k/\delta y_{k1}^*$ is a *vector* so $\delta E_k/\delta y_{k1}^*$ is the scalar product of these two. Hence the first part of (51) results and the second part follows from (48) and the first sum expression in (49).

Next note that the expression in braces in (50) is equal to $\delta E_k / \delta s_{k1}$ by the chain rule, so that 1: from this and 2: from combining (50) and (51b) (2) we get

$$1: \quad \partial E_k / \partial w_{12} = (\partial E_k / \partial S_{k1}^*) y_{k2}^{**}$$

$$2: \quad \partial E_k / \partial w_{12} = -\sum_{j=1}^{4} (\delta_{kj} w_{j1}) \, F'(S_{k1}^*) y_{k2}^{**}$$

From 1: and 2: it follows that $\delta E_K / \delta S_{k1}^* = -\sum_{j=1}^{4} (\delta_{kj} w_{j1}) F(S_{k1}^*)$. Besides by the definition of δ_{k1}^* we have $\delta E_K / \delta S_{k1}^* = -\delta_{k1}^*$, so therefore we end up with

$$\delta_{k1}^* = \left\{ \sum_{j=1}^{4} \delta_{kj} \, w_{j1} \right\} F'(S_{k1}^*) . \tag{52a}$$

and next that

$$\partial E_k / \partial w_{12} = -\delta_{k1}^* y_{k2}^{**} \tag{52b}$$

so that we get for the update of w_{12}

$$\Delta w_{12} = -\eta \, \partial E_k / \partial w_{12} = \eta \delta_{k1}^* y_{k2}^{**}$$

which for any weight *in the second layer of weights* generalizes to

$$\Delta w_{rs} = \eta \delta_{kr}^* y_{ks}^{**} \tag{53}$$

THE FINAL CONCLUSION

We now have computed the update of the weights in the first and second layers of weights. After we have done the second layer, the updating of the weights in the third and later layers of weights follows the same pattern that we have for the second layer of weights. We shall describe this a little later.

But first let us underline that some of the information of the first step, is passed on to the next. This information is what you use to update the weights. Here we use the words first step, second step and so on to refer to what is done when we update the weights in the first weight layer, in the second weight layer *etc.*

We should also make it clear that in the first step, the first layer is involved in addition to the output of layer 2. In the second step the two first layers are involved in addition to the output of layer 3, *etc.* Let us call this the first section and the second section. (Figs. **2** and **3**).

And when we come to the third step, the corresponding section comprises the second and third layer and the output of layer 4. But this we have not shown by computations, however it will be explained further down when we talk about the patterns underlying the updates of weights.

Now let us repeat the central formulas. The update of the weights *in the first weight layer*, $\Delta w_{rs} = \eta\,\delta_{KR} Y_{KS}$ uses the error signal $\delta_{KR} = (d_{kr} - y_{kr})\,F'(S_{kr})$, and this information, this error signal, is passed on to the second step where we get a new error signal δ^{*}_{kr} where $\delta^{*}_{kr} = \{\sum^{4}_{j=1}\,\delta_{kj}w_{jr}\}\,F'(S^{*}_{kr})$.[16] This quantity δ^{*}_{kr} is *defined* as minus the derivative $\delta E_{K}/\delta S^{*}_{k1}$, see (48). Also δ_{kr} is equal to minus the corresponding derivative of the first step, $-\delta E_{k}/\delta S_{k1}$.

The update of the weights *in the second layer*, $\Delta w_{rs} = \eta\delta_{kr} Y_{ks}$, uses the new error signal. In fact, computing the update of this weight is what brings this error signal to the surface. This happens through the derivative $\delta E_{k}/\delta S_{k1}$. The error signal δ_{kr} is just another name of $-\delta E_{K}/\delta S_{K1}$.

This procedure continues, that is the error signal δ^{*}_{kr} is passed on to the third step, through the formula $\delta^{**}_{k\,r} = \{\sum^{3}_{j=1}\,\delta^{*}_{kj}w_{jr}\}\,F'(S^{**}_{k\,r})$ which originates from $-\delta E_{k}/\delta S^{**}_{k\,1}$ to which it is equal. So we might just as well say that it is these derivatives that are passed on.

PROPAGATION OF THE ERROR SIGNALS

In (52a) we see that the error signal of neuron 1 in layer 2 is computed by a linear combination of the error signals in layer 1 weighing them with the weights to all the neurons in layer 1 from neuron 1 in layer 2, *and multiplying* this linear combination by the derivative of the transfer function taken at the activation of neuron 1 in layer 2.

The error signals of any other neuron *k* of layer 2 are found likewise, replacing the phrase "neuron 1" above with neuron *k*.

We are then justified in saying that the error signals in layer 1 are propagated *backwards* to layer 2, whereas the original (output) signals are propagated *forwards*[16] from layer 2 to layer 1, that is in the opposite direction, *both using weights between the two layers* (Fig. **4**).

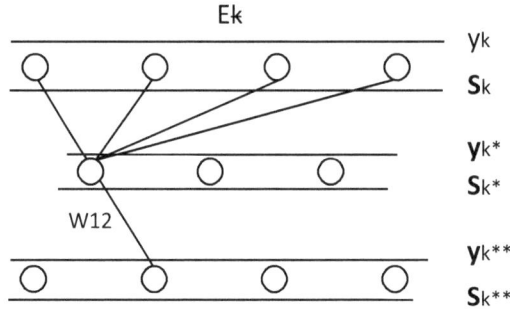

Fig. (4). Updating the second layer of weights.

Finally, as we know, the signal propagated forward from layer 2 to the first neuron in layer 1 is found as a linear combination of the (output) signals from layer 2, weighing them with the weights to the first neuron in layer 1 from the neurons in layer 2, and next apply the transfer function to the activation of neuron 1. Here of course, the activation is equal to this linear combination.

Updating the Weights for all Layers of Weights

Now let us explain why we can say that updating the weights in the second and third layer of weights follow the same computational pattern. And in fact the same thing goes for all layers of weights except the first one.

But let us think of updating the weights of the third layer of weights, choosing w_{24} to have a concrete example. Then we look at (49) where we start by considering the error E_k to be a function $E_k(y_k)$.

Now we start by considering E_k to be the function $E_k(y^*_k)$.

This is the composition of the three functions $E_k = E_k(y_k)$, $y_k = F(S_k)$ and $S_k = S_k(y^*_{k1})$. The last function here is $R^3 \rightarrow R^4$ whereas the third function in (49) is $R \rightarrow R^4$.

The composite functions with which we now work consequently is obtained from (49) by adding one star * in the superscripts. The quantities y_k and S_k which have no superscript, get a star * added as superscripts. That is we get, (see Figs. **5** and **6**).

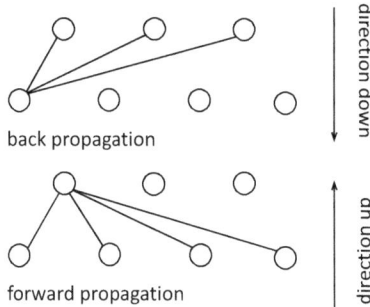

Fig. (5). The Backpropagation algorithm.

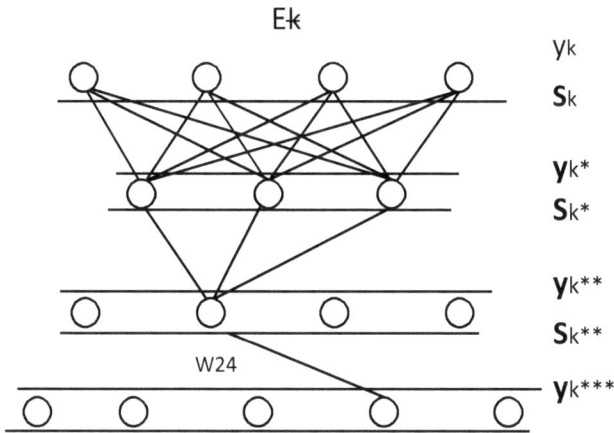

Fig. (6). Different composite functions.

$$E_k = E_k(y_k^*) \quad y_k^* = F(S_k^*) \quad S_k^* = S_k^*(y_{k2}^{**}) \quad S_{ki}^* = \tag{54}$$
$$\sum_{j=1}^{3} w_{ij} y_{kj}^{**} \quad i = 1 \cdots 4 \quad y_{k2}^{**} = F(S_{k2}^{**}) \quad S_{k2}^{**} = S_{k2}^{**}(y_{k4}^{***}) \quad S_{k2}^{**} = \sum_{j=1}^{4} w_{2j} y_{kj}^{***}$$

The computations that will follow, will be exactly the same as for the second layer of weights, because the structure of the neural network is the same throughout.

For the update of the weights *in the third layer of weights* we therefore get

$$\Delta w_{rs} = \eta \delta_{kr}^{**} y_{ks}^{***} \quad \text{with} \quad \delta_{kr}^{**} = \left\{ \sum_{j=1}^{3} \delta_{kj}^* w_{j1} \right\} F'(S_{kr}^{**}) \tag{55}$$

As long as there are more layers of weights, we continue to update these, one at a time. And having arrived at the weights of the connections from the input layer, we are done.

Using Number Indices

Finally we remark that we could use number indices instead of stars * to keep track of the layers. Our system has been such as to let an index p be equal to the number of stars * plus one. Then we see from (46), (53) and (55) that the weight updates of the layer number p of weights is:

$$\Delta w_{rs}^p = \eta \delta_{kr}^p y_{ks}^{p+1} \quad p = 1 \cdots h \tag{56}$$

Where $h + 1$ is the number of layers, and h is the number of layers of weights. See the discussion just before (7), that is w_{rs}^h are the weights from the input layer to the next layer. And the error signals in δ_{kr}^p (56) we get from the recurrence relation

$$\delta_{kr}^1 = (d_{kr} - y_{kr}) F'(S_{kr}^1) \tag{57a}$$

$$\delta_{kr}^{p+1} = \left\{ \sum_{j=1}^m \delta_{kj}^p w_{jr}^p \right\} F'(S_{kr}^{p+1}) \quad p = 1 \cdots h - 1 \tag{57b}$$

The upper limit of the summation is equal to the number of neurons in layer p.

Finding the Weights Themselves

So far we have not explained how to use the result in (56) and (57) to find new weights, given that we start out with a set of weights.

To be precise, suppose you have a set of start weights for the network. Then consider the first input vector x_k with $k = 1$. The weights of the first layer of connections, that is for $p = 1$ in (56) then can be found by adding Δw_{rs} to the start weight for layer 1 of connections. However if you next use (56) for $p = 2$, the new weights that you now find, will not be based on the *start weights* of he second layer of connections, but it is based on the *new weight* that you found for p = 2 in (56).

So we do not find new weights for the network based directly on the start weights.

If you find this to be satisfactory, we just continue in this way completing the scheme (56), (57) for and start over again for and so on.

But we can also let the weights in (57b) be the start weights and not the weights that we compute from (56) for each step. Then, as we get error signals from (57), we put them into (56) to use (56) and get a new set of weights that results from introducing x_1 to the network. Then we continue introducing a new training example, that is x_2, and use the weights we found based on x_1 as a new set of start weights for x_2.

We do not intend to complete this discussion, since continuing it, will be more a question of what can be turned into code that could run without using too much computing time and space. Again, reference [4] will be a place worth of study. They find new weights in a still different way.

CONCLUSION

In this chapter we have given a detailed mathematical description of a *feed forward* network. We described the *structure* of this network, but did not give any applications. However we have given some simple detailed examples for the sake of illustrating *the principles* according to which a feed forward network is working. In this respect we have treated matters from logic, classification and regression, using the *perceptron*.

However, to be able to carry through more "realistic" applications, hidden layers must be included, so we studied the *multilayer perceptron*, being trained by the backpropagation algorithm. This we have treated using only elementary mathematical theory.

NOTES

[1]The *activation* often seems to refer to the *value* that the function F gives, when the argument is S_i whereas we here use this word to denote the argument itself.
[2]Actually Y^2 is a matrix and not a number of course, it is 1 x 1 matrix. But since a 1 x 1 matrix just contains one element, we think of the matrix as this number and we treat it as a number. This is a standard way of doing things.
[3]We use the letter d for the correct function value, the letter d stands for «the desired function value» of f, the ....
[4]The learning rate is set equal to 1 to make the computations proceed with simpler symbols, just the numbers 1 and 0. It has no influence on whether the intcrations converge or not.
[5]If the transfer function F is nondecreasing, which it is.
[6]A line in R^2 is a «hyperplane» in R^2
[7]An affine function is a constant plus a linear function, so that the graph of an affine function is a hyperplan.
[8]This is a standard result og vector analysis.
[9]In R^3 an ellipsoid and a sphere are examples of closed surfaces. In R^2 ellipses and circles are examples of closed surfaces.

[10]How can a vector be a point? Mathematicians have a tendency to call any sort of elements that seem to have some relation to geometry, for points.

[11]However if we have a perceptron with more than one neuron in the output layer, we shall have to consider matrices as well, (a case that we have not included in our study), but these can be treated as a sequence of vectors, so when it comes to updating the weights, this case end up with the same conclusion as for a simple perceptron.

[12]We repeat that if we start counting the input layer as layer 1, then the output layer will be layer number $h+1$, and there are $h-1$ hidden layers.

[13]We use a star in y^*_{kj} to denote that it is the output from a neuron in layer 2.

[14]Note that a superscript always refers to a layer and a subscript to a neuron. The subscript k in (47) refers to the iterations, the repetition of input vectors, and is not needed in the general definition (48),

[15]For the chain rule here see [5]

[16]We repeat that when a quantity like δ^*_{kr} and S^*_{kr} bears a star * as superscript, it belongs to the second step. When there is no star, it belongs to the first step *etc*. However we have no such markings of the weights because it can be inferred from the context to where they belong.

[17]We mentioned this term in the text between equations (12) and (13).

CONSENT FOR PUBLICATION

Not applicable.

CONFLICT OF INTEREST

The author declares no conflict of interest, financial or otherwise.

ACKNOWLEDGEMENTS

I would here like to thank my colleague Terje Solsvik Kristensen for interesting discussions in connection with this work.

REFERENCES

[1]   H. Abdi, D. Valentin, and B. Edelman, *Neural Networks*. Sage Publications, 1999. [http://dx.doi.org/10.4135/9781412985277]

[2]   J. Lawrence, *Introduction to Neural Networks*. California Scientific Software, 1991.

[3]   S. Haykin, *Neural Networks and Learning Machines*. 3rd ed. Pearson, 2009.

[4]   B. Nikhil, *Fundamentals of Deep Learning*. O'Reilly, 2017.

[5]   E. Kreyszig, Advanced Engineering Mathematics, Chap. 9, Tenth Edition, Wiley & Sons, 2011.

SUBJECT INDEX

www.ingramcontent.com/pod-product-compliance
Lightning Source LLC
Chambersburg PA
CBHW041706210326
41598CB00007B/555